N.F. Southwick '88

4/20/24

KENYON COLLEGE

Its First Century

BISHOP CHASE

KENYON COLLEGE

Its First Century

BY

GEORGE FRANKLIN SMYTHE

NEW HAVEN

Published for Kenyon College by the
Yale University Press

1924

PREFACE

I PRESENT this book, which has been written at their request, to the Board of Trustees of Kenyon College. No one who has not gone through the records can duly appreciate the fidelity and care with which this Board, ever since its creation one hundred years ago, has watched over the affairs of the college and sought to promote its interests. A very great amount of thought, time, and patience has been devoted, year after year, by members of the Board to the task—often very wearisome and discouraging—of administering the trust committed to them. The ultimate responsibility has always been with them, and to them is due the ultimate praise.

This book does not pretend to be a complete, or even a very full, history of the college. Although it contains much information, still it is not a storehouse of facts. It is only a sketch, drawn chiefly with an attempt to show in outline the features and expression of Alma Mater, as they have changed through the century. There are omissions which I regret; but the limits of the book required brevity and condensation, and doubtless some things have been unwisely omitted simply because I did not know of them, or did not rightly estimate their importance.

Some readers may complain because these pages are so scantily "documented"; but it seems pretentious and senseless to cumber a book with footnotes and references of which very few can make use. The chief documents are at Gambier, and nowhere else, and many of them are private papers to which I have had access only by special permission. However, I intend to make full notes and references upon the margins of two or three copies of this book, and place them in the college and seminary libraries at Gambier, where those who care to do so can examine them and consult most of the documents.

Though I have taken pains to be accurate in every statement, yet it is probable that errors will be found here. I hope that these will be regarded with forbearance in view of the great difficulty which an inexperienced historian, working for the most part at a distance from his sources, has to encounter, first, in acquiring information, and second, in keeping it where he can find it when he wants it. To all those persons who have answered my letters, and have sent me, so far as they could, the facts for which I have asked, I express my hearty thanks; and I am grateful also to all who have read portions of the manuscript, or proof, and have given me the benefit of their corrections and suggestions.

The illustrations which are scattered through these pages are to me a source of pride. Some of them were obtained only with difficulty. About half of them have probably never before been published. Now for the first time, I think, appear in print these striking pictures of Bishop McIlvaine, Bishop Bedell, Lord Kenyon, Lord Bexley, Mr. Marriott, and President Short—pictures which show them at their best. The pictures of old-time Gambier will be especially interesting to those who have known the village only within the last forty or fifty years. I have thought it better to put these pictures in, rather than to fill my allotted number of pages with existing buildings with which the great majority of readers of this book are perfectly familiar. For many of the Gambier pictures I am indebted to Mr. Wagoner, the photographer, of Mount Vernon, who found the ancient negatives in the attic of his gallery and generously gave them to the college. To persons who have lent me precious pictures to reproduce here, I express my gratitude, as well as to Mr. F. L. White for his map which shows the earliest group of Kenyon buildings.

G. F. S.

Cleveland, Ohio,
  January 1, 1924.

CONTENTS

CONTENTS

ILLUSTRATIONS

Facing page

CHAPTER I

PHILANDER CHASE

THE story of Kenyon College must begin with the story of Philander Chase; for not only was he its founder, but he so stamped his ideas upon it that it has been, and always must be, very largely what he made it. He was the first "Kenyon man"; and he still rubs up against everyone who, dwelling upon the Hill, shares in the life of the college and of the place.

In the year 1775 Dudley Chase and Alice Corbett, his wife, were living at Cornish, New Hampshire, whither they had come, ten years before, from Sutton, Massachusetts. Already they had thirteen children, when, on the fourteenth of December of that year, another son was born; and his father, who loved to read *Young's Night Thoughts*, named him *Philander*, after one of the characters of that sententious poem. The boy grew up on the farm and in the woods, among a pioneer people, and learned the arts of the farmer, the woodman, and the pioneer. He was as much at home on horseback as on his feet. He could swim, he said, "like a duck." All his life long he wanted to have plenty of room about him. His people were Congregationalists, and he was very religiously brought up.

Only a few miles from Cornish, at Hanover, was Dartmouth College; and several of the Chase boys graduated there. Thither went Philander in 1791, rather to gratify his parents than because he had any desire for an extended education. Nothing is known of his course in college, but he acquired a good deal of knowledge that was useful to him in later years. He graduated in 1795.

While he was in college a Prayer Book somehow fell into young Chase's hands. It impressed him so profoundly that he went over to the Episcopal Church, and decided to enter the Episcopal ministry. In those days there were no theological seminaries; he who would study to be a minister betook himself to some clergyman, and learned from him what he could. Chase went to Albany and put himself under the kindly and scholarly direction of the Reverend Thomas Ellison, rector of St. Peter's Church. He studied the books that Mr. Ellison lent him, and at the same time he taught school in order to earn money. He needed money, for in 1796 he had married Mary Fay, a beautiful girl, and in 1797 a son was born to them.

After he had been ordained deacon, in 1798, Chase served for a year and a half as a missionary in central and western New York. This was a new region, recently opened, and great numbers of settlers were pouring in. Traveling among them, sharing their life and their hardships, preaching, founding churches, the young minister gained experience that was of value to him long after, in Ohio and Illinois, where he dealt with similar conditions. In 1799 he was ordained priest, and thereafter, until 1805, was rector of Christ Church, Poughkeepsie. Here also he taught a school; not because he liked to teach, but because in that way he could eke out an inadequate salary. He had no great predilection for the schoolmaster's business; but it was a resource to which he could turn in case of need, as he could to so many other businesses; and, except when he lived at Hartford, his salary was small, and schoolmasters were in demand wherever he was.

From 1806 to 1811 Chase was in New Orleans, where he founded Christ Church and became its rector. He had a very successful school in that city. In 1811 he removed to Connecticut, and was soon called to be rector of Christ Church, Hartford. Here his position was prominent and important, both in the Church and in society, and his relations with his people were most happy; but in 1816 something occurred in the Diocese of Connecticut that occasioned so great dissatisfaction in his mind that he determined to leave the state. "I am persuaded," he said, "that I can be more useful to the Church of Christ and more happy in my own person *elsewhere* than in the Diocese of Connecticut." This unhappiness in his own person was connected with the coming of Bishop Hobart, at the invitation of the diocesan convention, to take temporary charge of the diocese. These two good men—Chase and Hobart—never did or could agree. Friction arose between them, and Chase decided to leave Connecticut. As were all his decisions upon important matters, this determination was made quickly and irrevocably; and at the same time he made up his mind where he would go.

In the year 1817 the tide of emigration from the older states to Ohio, after suffering a check by the War of 1812, set in again, with much greater volume. Thousands and thousands came into the new state every year. The population, which had been 231,000 in 1810, rose to 581,000 in 1820; and two-thirds of that increase came after 1815. Ohio was evidently destined to be a great state, and whatever forces took possession of it in its formative years were likely to remain dominant for a long time. Of the thousands who were making new homes in Ohio, a large part came from New England, and especially from Connecticut. Some of the towns in that state were seriously depleted of population, and many country parishes saw their strength departing in that exodus.

Philander Chase, living in Connecticut, was deeply impressed by the emigration that was going on all about him. He knew many of the emigrants. He saw the wagons lumbering through Hartford day after day, bound for the West, loaded with household goods, amidst which were bestowed wife and children; while the goodman of the moving house walked beside it, guiding the horses or oxen. Sights like this,

and the thought of the new homes on the far-distant frontier
to which these vigorous, hopeful, adventurous young people
were going—for most of them were young—could not fail
to stir the soul of a man so imaginative, so emotionally susceptible, as Chase. It must have carried him back to the
days of his own youth, when he grew up on a frontier
farm, among pioneers, and to the times of his first travels,
when as a young missionary he had pushed westward
through New York, along the very roads—then scarcely
more than trails—that these emigrants were to travel slowly
and laboriously. Who, being of a romantically reminiscent
spirit, as was he, would not feel a mighty pull towards the
West? When, therefore, just at this time, he was resolved
to leave Connecticut, it is not strange that he thought of
going to Ohio; but such fancies as these could not alone have
drawn him away from the comforts and amenities that he
loved, and driven him into the wilderness, with his wife, a
woman in delicate health, bearing an infant in her arms. The
pioneer instinct was not so strong in Philander Chase as some
have thought. For seventeen years he had lived in long-
settled towns, Poughkeepsie, New Orleans, and Hartford,
among prosperous and cultivated people, and had not found
civilization uncomfortable. But within him, both then and
afterwards, was a strong desire for freedom to do, in accordance with his own ideas, a work for God that should be
commensurate with what he felt to be his strength and
abilities. If now he heard "the call of the wild," it was
because to him it was the call of God to such freedom and
such work. He was in his forty-second year, at the height of
his physical manhood, with an experience of twenty years
of remarkable success in the ministry, extraordinarily capable, versatile, and energetic. He was able, and felt himself
able, to do a much harder and greater work than any that
he had yet done; he was fitted to exercise a larger leadership.

sympathy and admiration. This account of Mr. Morse's cheers me, Dear Father, beyond all the comforts I have received for many a day."

I raised myself from the couch and poured out my thanks with my whole heart.

"It pleases & comforts you, I perceive," said my son, "as well as me; and I think the news that there are those who sympathize with us in our deprivations and troubles is a comfort that we did not expect—too exquisite to be described. It is felt however, and we will sleep the sweeter for it; & I am glad I have told it you."

"But, my Dear Son," said I, "a thought has struck me as from Heaven, which, from this sympathy felt by others, opens to me a door of hope, thro' which there pours in upon our dark and benighted prospects a flood of light that overwhelms me."

"What do you mean, Father. Pray explain yourself."

"*I will apply to England for assistance.* If from what they have seen they think kindly of us, when the whole truth is known they will help us."

"You are crazy, Dear Father to think of it. Pardon me for such an expression, but the thought of such a measure seems not the result of reason."

"With God's assistance it can and shall be attempted, and you shall go. A sea voyage may be the means of recovering your health, as it was that of your Mother."

"Oh, I have not strength to undertake it."

"Don't say so; God will help you."

Thus the conversation went on, alternately making, obviating, difficulties.*

The reader will perceive in this something analogous to the experience of "sudden conversion." Here was a swift passage from a state of depression to one of great exaltation. Suddenly a thought struck him "as from Heaven," a "door of hope" flew open, through which an overwhelming flood of light poured in, and a new resolution was formed within him. From this time forward for eight years, every purpose, every effort, of his life might be traced back to this moment. But his mind was not instantly clear as to just what was

* Letter in Kenyon College Library, K. Ch. J. 240106.

involved in the thought that had struck him like a bolt out of the sky—*I will apply to England for assistance.* How would he apply? And for what object should he ask assistance? At first he thought that he would send his son across the sea; but the son was an invalid, near to death, and his rapid failure within the next few days made it evident that he could not go. Then it was that, as Bishop Chase said, "the great truth was realized" that he "must put his trust in God, and go himself to England." This decision also, like the first, "was like the light pouring into a dark and desolate room; it filled every cubic inch with splendor." Again, Bishop Chase did not at first see exactly what it was for which he would solicit aid. In the conversation with his son, as related in this early account, nothing was said about obtaining means to found a school for the education of ministers; nor again, two days later, when the matter was acted on by the Missionary Society of the diocese—it was never laid before the diocesan convention—was such a school thought of, so far as the minutes of the meeting show. The society had already held its annual meeting and adjourned *sine die*, when, on the fifth of June, 1823, the Bishop called its members together again in special session. He tells us in his *Reminiscences* that "the project, though opened with great seriousness and the entreating of divine direction, was at first opposed by nearly all. It was considered as visionary, though at last agreed to by the clergy, and silent consent was impliedly given by the laity." We have no means of knowing what this "project" was which was laid before the society, except as it is disclosed in these resolutions passed at the ending of the discussion:

Resolved, that this society appoint the Rev. Philander Chase, jun. to cross the Atlantic, with proper credentials, for the purpose of soliciting aid in Great Britain, for the support of the Protestant Episcopal Church in the Diocess of Ohio: and that he be allowed five hundred dollars for his expenses.

Resolved, that the Rt. Rev. the Bishop be respectfully requested to furnish the proper credentials, and also to furnish an address, setting forth our condition, our wants, and our prayers, to the Rt. Rev. the Bishops, Clergy, and members of the Church of England.

Nothing in these resolutions indicates that a school for the education of ministers was included in the "project" which Bishop Chase laid before the Missionary Society, and it is probable that no plan to establish such a school had yet taken distinct form in his mind. It is sometimes said that when he first came to Ohio part of his intention was to found a seminary and college; but no one has told where trustworthy evidence of such an intention may be found. It is, however, very likely that the thought of a diocesan theological seminary had sometimes crossed his mind, and that he had wished that there might be one in Ohio; and it is not strange that when his eyes became accustomed to the overwhelming "flood of light" which had so suddenly poured out upon him, he discerned such a seminary as the principal object disclosed within the "door of hope." Henceforward, so long as he appears in our history, we shall see him engaged in nothing else but in trying to make that vision real.

In the next chapter we shall follow Bishop Chase into the great cities of England and the United States, shall see him associating with persons high in rank, in social position, and in learning, and shall find him everywhere making an astonishing impression, winning ardent friends and strong supporters, yet also offending and alienating some good men. It will, therefore, be well to pause here and look at this remarkable man, and see what he was, as he presented himself to the eyes and minds of his contemporaries. He was a man whom, whether you liked him or disliked him, you could not ignore. It almost seems as if everyone that met him left some account of his appearance, or of the impression he made. Many such accounts have come down to us; and, making allowance for the different points of view of the writers, they are in a high degree consistent with one another.

Bishop Chase was a man of very large physical build. He was considerably more than six feet in height, and his breadth was in proportion. He inclined to corpulency, yet never, until he was an old man, was his form at all unwieldy or his step other than firm and quick. His size and figure impressed men; such terms as "massive form," "majestic height," "commanding figure," "a stalwart giant," abound in the descriptions of him. Doctor Sparrow, telling of the first time he saw him, said: "I tho't as my eye fell upon him he was the most majestic man I had ever seen. He filled the whole door."

According to the most competent testimony, Bishop Chase's features and customary expression were admirably portrayed by the artist J. G. Strutt in his first picture of him, painted in London in 1824. When Hubbard Hall was burned, in 1910, this picture was destroyed, and the loss of it was grievous; yet, fortunately, there are in existence copies of a fine engraving of it, made by J. P. Quilley, and there are also photographs of it. The portrait now hanging in Norton Hall, presented to the college by William M. Evarts, is by the same artist; but it is not a replica of the other, although resembling it in a general way, and it is not so good a likeness. The portraits by Strutt, and a pencil sketch by John Cranch, in possession of the college, are our principal means of knowing how Bishop Chase looked in the years when he was the chief figure in our history. Pictures that show him bespectacled, and wearing a strange black cap on his head, all belong to later times.

Strutt's pictures show the head and features of a handsome and very masculine man. His hair was of a dark brown color. His eyes were blue, with a penetrating glance, and had a slight "cast"—just observable in the pictures—which added to the piquancy of his expression. His countenance was never so calm that you did not feel that something was going on within, likely to find outward expression at any moment. In his genial moods there was a kind of archness in his looks, a slight expression of amusement—"as if he were holding something queer within," said Bishop B. B. Smith.

Bishop Chase's bearing and manners were those of a gentleman accustomed to good society and perfectly at home in it. The idea is wholly incorrect, and most absurd, that he attracted attention in England as a sort of wild-western bishop. He possessed unusual social gifts. He was dignified, and, when in a happy frame of mind, exceedingly affable. Few men could equal him in conversational charm when he was at his best. Professor John Kendrick, who knew him well, said:

It was the verdict of Washington society the last winter he spent there, that the Bishop excelled Henry Clay in conversations. It was said that, let Clay have the "floor," and no one could equal him; but that in conversation among equals, in the quickness of speech, in the rapid question and answer, in the wit, repartee, and anecdote that characterize the highest style of conversation, the Bishop excelled him.

Bishop George Burgess said of him:

In conversation his powers were singular, versatile and exceedingly effective. He was profoundly serious, and he was irresistibly humorous, with the varying tide of the discourse.

And it must be remembered that he exercised these fascinating gifts not only among persons of cultivation, but also among the uneducated and the rude, and with equal effect.

But there were times when Bishop Chase lost this affability. We cannot do better here than quote the words of Bishop Burgess, who honored and loved him:

It was given him to lead, and he was impatient when men were slow to follow. He identified himself with his work; and if he were thwarted or contradicted, it was not always easy for him to feel that it could have been in Christian sincerity. . . . The very warmth with which he laid hold on a good cause, and the consciousness of his own simplicity of purpose, would not permit him to regard otherwise than as personal opponents some who wished well to his undertakings, but withheld their confidence from some of his decisions. From such he maintained somewhat too readily a distance, the penalty of which he was willing to pay in laboring without their coöperation.

The Reverend Henry Caswall, one of the earliest of the Kenyon alumni and closely connected with Bishop Chase by marriage, said:

The same sanguine temperament which led the Bishop to design great things for the Church, often hurried him into vehement expressions of feeling, and produced an apparent want of deference for the opinions of others, which could hardly fail to give offence. His own zeal . . . led him to expect the same zeal in others, and occasioned vexation and annoyance when those expectations were disappointed.

Bishop Chase's zeal in any cause to which he devoted himself was intense and impetuous. It was said of him that "his blood was at fever heat for forty years together." He was most tenacious of purpose, could not be daunted or intimidated; could not, indeed, be dissuaded. "His opinions once made up, they become principles of action," said one of his presbyters. This inflexibility of his was often called *obstinacy*, and, indeed, he was obstinate; but this was only one side, one manifestation, of a quality without which none of his great accomplishments could have been brought to pass. When he entered upon a course of action, it was with the firm conviction that in so doing he was following the will of God; and very seldom did he afterwards see reason to think that he had been mistaken. Moreover, he was accustomed to decide and act for himself. No man was ever more independent than he, and he had that self-confidence which every successful man must have. Within his own field he felt that he *knew;* and if others differed with him, then they did not know so well as he. Therefore he must follow the light which he saw, even though to others it seemed darkness. Undoubtedly it was a weakness in him that he was so little inclined to have confidence in others, or listen to them, unless they agreed with him; and this was the cause of some great disasters; but, on the other hand, all his large accomplishments were due to this certainty that he was right, and this pertinacity in pursuing his own course. At any rate, Kenyon men must rejoice that he possessed these qualities in a very high degree, for had he not, there would have been no Kenyon College. Whatever good the college and the theological seminary have done, whatever pride we have in them, whatever affection we feel towards them, all these cry out in thankfulness to Heaven for Bishop Chase's indomitable obstinacy.

One other quality remains to be spoken of, the crown and complement of all the rest; this was his absolute devotion to God and his sure trust in Him. His nephew, Salmon Portland Chase, has stated it well:

Thoroughly religious, he always looked to God. His motto was, Jehovah Jireh—God will provide. But his faith in God only animated him to most strenuous personal labor. It was not passive, but active. If anything was to be done, he felt that he must do it; and that, if he put forth all his energy, he might cheerfully and safely leave the event to Divine Providence.

Such was the man who founded Kenyon College.

CHAPTER II

THE THEOLOGICAL SEMINARY AND KENYON COLLEGE FOUNDED

ALTHOUGH in the first flash of his inspiration to go to England Bishop Chase probably had not thought of applying there for aid to establish in Ohio a training school for ministers, yet it was but a short time before such a purpose was definitely formed in his mind, and within a month the main outlines of his plan were fully drafted, and the arguments in its favor were worked out. On the twenty-ninth of July, 1823, he addressed a letter to his brethren of the House of Bishops, informing them of his intention to "proceed immediately to Old England, to solicit means for the establishment of a school for the education of young men for the ministry." He stated the situation forcibly.

Unless we can have some little means of educating our pious young men *here*, and *here* being secure of their affections, station them in the woods and among our scattered people, to gather in and nourish our wandering lambs, we have no reason to hope in the continuance of the Church in the west.

Every effort had been made to procure clergymen, but the results had been wholly disappointing. Already they had waited too long.

For one, I feel disposed, by the grace of God, to amend my ways in this respect. I will endeavour to institute a humble school, to receive and prepare such materials as we have among us. These we will polish under our own eye, to the best of our power; and with these we will build the temple, humble as it may be, to the glory of God.

Having entered on this resolution, under the guiding and directing hand of Providence, I shall make my best way to the land of our fathers—to the Church of England—to that generous people, who will not turn a deaf ear to the cries of those who are ready to perish,

LORD GAMBIER

especially if in them she identify her legitimate children. Thus under God being resolved, the Episcopal Church in the west will not, must not die, without a struggle.

He asked the bishops to write him letters of approval and commendation, and begged that prayers might be offered that God would prosper his endeavors.

On the fourth of August Bishop Chase put himself, his wife, and his children into a great carriage, took up the reins, and set forth on the long drive from Cincinnati to Kingston, New York, where he would leave his family, at the home of his wife's mother, while he was away. By this time it had occurred to him that he should have some better endorsement than the resolutions of the Missionary Society, to show that he went upon his mission with the approval of his diocese. He could not reassemble the diocesan convention, but he procured a letter, signed by the Reverend Samuel Johnston, of Christ Church, Cincinnati; and by stopping at Chillicothe, Steubenville, and Ashtabula, he got the signatures of the other clergymen, in all, seven names. This letter—doubtless composed by Mr. Johnston—beginning with the words, "We, the presbyters and deacons of the diocese of Ohio, North America," told briefly of "the gloomy prospects of the Church in the states west of the Alleghany mountains." "At the impulse of hard necessity," they turned to the land and Church of their fathers for help. They humbly introduced their "venerated and beloved Diocesan" as the messenger of their wants, who would make known "the precarious condition and needy circumstances" of their diocese. They concluded by saying, "We wait, therefore, anxiously, but submissively, the sentence of the Lord on the destiny of our infant Church."

After a journey of nearly six weeks, the Bishop arrived with his family at Kingston. There he found awaiting him letters from several of the bishops, written in answer to his request for recommendations and prayers. Two or three of these letters were very encouraging and sympathetic, but the letters of Bishop White of Pennsylvania, the presiding bishop, and of Bishop Hobart of New York, expressed strong disapproval of his undertaking. Bishop White objected to any application from the American Episcopal Church to that of England for financial aid. He said with much asperity that nothing was so annoying as a beggar. Such words from Bishop White, whom everyone held in veneration, were discouraging indeed; probably no bishop except Chase would have stood out against them. Bishop Hobart's letter went much further. He was deeply interested in the General Theological Seminary, established in New York by the General Convention a few years before. No other theological seminaries, he thought, should be allowed in the Episcopal Church, for they were likely to breed differences of theology and churchmanship, and thus imperil the unity of the Church. The Diocese of Ohio, he said, did not need a seminary, for it had scarcely any candidates for Holy Orders, and probably never would have many; but if such a need should arise, the General Seminary would establish a branch school there. He declared that the weight of opinion in the Church was heavily against Bishop Chase's project. He said that he was himself about to go to England for his health, and should there oppose Bishop Chase, if he persisted in carrying out his purpose; and in the face of such opposition nothing but mortifying failure could result.

Not content with these threats, Bishop Hobart convinced many friends of Bishop Chase that the proposed visit to England would prove disastrous; and they added their alarmed expostulations. From the Missionary Society of the Church, and from the General Theological Seminary he procured the passage of resolutions condemning Bishop Chase's design, and he induced influential persons to withhold letters of introduction. Fortunately Henry Clay was beyond his reach; and from him Charles Hammond, an influential lawyer, editor, and Churchman of Cincinnati, obtained a letter introducing Bishop Chase to Lord Gambier, a distinguished British admiral, with whom Mr. Clay had become well acquainted when they both were members of the commissions that drew up the Treaty of Ghent, at the close of the War of 1812.

Imagine what Bishop Chase had before him. He, a man almost wholly unknown in England, bishop of a far-western diocese of which few Englishmen had ever heard, carrying with him only a single letter to any person of prominence— he was to go to England and ask money in behalf of a project that was condemned by the presiding bishop of the Church, and by the official missionary society, and by the General Theological Seminary, and, so it was asserted, by American Churchmen generally. And he was to be confronted in England by Bishop Hobart, the most influential man in the American Church, who had notified him that he should leave no stone unturned to thwart his efforts. To almost any man it would have seemed folly to proceed in an undertaking so feebly supported, so generally condemned, and so powerfully opposed. Even the stout heart of Mrs. Chase failed for once, and she proposed that they "go back to Ohio, and there expire." The Bishop says: "The rejoinder was '*Never!*' From that moment there was mutual firmness of purpose."

To Bishop Hobart's letter Bishop Chase deigned no reply. To Bishop White he addressed a long answer, and printed it in a pamphlet, with many appendices. He explained and justified his purpose. The Church in Ohio and in all the West would perish if it were not soon supplied with clergymen. These could not be obtained in sufficient numbers from the East, as experience had amply shown. Therefore the Church in Ohio must educate the "sons of the soil" to minister at her altars; and she must educate them in Ohio, because the expense of sending them to the General Seminary in

New York was too great, and because, once they had grown accustomed to the East, it would be difficult to induce them to return and labor in the wilds of Ohio. There was "an imperious necessity of having an institution for the education of young men for the ministry, among those who are benefited by their labors." This institution must not be a "branch" of the General Seminary, but must be governed by persons "on the spot," who know the western people; "and to this end their funds should be at their own control."

To prevent the possibility, however, in any future generation, of a diversion of their funds to things foreign from their original intention, and to secure the unity of the Church to all intents of the constitution and canons of the general convention, it was and is our purpose to insert in the legal act of incorporation a proviso, that, on evidence of a malapplication of funds the General Theological Institution, or the Bishops, as a committee of that body, should be authorized by law to make inquiries, and set things right. [And, furthermore] It is understood that the institution is to be under the immediate care of the Bishop for the time being, or his substitute, assisted by two or more professors of sacred learning, and a grammar-school teacher.

In defence of an application to England for money to carry out this project, Bishop Chase said that nowhere else could money be obtained, since the General Seminary had need of all that the Episcopalians of the Atlantic states could give. Whither, then should he turn, if not to "that land whose enlightened inhabitants are spreading the glorious gospel throughout a benighted world"? Replying to Bishop White's pointed observations on the nuisance of begging, Bishop Chase remarked that if it was commendable in St. Paul to make collections for the poor, he did not see why it should be thought a criminal thing in *him* to do so. But whatever difference of opinion there might be as to the expediency of his going to England on such an errand, he trusted that they would grant that it was his duty to obey the dictates of his own conscience and proceed without delay.

"Accordingly," he said, "my passage being taken on board the packet, if the Lord permit, I shall, according to the time fixed on while in Ohio, sail on the first of October."

Bishop Chase did not use the five hundred dollars voted by the missionary society to meet the expense of the application to England. His uncle, March Chase, had left him a small legacy; Intrepid Morse, his nephew, lent him something; and a little piece of property in Poughkeepsie, which he sold at this time, probably added to the fund. After his return the trustees of the new institution borrowed one thousand dollars from the funds of the missionary society to reimburse him, and ultimately this was repaid out of the money raised in England.

Bishop Chase sailed from New York on the first of October, 1823, in the packet ship *Orbit*, and after a long and stormy passage, landed at Liverpool on the third of November. He went at once to Manchester, and spent a few days with his "old friend and college companion," Timothy Wiggin, an American, who had married in England and was engaged in prosperous business there. Mr. Wiggin invited several prominent clergymen to meet him, and they gave him much practical advice as to how to conduct his campaign, and furnished him with letters to clergymen in London and elsewhere. In Mr. Wiggin and his family Bishop Chase found "friends, the first, and of the truest and best in England." To them he repeatedly turned for counsel and encouragement, and never failed to find it.

On his way from Manchester to London he stopped at Oxford, where his reception was chilly. Arriving at London, he took lodgings in Holborn. Not a soul did he know in all that city, yet there it was that he must make friends and strong supporters if he was to accomplish the end for which he had come to England. He had a few letters of introduction, but when he delivered them, he found that, in every instance, the minds of those to whom they were addressed had been prepossessed against him. Bishop Hobart, who had arrived in England before him, had immediately set going a "whirlwind campaign" to frustrate Bishop Chase's plans; had called on many persons, written many letters, and printed a pamphlet which he distributed widely. In this pamphlet, which he entitled *Notes*, he informed the reader that the Protestant Episcopal Church in the United States had not, in any way, authorized Bishop Chase's appeal; the diocesan convention of Ohio had not approved it, and had not adopted any plan for the organization of the proposed seminary; nor was there any incorporated body to hold and manage funds that might be given to it. In short, it was entirely Bishop Chase's own project and enterprise. He said that he was persuaded that the great body of the bishops, clergy, and laity in the United States were opposed to an appeal to England in behalf of any particular diocese, but added that if English Churchmen had money to give to any American cause, the General Seminary should be the object of their generosity. In a supplement he declared, with great emphasis, that many other dioceses were as needy as Ohio, and that other bishops were as laborious as Chase. It is improbable that Bishop Hobart was directly responsible for the reports that circulated among London Churchmen that Bishop Chase was not to be trusted with money; but he had partisans who were quite ready to do work of that sort. Chief among these in importance was the Reverend H. H. Norris, a clergyman of great influence, who controlled the powerful *British Critic*. He was Bishop Hobart's warm friend, and more than seconded all his efforts to discredit Bishop Chase, whom he conceived to be—dreadful to say— little better than a Methodist.

Bishop Chase had but one hope, and that was in Lord Gambier. He dispatched to him the letter of introduction from Henry Clay, received a courteous acknowledgment, and then waited two weeks before Lord Gambier was able to see him. These two weeks were, perhaps, the most disheartening period he ever passed through. He felt no interest to go about and see London, but remained at his lodgings, praying, reading, writing letters to his wife. The words came home to him with consoling, strengthening power—"O tarry thou the Lord's leisure; be strong, and He shall comfort thine heart; and put thou thy trust in the Lord."

One wise, though blunt, counselor he did find, the Reverend Mr. Crosby, to whom he had brought a letter of introduction from a brother in Zanesville. Mr. Crosby told him that his cause was good, but that there was great prejudice against it and him. The purity of his motives was doubted. He must make it unquestionably appear that the money which he solicited would be faithfully applied; "and to ensure this," he said, "there must be those in England who will stand pledged." Bishop Chase appreciated the force of Mr. Crosby's words, and within a day or two he drew up a paper intended to meet these objections. He sent it to Mr. Wiggin for his judgment and advice, and Mr. Wiggin heartily approved it. This paper* merely put into practical shape the plan which Bishop Chase had formed before he left Ohio, and which he had outlined in his letter to Bishop White. He called it now a "Deed of Gift," or a "Deed of Donation." This is the fundamental document in the history of Kenyon College. It gave shape to the institution, satisfied the natural demands of Englishmen for the security of the money they might give, and at last, by a strange turn of things, drove Bishop Chase from Ohio. Very slowly has the college released itself from the bands with which this document tied it up.

In the Deed Bishop Chase bound himself to give to the proposed seminary his farm at Worthington "and all things

* See Appendix I.

thereunto pertaining," provided ten thousand dollars should be contributed in England. From this obligation he was to be released if the convention of the Diocese of Ohio should prefer some other location than Worthington, and should "give, or procure to be given a farm, equal or superior in value in buildings and conveniences" to that which he offered. All moneys given to this school were to be deposited in England, in the hands of men who had the confidence of the English people, and should not be transferred to America until Henry Clay should certify that all the conditions had been fulfilled in good faith; or, if Mr. Clay were unable to attend to the business, then the governor of Ohio should act in his stead. The institution was to be legally incorporated, and the bishops were to have visitatorial power to see that everything was done in accordance with the doctrines and canons of the Church. This document he signed and executed on the twenty-seventh of November, naming Lord Gambier as trustee, and added to it a careful inventory of all buildings, fruit trees, and animals on the Worthington farm.

Everything now depended on what Lord Gambier would do, and that depended on the impression which Bishop Chase might be able to make upon him when they met. This long delayed event took place on the fourth of December. Lord Gambier was very courteous, but Bishop Hobart had written to him, and had sent him his *Notes*, and these, he confessed, had produced "an unpleasant effect on his mind," so that he was unable to take a very favorable view of the proposed Ohio seminary. However, he conveyed Bishop Chase to his home at Iver Grove, near Uxbridge, and entertained him for four days. The Bishop asked only for an opportunity to present his cause, and this Lord Gambier granted him. Nearly one whole day was spent in examining papers and documents, including Bishop Hobart's *Notes*, and in considering conditions in Ohio, and the need of a theological seminary there, and the adequacy of the proposed Deed of

Gift—if it should be accepted—to preclude all danger of schism and of misappropriation of funds.

To this presentation of his cause Bishop Chase bent all his powers, well knowing that everything depended upon his ability to demonstrate its soundness and justice, and the purity of his own motives. Lord Gambier was surprised and impressed by the facts and arguments that were laid before him; and he said, with some emphasis, that the situation was quite different from what he had been led to suppose. Later he assured Bishop Chase that he would support the Ohio cause, but told him that it would be no easy thing to overcome the prejudice that had been created against it. He gave him a letter to the Reverend Josiah Pratt, secretary of the Church Missionary Society, of which he himself was president.

Mr. Pratt, who had read Bishop Hobart's pamphlet and had been prejudiced by it against Bishop Chase, received him at first with mere civility; but upon reading Lord Gambier's letter he became cordial, listened to what his visitor had to say, promised to read the papers left with him, and said that he would call on him soon. He became one of Bishop Chase's most energetic helpers. As secretary of the great Church Missionary Society his acquaintance among the clergy of the Evangelical party was extensive, and he had thorough knowledge of the ways of conducting a religious campaign for raising money. He called together a number of clergymen, had Bishop Chase tell them his story and present his cause, and then he organized them into an informal committee of propaganda which worked with great efficiency. He composed a pamphlet entitled *Appeal in Behalf of the Diocese of Ohio in the Western Territory of the United States*. It was made up largely of extracts from the Bishop's addresses to the diocesan convention and from his letter to Bishop White, with explanatory matter. No mention was made of Bishop Hobart and his opposition to the

Ohio cause; for it had been agreed that the best course was to maintain silence on this subject—a policy that proved a very effective counter to the attacks which at first had been so formidable. The *Appeal* closed with a most hearty endorsement of Bishop Chase, and with the names of persons to whom subscriptions might be sent. The Bishop while in England did not personally solicit money or receive it.

To compose and publish this pamphlet took a number of days, for Mr. Pratt was an exceedingly busy man. These days dragged heavily with Bishop Chase, until one morning —it was the Festival of the Epiphany, 1824—there called at his lodgings a gentleman who was to prove one of his most devoted friends. This was George Wharton Marriott, a lawyer, a man of the best social position, belonging to a family that had furnished many able clergymen to the Church. Mr. Marriott called merely out of curiosity and the desire he had to meet a man of whom he had heard so many things favorable and unfavorable. It was fortunate for Bishop Chase's cause that this new friend was of the High Church party; for, owing to the ecclesiastical connections of Lord Gambier, Bishop Chase had thus far come in contact only with Evangelicals, or Low Churchmen; but Mr. Marriott's friendship and zeal secured for him acquaintance with men of the other party also, some of whom became his enthusiastic supporters. Most prominent among these was Doctor George Gaskin, canon of Ely, an eminent clergyman, and Lord Kenyon, for whom the college is named. It was regarded as a remarkable result of Bishop Chase's visit to England that he brought together into harmonious coöperation men, such as Gambier and Kenyon, Gaskin and Pratt, who had previously stood apart because of difference in churchmanship.

The early months of the year 1824 were spent by Bishop Chase in northern England, where he followed an itinerary supplied by Mr. Pratt. He made no public appearances of any kind, preached no sermons, delivered no addresses, but

GEORGE WHARTON MARRIOTT

HARCOURT PLACE

met people in their houses and in small companies at dinners
and breakfasts given in his honor. In every town someone
undertook to distribute the *Appeal* and ask for subscriptions.
The impression which the Bishop made was immense. His
noble proportions and handsome face, his affability and
good manners, the gift of fascinating narration which he displayed as he told of his missionary labors in the wilds of far-
distant Ohio, the elevation of his spirit, the fervor of his
piety, the thought of the sacrifices he was making for the
cause of Christ and the Church, the dignified silence with
which he had met the sharp attacks upon himself—all these
combined to raise him high in the opinion of those who met
him. The letters which he received in great numbers were
full of admiration and of gratitude for the good he had done
in coming to England and letting men see and know him.

"Every one of my guests," wrote the Reverend Charles
Crawley, "were full of his praises, & astonished at his ability
at the same time to delight and interest." The Reverend
Robert Marriott wrote, "I am certain that the good you do
is incalculable among us; so much so, that I am sure you
would have reason to rejoice and be glad all the days of your
remaining stay upon earth, even though your journey were
quite to fail as to the immediate object of it." "I thank God
that you came to England," wrote the Bishop of Durham.
Lord Kenyon said of him, "He will return from among us
venerated and beloved by all who have the privilege of
knowing him and his proceedings; and leaving a deep impression on our minds of the blessings which that distant
branch of the Episcopal Church enjoys in possessing such an
Ecclesiastical Governour. Our sister Church has been raised
by him in the esteem of great numbers among us." And to
the Bishop himself Lord Kenyon wrote, "I cannot help
thinking my affectionate intercourse with you among my
primest blessings."

Not less notable was the impression which Bishop Chase

made upon young people. The girls of the Wiggin family
were devoted to him. Mary Ward, at that time thirteen years
of age, whose father was not long afterwards made Bishop
of Sodor and Man, assumed the middle name Ohio, and
thenceforth was "Mary Ohio" in Bishop Chase's correspondence. He gave her some melon seeds which, perhaps, he
found in his pocket; and she wrote to him formally, and in
the third person, that he had

left in her possession not merely the seeds of a perishable Mellon,
which however prized by her for the sake of the Donor and the soil
in which they grew, are yet not comparable in value with the
heavenly seeds which he has dropped upon her heart by his conversation and example.

There grew up also a very beautiful friendship between
the Bishop and Margaret Kenyon, Lord Kenyon's eldest
daughter. They saw each other but once, and only for an
hour, yet the girl felt that he had greatly enriched her life.
She remembered and cherished every word he said, and knelt
to receive his benediction as he was departing. After he had
returned to America, she devised an "Ohio garden," for
which he supplied her with seeds of our native plants and
slips from trees and vines. She wrote to him that she wished
to build in the midst of it "something in the way of a summer house in imitation of the cottages or usual habitations"
in Ohio. Accordingly she had a primitive cabin built of logs,
cut from trees which her father selected for that purpose.
The cabin still stands, apparently in unimpaired integrity,
having been affectionately cared for through nearly a century. A year from the day the Bishop left England she wrote
to him:

My Ohio house is finished, and when I have furnished it with your
print, and some Ohio papers, etc., I shall often be in it to think of
you. I have had it put near the bottom of a steep bank, by way of
representing in a humble manner the Alleghany mountains.

In April Bishop Chase returned to London from his northern trip, and thenceforth he made the city his headquarters until he was about to depart for home. Here, and in Cambridge and Oxford, which he soon visited, he was regarded with the same admiration and reverence as in the North. It was during this time that Mr. Marriott brought about a meeting of Lord Kenyon and Bishop Chase; and thereupon a lifelong and most affectionate friendship began between these two men. Money was coming in. A board of trustees, consisting of Lords Gambier and Kenyon, Doctor Gaskin, and Mr. Henry Hoare, took charge of it, to hold it until the terms of the Deed of Donation should be fulfilled. Meanwhile, Bishop Hobart's opposition had entirely ceased. Indeed, he sought repeatedly to enter into some agreement with Bishop Chase whereby they should work together in one campaign for funds, and divide the proceeds between the General Seminary and the new seminary that was to be in Ohio. Many forms of this proposition were made, but none that both bishops were willing to sign; and finally Bishop Hobart let Bishop Chase and his seminary alone.

At the end of June interest in the Ohio cause was at its height. The list of subscribers was rapidly lengthening. Bishop Chase's popularity was such as almost to embarrass him with invitations to dinners and breakfasts, and with other attentions. But he had begun to long for home. Since he left America his beloved son Philander, who had for years been an invalid, had died of consumption, and another son had been born. Very little news had come from Ohio, and his anxious thoughts dwelt upon the field which God had given him to cultivate, and from which he had been absent so long. Therefore, despite all urging, he left London on June 29, bidding a sad adieu to his dear and generous friends there. He made a short visit to western and southwestern England, to see Sir Thomas and Lady Acland, and Lady Rosse, and Hannah More, all of whom had contributed liberally to his funds; he went to Manchester to say farewell to the Wiggin family, and then came to Liverpool where Lord Kenyon brought his children to receive his blessing and say good-bye. Other friends came for a last greeting. Mr. Adam Hodgson, a loyal supporter, had all the Liverpool clergy in to take tea with him. Letters came in great numbers. So every token of affection and esteem was bestowed upon this man who, eight months before, had landed in England a stranger, opposed and discredited by the most influential Churchman of his native country, and distrusted by everyone that had heard of him.

The ship *Orbit* sailed on the seventeenth of July, 1824, and on the twenty-ninth of August landed her passengers at New York. The Bishop went at once to Kingston, where he had left his family, and a month later he and they were in Worthington.

The annual convention of the Diocese of Ohio met at Chillicothe on the third of November, 1824. Bishop Chase had already been in that village for several days, in consultation with Charles Hammond, the eminent lawyer and Churchman of Cincinnati, whom he had, by a most urgent letter, summoned to meet him there, and aid in drafting a constitution for the proposed seminary, to be submitted to the convention for its approval.

I want to see you more than any man breathing [so he had written to him]. The donations to the seminary are but *commencing* if all be conducted right, & that they may be so conducted I have great reliance upon you. . . . Come up before all others and let me see your face and talk matters over.

In his address to the convention the Bishop glanced briefly at the history of his recent activities. He reminded his hearers of the almost hopeless aspect of the Episcopal Church in Ohio when they last met. He referred to his determination to go to England for aid, and to the opposition he had encountered. He told of the generous manner in which English Churchmen had received him. "Never was benevolence more disinterested: never was christian zeal more active."

It was now necessary to provide an organization for the seminary for which the Bishop had procured the money. Mr. Hammond's draft of a constitution was laid before the convention and was adopted, and a committee was appointed to procure from the legislature the incorporation of the institution thus created. The constitution, first of all, gave a name to the seminary, "The Theological Seminary of the Protestant Episcopal Church in the Diocese of Ohio"; and the purpose of the seminary was declared to be "the Education of Ministers of the Gospel in said Church." No thought was then entertained of establishing a college, or of giving instruction in any secular branches, save as such instruction might be needed by young men who were preparing to take theological studies. Bishop Chase, in his letter to Bishop White, had described his proposed faculty as consisting of "two or more professors of sacred learning, and a grammar-school teacher."

The second article of the constitution declared that

the said Seminary shall be established by the Convention of the Diocese at such place within the same as shall be consistent with the deed of donation executed by the Bishop of Ohio, in England, on the 27th day of November, 1823; and when once established, shall forever after remain in the same place.

Bishop Chase, in his letter to Bishop White, had promised to give his farm near Worthington as a site for the institution. Apparently he then thought of no other location but that; and since he was about to ask gifts for the cause, he was moved himself to make to it a most generous gift. This proved to be in England a very impelling example, and the Bishop's munificence was warmly spoken of; yet the promise was decidedly modified in the Deed of Donation. The right was there reserved, as has been said, to substitute another place, under certain conditions; and in that case the Bishop was to be exonerated from his promise concerning the farm. The constitution provided that these engagements with regard to location should be kept.

By the third article the "direction and management" of the seminary was vested in a board of trustees, to consist of the Bishop of the Diocese, and four clerical and four lay members, to be chosen by the convention for a period of three years. The number might be increased. The Bishop was to preside at the meetings, when he was present.

> The board of Trustees shall have power to constitute professorships, and to appoint and remove professors, and to prescribe the course of study, and to make all rules, regulations and statutes which may be necessary for the government of the seminary, and to secure its prosperity.

It would not naturally occur to Bishop Chase to propose such a body of managers, for he expected to manage everything himself. Nothing had been said about a board of trustees, either in the letter to Bishop White, or in the Deed of Donation; and, no doubt, these constitutional provisions were wholly the work of Mr. Hammond, who, as a lawyer, saw that they were necessary.

In the letter to Bishop White it had been stipulated that the Bishop of Ohio, "or his substitute," was to have "the immediate care of the institution"; and article five of the constitution granted him "the immediate charge and superintendence" of the seminary "as principal professor and President."

Bishop Chase had from the first seen clearly that in going abroad to solicit funds he must be able to offer some guarantee that the money which he might secure should forever be used for the purposes for which it was given; and also that his independent school in the far West should not foster independent and schismatical teachings, and so endanger the peace and unity of the Church. He must provide safeguards which would satisfy English Churchmen. Therefore in his letter to Bishop White he had outlined a plan to accomplish this end.* But after Bishop Hobart had stirred up so much apprehension lest the existence of an independent school in the West should lead to schism, Bishop Chase in the Deed of Donation strengthened and made more definite the guarantees which he had included in his letter to Bishop White. These provisions appear, in substance, in the constitution. All "rules, regulations, statutes, or other proceedings" prescribed by the board of trustees must forever "be in conformity to the doctrine, discipline, constitution and canons" of the Church, and the course of study must conform to that marked out by the bishops; and if the General Convention should deem any of them contrary to the doctrines, discipline, constitution, or canons of the Church, then they should be "considered as abrogated and annulled." The bishops of the Church were declared to be

visitants of the Seminary, to take care that the course of discipline and instruction be conformable to the preceding provisions. And it shall be lawful for any one of the Bishops aforesaid, at any time, to institute in his own name and character of Bishop, any proper legal process to enforce and secure the administration of the Seminary according to the foundation herein prescribed.

Thus was the seminary, in order to guarantee to the world its orthodoxy and its loyalty to the Protestant Episcopal Church, tied hand and foot to the will of the General Convention and the bishops, if they should ever choose to exert that will. But these elaborate provisions were never called into practice, since no General Convention, and no bishop, ever cared to assume responsibility or authority with regard to the Theological Seminary of the Diocese of Ohio; and its orthodoxy and loyalty to the Church have never been seriously called in question.

* See page 20.

On the twenty-ninth day of December, 1824, the General Assembly of Ohio passed "An Act to incorporate the Theological Seminary of the Protestant Episcopal Church in the Diocese of Ohio." By that act, upon that day, came into being not only the theological seminary, but also the grammar school and Kenyon College, which were soon to be evolved from it as its natural developments. The institution was a going concern from the day of its birth. Already it had a home—Bishop Chase's house near Worthington—a board of trustees, an endowment, a library, a faculty—the Bishop —and a "student body" in the person of a youth named Hunter, who was supposed to be studying with the Bishop preparatory to becoming a candidate for Holy Orders. From that day to this it has proceeded with its work, through many vicissitudes, yet without suspension or lapse.

BIOGRAPHICAL NOTES

LORD GAMBIER

JAMES GAMBIER was born in the year 1756 at New Providence in the Bahamas, where his father was lieutenant-governor. He entered the British navy when but a young boy, rose rapidly in rank, and participated in the naval actions of our Revolutionary War. He served with distinction in the wars with France, and in 1795 became rear admiral. In 1807, in recognition of his services at the siege of Copenhagen, he was raised to the peerage as Lord Gambier. He was one of the chief commissioners of Great Britain in the negotiations which led to the Treaty of Ghent, by which the issues of the War of 1812 were settled. In these negotiations he met Henry Clay, one of the commissioners for the United States; and it was the friendship thus formed that enabled Mr. Clay to write to Lord Gambier that letter of introduction which opened the way for Bishop Chase's successful campaign in England. In 1830 Lord Gambier was advanced to the highest naval rank, that of Admiral of the Fleet. In 1833 he died, having in the course of a long life attained every possible distinction and rank that his profession could afford. Along with this he was equally distinguished for his interest in the religious enterprises of the Evangelical party in the Church of England, of which he was among the foremost leaders. For many years he was president of the great Church Missionary Society.

LORD KENYON

GEORGE KENYON, born in 1776, was the son of Lloyd Kenyon, the Lord Chief Justice of England, who, upon attaining that office, had been created Baron Kenyon of Gredington. Upon his father's death he succeeded to the title and estates. He had already graduated at Christ Church, Oxford, and had studied law, having chambers in Lincoln's Inn. Subsequently he became a bencher of the Middle Temple. He was most devotedly attached to his wife, a woman of extraordinary beauty of face and of character, and to his children, three sons and three daughters.

Lord Kenyon was deeply interested in the cause of religious education, and was one of the earliest and most active members of the National Society, which was formed to promote that cause. At one time he had seven of its schools under his immediate supervision, visited them constantly, and took part, as he was able, in instructing the children. He was interested also in railways in the early days of their history, and both in the House of Lords and elsewhere he successfully fought the strong opposition with which they were at first met.

Yet though in these important matters he took a stand in advance of the generality of his age, in things political and personal he was decidedly a conservative. He described himself as "an old Tory." He was strongly opposed to most of the reform bills, although he was not without sympathy with many of the objects they were intended to secure. He is said to have been the last man in England to wear a pigtail, and to have cut off this adornment when the Catholic Emancipation Bill was passed, since, as he said, "there was nothing left to wear a pigtail for."

Lord Kenyon was a man of sincere piety, a gentleman of the highest type of honor and magnanimity; he was full of good works both in London and about Gredington, and there are few noble traits of character which he did not in some measure illustrate. He died in 1855, being then in his eightieth year, and is buried in the parish church at Hanmer, near Gredington.

CHAPTER III

KENYON COLLEGE AT WORTHINGTON

BISHOP CHASE had at first intended to locate his school permanently upon his farm at Worthington. This is implied in his letter to Bishop White, of September 23, 1823, and in the reference in the Deed of Donation to his occupancy of "the Mansion house, as usual, during his life-time." Nevertheless, in this deed he also made, as we have seen, provision for establishing the school elsewhere than at Worthington, should the convention prefer a different location, and procure for that purpose the gift of a farm of equal, or greater, value. There were reasons why Bishop Chase inclined to prefer some other site, and these increased in cogency as time went on. He was no longer on friendly terms with all the leading families at Worthington; and Mrs. Chase felt isolated and unhappy there. He thought that there were personal influences abroad in the village that were injurious to the morals of the young men. Again, while he never repented of his offer to give his farm to the seminary, yet he may well have come to feel, on mature consideration, that he ought not to bear the whole expense of providing a location for an institution that belonged to the diocese. The property at Worthington was practically all the wealth he had. Many towns were eager to have the seminary established within their borders, and were offering buildings and money to secure it. In view of all these considerations Bishop Chase early gave up the idea of planting the seminary permanently at Worthington, and began to look about for a suitable location elsewhere. To the diocesan convention of 1824 he said:

When and how to settle the question where to fix permanently this our favourite Institution, you, my Brethren, are better judges than

LORD KENYON

myself: But one thing it is my duty to observe, that this question is too vast in its consequences, it is too holy in its nature, it involves the interests of too many thousand souls to be determined hastily, without due consideration, or to admit, in the least, of local prejudices or sectional interest. . . . Wherever the real interests of the Church require, there doubtless it is your wish, the Seminary should be fixed. To ascertain this you will use the most proper means and exercise your best judgment.

In accordance with a resolution offered by Mr. Hammond, a committee was appointed "to receive propositions for fixing the seat of the Seminary," with instructions to report on the first day of the next convention, which was to meet at Zanesville on the first day of the following June.

It was therefore with the presumption that the location was but temporary that Bishop Chase opened the school at his farm near Worthington, at what is now the "Chaseland" stop on the interurban railway. The farm of one hundred and fifty acres lay on both sides of the Columbus road, half a mile south of the village. The Bishop had purchased it in 1817, and had labored very hard, yet with delight, in planting trees and vines, that it might be both fruitful and beautiful. He had built at first a small house, of but two rooms below; but soon he erected the fine, spacious residence that still stands, overhung by great trees, several hundred feet east of the main road. That was his home in 1824, and that was the first home of Kenyon College. But as numbers increased he made use also of the small, older house, and constructed, one after another, four rude, temporary structures of unhewn logs. One of these was a dining room, adjacent to the kitchen of his house. Another contained the large room that served as schoolroom and chapel. The other two provided rooms for the students.

Mr. Hunter, the first pupil, did not stay long; but during the early months of 1825 a few students arrived. One of these was Erastus Burr, to whose "recollections," printed in the *Kenyon Book*, we are indebted for much of our information about the school. Bishop Chase was at first the only teacher; but being busy with a farm and a heavy correspondence, and having upon him the care of all the churches, he could not give much attention to his pupils. One boy, at least, found the course of study too strenuous. The Bishop, in a letter to a friend, tells how this young man

went on with his studies of the *Latin Grammar* and got as far as *Sum & Nolo*. There he stopped short & said he could not & would not pursue his studies any further.

So he went home. This youth will not wholly fail of sympathy.

On the fifth of April Bishop Chase wrote that he was expecting Mr. William Sparrow, and that when he came the school would "commence with great regularity and assiduity." Mr. Sparrow had assisted him for a short time in the old Worthington College, had accompanied him to Cincinnati, and later had accepted a place as professor at Miami University. This position was agreeable to him, and paid him very well; but when Bishop Chase appealed to him to come and help him at Worthington again, he yielded to a sense of duty and loyalty, and took the work, although it was much more laborious and much less remunerative, than that which he gave up for it. He was the principal of the school and the chief teacher; for after his arrival Bishop Chase ceased to teach, and gave but occasional attention to matters of conduct and government, leaving all such things to Mr. Sparrow and Mrs. Chase. When Mr. Sparrow arrived studies began in earnest. Another teacher was added soon, Mr. Gideon McMillan, who taught the elementary branches. Later came Mr. C. W. Adams; and in 1827, when Mr. McMillan withdrew, Marcus Tullius Cicero Wing took a place in the faculty, which he was to retain—with one short intermission—for nearly forty years. William Preston taught for a short time in 1828.

The school grew rapidly. In April, 1826, Bishop Chase wrote, "We are as thick as pigeons in a nest." The chief care of the household affairs fell upon Mrs. Chase. She also kept the accounts of the institution, and looked after the library. In the Bishop's absence the more important matters of discipline were in her hands, and only with her consent might disorderly and undesirable pupils be dismissed. In 1828 there were fifty pupils in the school, coming from many parts of the country. As the Bishop traveled about, soliciting money for his great projects, he picked up boys here and there, and sent them on to Worthington, or took them back with him. One of the inducements that led parents to send their young sons to his school was the "unexampled and almost incredibly reduced rate" of charges. Candidates for Holy Orders paid fifty dollars a year, "collegians" seventy dollars, grammar school pupils sixty dollars. These prices covered all expenses for forty weeks, except stationery, books, and clothing.

At one time there were five Indian boys in the school, Mohawks from northern Ohio, four of whom were supported by the government. They were well behaved, and were susceptible to Christian teachings, but did not remain long. They served a useful purpose by adding a picturesque interest to the school, especially in England, and by giving to it something of a missionary character—though these Mohawks were, in fact, Christians and Churchmen, their tribe having had, in their New York home, Church of England ministers and teachers.

There is in existence a letter, written by a young student at Worthington in June, 1827, which shows what was the daily life of the school:

I arise in the morning at five, dress myself, and after prayers in my chamber, go into the school room and remain there until seven o'clock, when all the students attend to hear the scriptures and prayers read, and in conclusion all join in repeating the Lord's

Prayer. We then breakfast, and by nine o'clock return to school and continue our studies until twelve, when we are dismissed, eat our dinner, and resume our studies from two to five o'clock. We have then an hour or two of recreation, after which we have supper, and close the daily regulations of the institution by hearing the Holy Scriptures read and conclude with prayers.

The institution at Worthington was officially known as a theological seminary, yet but one or two of the students there pursued what is ordinarily called a theological course; most of them were doing work of preparatory grade, and a few took college studies. This anomaly calls for explanation.

Beyond question, Bishop Chase's first plan had embraced nothing more than the establishment upon his farm at Worthington of a small school for the education of "the sons of the soil" for the ministry of the Protestant Episcopal Church—"a humble school," he called it, "to receive and prepare such material as we have among us." His letter to the bishops, telling them of his intended visit to England, and his letter to Bishop White, speak of no other purpose than this. The "Appeal in Behalf of the Diocese of Ohio," which was issued in England, and widely distributed there, speaks only of "the establishment of an Institution on the spot, in which the natives of the country may be prepared for the Ministry." The Deed of Gift speaks of the institution as a "School, or Theological Seminary, for the education of young men for the Christian ministry." This term, "School, or Theological Seminary," is used five times in the Deed, and the term "School, or Seminary" is used three times; and the only other equivalent term in the document is "the Institution," used once. The constitution of the seminary, and the articles of incorporation, contemplated no other object than the education of ministers.

But Bishop Chase never intended that the institution should provide instruction only in studies that are technically known as "theological." He knew very well that

among the sons of the soil whom he hoped to prepare for the
ministry there would be but few that had received that training in collegiate and grammar school studies which the
canons of the Church required of all candidates for ordina-
tion. In educating those men for the ministry, it would be
necessary, in most cases, to begin with elementary, or second-
ary, studies; and this work must be done in the theological
seminary. Hence, in his letter to Bishop White, he had included a grammar school teacher in his proposed faculty.
In his address to the convention of 1825 he spoke of his
house at Worthington, and said:

Here the Seminary in all its branches, from the grammar school
through all the courses of collegiate instruction to those of theology,
as required by our Canons, might proceed.

And again, he spoke of "our plan of founding a christian
College containing all the means of full instruction for the
ministry." It is very important to observe that he here speaks
of the seminary as a college. To him the two words were
synonymous, although he preferred to use the latter word.

In the summer and early fall of 1825 students began to
arrive in considerable numbers, and within a few months
there were twenty-five enrolled, including the Indians. Doctor Burr gives the names of the students in the school on the
first of January, 1826; and as we read them we are impressed
by the fact that few, if any, of these lads, except Erastus
Burr himself, ever entered the ministry. They seem to have
been youths of the same sort that had attended Bishop
Chase's Worthington College a few years before, and to have
come for the same purpose, that is, to gain an academical
education. It was easy to gather many such pupils, and the
Bishop thought it well worth while. He had been deeply
impressed with the belief that great numbers of Ohio children were growing up in illiteracy. A law had just been
enacted, enabling communities to levy a tax for the support
of schools; but the effect was likely to be nugatory, for it was

hard to find competent teachers for these schools. The
thought grew upon Bishop Chase that schoolmasters were
almost as sorely needed in Ohio as ministers; and he felt
that his seminary would be doing a good work if it fitted
young men for that profession. And why should not the
grammar school and collegiate classes, which he must maintain for the canonical education of prospective ministers,
be open also to any young man who desired a liberal education? Bishop Chase's ideas, once started, always grew
rapidly; and he was soon convinced that it was of the utmost
importance to develop the collegiate work of the school, and
provide for all who sought it a liberal education on terms
of "unexampled cheapness." Addressing the convention of
1826 he said:

Much of the field of art and science, is open alike to the physician,
civilian and the divine. What one studies the others must not neglect.
The knowledge of the languages, philosophy and Belles letters, is
necessary to all, and in the attainment of this, the ability and number
of the professors and teachers, the quality and extent of the libraries
and the use and value of an astronomical and philosophical apparatus
may be greatly enlarged, for the benefit of each, by a junction of the
funds of both. It was therefore to *promote*, and not to impede the
original design of our institution, that I have endeavoured to annex
a college of general science to our Seminary, and to open our doors
to students designed eventually for all the learned professions.

From this time forward the center of interest in the
Bishop's mind shifted over, more and more, from the theological part of the institution, in which there was little
doing, to the collegiate and preparatory annex which enrolled nearly all the pupils he had, and for which he saw a
great future—so great that, a few years later, he told the
diocesan convention that the purpose of his labors was

to cherish an institution of christian education at a rate of unexampled cheapness, bringing science with all its blessings within the
reach of thousands and tens of thousands of persons, who, by reason
of their straightened circumstances must forever remain in compara-

tive ignorance. It is to teach the children of the poor to become *school-masters*, to instruct our common schools throughout the vast valley of the Mississippi. It is to teach the children of the poor to rise by their wisdom and merit into stations hitherto occupied by the rich; to fill our pulpits, to sit in our senate chambers, and on our seats of justice; and to secure in the best possible way the Liberties of our country.

This was indeed a great and splendid vision, to fill the vast Mississippi Valley with schoolmasters, besides doing all the other things. It would require a great output of graduates; but the Bishop was sure that, if he could have the necessary buildings, "our young men graduated in this Seminary yearly, will exceed two hundred." The more he thought of it and labored to bring it to pass, the more certain he was that, as he wrote to his brother Dudley Chase, a member of the United States Senate,

there is no other method or plan by which our Western World can be kept from going back into a vandal state, than the one on which our Institution is proceeding. . . . Give me then a college (I ask nothing but the buildings) out of which I can turn school-teachers, drawn from the poorer classes of society (and, therefore, not above their business), in sufficient numbers (no half-way business) and I will do more good—I mean you Congressmen will do more good, through God's grace given unto you, than by all your great speeches made this winter.

The name "Theological Seminary of the Protestant Episcopal Church in the Diocese of Ohio" which the institution bore in law, must have been very distasteful to Bishop Chase, who had a remarkable gift for bestowing fine names. Besides, it was unsuited to the institution in the new shape which it had taken in his mind. With his usual promptitude and directness he determined to change it, or, at least, to substitute for it in popular usage a name more practical and euphonious; and the prominence which the collegiate department had attained gave him his opportunity to do this. In October, 1825, he wrote to an English friend that he had decided to give to that department the name of Kenyon College; and on the twenty-fourth of the following January, entirely of his own motion and with no authority of convention or trustees, he procured from the General Assembly the following act:

An act, supplementary to the act, entitled "An Act, to incorporate the Theological Seminary of the Protestant Episcopal Church in the Diocese of Ohio."

Sec. I. Be it enacted by the General Assembly of the State of Ohio, That the president and professors of said Seminary shall be considered as the faculty of a College, and as such, have the power of conferring degrees in the arts and sciences, and of performing all such other acts as pertain unto the Faculties of Colleges, for the encouragement and reward of learning, and the name and style by which the said degrees shall be conferred, and the certificates given shall be that of the "President and Professors of Kenyon College, in the State of Ohio."

Explaining this matter to the diocesan convention in the following June, Bishop Chase said:

Having obtained the means to complete the education of young men for the reception of degrees, in the arts and sciences, it seemed no more than reasonable and just, that the President and Professors by whom they were educated, should have the power of *conferring* these degrees.

Of course, so far as the giving of degrees was concerned, no change of name was necessary; but here was an opportunity to be rid of a cumbersome and misleading name, and to substitute a good one. True, Kenyon College was by law only a title under which degrees might be conferred, but it soon became the popular name of the institution, and the long theological name was seldom used except when formality required it. The fact that the main building of the college bore the same name, helped materially in bringing about this change of usage. Bishop Chase never thought out clearly the relationship between the theological seminary and the college, and it is impossible to reconcile all his state-

ments one with another. By no means did he give up the idea
of educating ministers, and there was no time when he would
not have said that this was his chief purpose; yet certainly
the collegiate work occupied most of his thought, and it was
with reference to this that he shaped his plans. He knew that
he should never have many theological students, but he expected to have many hundreds in the collegiate and preparatory departments, if he could only have a suitable place to
put them; and towards the selection and preparation of such
a place he bent his energies.

CHAPTER IV

WHERE SHALL THE INSTITUTION
BE PLACED?

SEVERAL towns wanted the college. Offers of money, or of buildings, came from Zanesville, Chillicothe, Franklinton, and were expected from Cincinnati; but Bishop Chase had made up his mind that he would not plant his school in any city or populous place; for, he said, "in our City Colleges" the students are exposed to the temptations of "those who find it their interest or malicious pleasure to seduce them from their studies into vice and dissipation." Nor would he place it in any small village.

To establish our Seminary in a village [he said] with no more accessions to her fund, than a village can give, and yet expect that she will open her doors to students in general learning, and in all respects maintain the dignified character of a College, is an attempt to reconcile inconsistencies and accomplish that which is impossible.

Excluded thus from both city and village, the institution was evidently obliged to "take to the woods"; and that was just what Bishop Chase had resolved that it should do. To the convention of 1825 he said:

By placing our Seminary on lands of which itself is owner for some distance round, we might possess, and if we chose, we might *exercise* a power as effectual as salutary—a power, by right of soil, to prevent the evils which otherwise the best of collegiate laws cannot cure. . . . PUT YOUR SEMINARY ON YOUR OWN DOMAIN; BE OWNERS OF THE SOIL ON WHICH YOU DWELL, AND LET THE TENURE OF EVERY LEASE AND DEED DEPEND ON THE EXPRESSED CONDITION, THAT NOTHING DETRIMENTAL TO THE MORALS AND STUDIES OF YOUTH BE ALLOWED ON THE PREMISES.

In this address Bishop Chase mentioned two other advantages to be gained by placing the institution in the country. The first was the healthfulness of such a location. The second was of a financial nature; for it must be remembered that there was not yet in hand money to purchase land anywhere.

Wherever in the country our Seminary is placed, the land for many miles around will greatly increase in value. . . . Should therefore the Seminary by gift or otherwise, (previous to the determination to fix absolute on any place) be certain of being the possessor of some thousands of acres of the surrounding country, how surely and how innocently, yea, how justly might it share in the gains of which itself would thus be the parent. . . . Suppose four thousand acres were given us, and by purchase we became owners of four thousand acres more. If the Seminary were established on them, the former of these would now be worth $20,000, and the latter, after deducting the price of their purchase, would amount to $15,000; and a few years would see these lands doubled even in this valuation.

The Bishop, being without funds, is here proposing a land speculation, such as he saw going on everywhere about him in Ohio at that time—buying land without money, or with very little, and making it pay for itself, and more. Indeed, when he delivered that address he was already trying to negotiate such an enterprise. Without waiting for the action of the convention or the board of trustees, he had provisionally decided the question of a location for the school. A generous Churchwoman of Zanesville, Mrs. Betsy Reed, had given him, for the benefit of the Church, one thousand acres on Alum Creek, north of Columbus. This was a fine piece of land, sufficiently remote from city temptations; and the Bishop decided that here the college should be put. The tract was not large enough, but he expected that neighboring landowners would make additional contributions, which, as he thought, their sense of self-interest would lead them to do, since their land would be more than doubled in value by the proximity of the college. Assuming that they would be awake to their interests, he, with his customary precipitancy, caused the land to be surveyed, and a site for the seminary to be marked out, eleven acres to be cleared and fenced, seed to be sowed for a harvest in the fall, and a log cabin to be built. The labor involved in the improvements was cheerfully contributed by the people of the region, who were moved by the Bishop's enthusiasm and eloquence, and, in the true pioneer spirit, were ready to help a new neighbor "settle." They assembled in a "bee," and cut down the trees.

How sublime a sight [said the Bishop] to see a thousand men at work and for such a purpose, and the whole forest nodding obedience, yea bending low at God's commandment.

This commandment, however, was subject to revocation, as will shortly appear.

Such doings as these could not be kept out of the newspapers, and so Mr. Hammond, and other members of the board of trustees, became aware of what the Bishop was about. They were much displeased, and both Mr. Hammond and the Reverend Samuel Johnston wrote letters to him, protesting against his action. As they saw it, Bishop Chase was endeavoring to force upon the convention—with which the choice of a location resided, by constitutional provision—the acceptance of his own views. Mr. Hammond was strongly of the opinion that the school should be strictly for the education of young men for the ministry, as had been originally intended; and that the proper place to educate men for the ministry is a city. It could not be supposed, he argued, that candidates for Holy Orders would need the protection of a forest to keep them from idleness and vice; and, on the other hand, in a city alone could they acquire that knowledge of men, and manners, and affairs, which it is essential that a minister have. Bishop Chase was so offended at Mr. Hammond's letter that he left it unanswered. He wrote to the Reverend Samuel Johnston:

I have received several letters from you & one from Mr. Hammond lately, but the state of my mind & feelings at present is such as to preclude the possibility of giving them such an answer as would suit them & me : therefore must delay that duty.

"That duty" was never performed. Mr. Hammond soon withdrew from the board of trustees, and Colonel John Johnston, another of the ablest men on the board, followed him before long. Had their views prevailed there would have been no Kenyon College; but there might have been, in Cincinnati or Columbus, a strong theological seminary of the Protestant Episcopal Church. That was, really, the main issue. Bishop Chase stood his ground, feeling that, in this matter at least, the decision ought to be his, and determined that it should be.

I am almost alone [he wrote] in the project of placing our College in the wilderness, yet the fatigues thereof falling principally on the first beginners, I have a right to decide for myself what I would not do in the case of another.

Having tried in vain to induce the owners of lands adjacent to the Betsy Reed tract to give the thousand or more additional acres he wanted, Bishop Chase abandoned the plan of putting his school there. This change of view was greatly facilitated by the discovery of a location he liked much better. On the twenty-first day of July, 1825, he held service at Mount Vernon. The next day, in company with Mr. Henry B. Curtis, a young lawyer of that city, and several other gentlemen, he took a ride that proved of the utmost consequence to him, and to many others, then and in succeeding years. Mr. Curtis long afterwards wrote for the *Collegian* an account of this ride; and it is given here, somewhat abbreviated.

It was on a bright summer morning (July 22, 1825), that a party of gentlemen started from Mount Vernon with Bishop Chase, for the purpose of exploring the country eastward of and adjacent to this city, with a view to the selection of a suitable site for the Theological Seminary and Kenyon College. We were all on horseback.

It was well known that Mr. William Hogg, of Brownsville, Pennsylvania, owned a tract of 8,000 acres of land—two military sections of 4,000 acres each—lying a few miles east of here, which, from the varied character of its surface, and the beauties of its streams and valleys, it was suggested might offer a suitable location for the proposed Seminary and College.

We went out on what is called the Coshocton Road, and struck the land of Mr. Hogg, on the west boundary of what has since been called the "North Section," at a distance of about four miles. We proceeded through the section, noticing many pleasant features. Thence down the valley of "Schenk's Creek," to the junction of that stream with "Owl Creek," and thence turning again westward, and proceeding up that river, and generally near its margin, we again entered the lands of William Hogg, at the eastern boundary of the "South Section."

On this section there were several cabins, and a number of small farms opened.* The road lay across the beautiful valley, and again striking the river, followed its margin in a pretty straight line, until interrupted by the abrupt descent of what is now the "College Hill."

I had once, on a previous occasion, crossed over this hill, or promentory, and it was with reference to this spot that I desired the party to return by this route. Arriving, therefore, at the base of "the hill," on its south side, I called the attention of the Bishop and others of the party, to the elevation on the right, and its beautiful surroundings. But it was suggested by Mr. Norton that there was not room enough on the crown of the hill for the accommodation of the necessary buildings and grounds for the contemplated Institution. To this I replied that I had once crossed the hill, and that there was a level plain on top, of wider extent than was supposed.

Bishop Chase answered by saying, "Come, Mr. C., I will go with you up to the top of this hill, and we will see how it looks." The Bishop and myself proceeded alone to mount the hill. The side was thickly set with an undergrowth of oak bushes, frequently interlaced with rambling grape vines. We struggled through these tangles on our horses until about half way up the hill, when the Bishop, becoming discouraged with that mode of proceeding, proposed that we should take it afoot. We dismounted and hitched our horses, and then proceeded as well as we could until we emerged on the top of the hill, on the very spot where the old College building now stands.

* That is, by squatters, without a title, or by tenants at will.

The heavy timber that had once covered the crown of the hill, had principally, many years before, been prostrated by a storm, or otherwise destroyed, so that, excepting a more stunted growth of brush than that we had just come through, the place on top was comparatively open and free from obstruction to the view. Passing a little northward, the whole panorama of the beautiful valleys lay at our feet, the undulating line and varying surface of the distant hills, eastward, southward, and westward, with the windings of the river, all were brought into view, and presented a scene and landscape of unsurpassed loveliness and beauty. It certainly so appeared to me then, and so it seemed to strike our good Bishop. Standing upon the trunk of an old fallen oak, and permitting his eye to pass round the horizon and take in the whole prospect, he expressed his delight and satisfaction in the brief but significant exclamation: "Well, this will do!" He then pointed out the varied beauties of the spot, its extensive views, and the advantages that would be obtained by opening some parts of the contiguous forest—improving the prospect in certain directions.

We then returned to the foot of the hill, and found our companions amusing and resting themselves where we had left them. The Bishop expressed himself to them in strong terms of satisfaction and delight in respect to the spot he had just examined.

We all returned to Mount Vernon together. The Bishop came with me to my house to tea, and from the circumstance of my wife being a near relative of Mr. Hogg—the owner of the land where the site had been selected—the conversation turned very much upon the hope of making that the permanent location, and the probability of obtaining the land at a price within the means of the young institution and its then limited endowment. When he left my house, Bishop Chase expressed to me his intention to visit Mr. Hogg at an early day, with a view of securing a contract for the purchase of the land. And he took with him a letter from me to that gentleman strongly recommending the objects of the Bishop's proposed visit.

CHAPTER V

THE KNOX COUNTY LAND PURCHASED

AT the time when Bishop Chase decided to purchase the land in Knox County he was without money. The English funds had not yet been transferred to America, and no money had been given here. Nevertheless, he had the courage to negotiate for the purchase of the tract that had so charmed him. From the moment when he first climbed the hill and looked about him, and said, "This will do," his mind was made up that here, and nowhere else, should his school be planted. Here was an ample, beautiful, "domain," with a rich soil, pastures for flocks and herds innumerable, inexhaustible springs and streams of clear water, the best of building stone and of timber, limestones in the creek for mortar, coal in the hills, mill sites here and there. And the place was remote, walled about with forests impenetrable to vice, and yet it was very accessible, too. It was almost in the center of Ohio; through Mount Vernon, but five miles away, stages ran "constantly" to Newark, Columbus, Cincinnati, Cleveland, and especially to Sandusky, where steamboats to and from Buffalo "touched constantly." The great National Road and the Ohio Canal, then under construction, would pass within twenty-five or thirty miles of this favored spot. Where else could so many conveniences be found? It was absurd—almost impious—to compare other places to it. Bishop Chase's heart went out to it, as the heart of a lover to his bride.

The price of the eight thousand acres was $24,000, but Mr. Hogg reduced it to $18,000, and on these terms Bishop Chase made a contract with him to purchase them, subject to the action of the diocesan convention. He wished that the members of the convention should see the place before going to the meeting, which was to occur at Columbus on the seventh of June, 1826. He therefore published a "Notice to the Friends of Religion and Learning, Especially to the Members of the Protestant Episcopal Church," dated at Portsmouth, Ohio, March 23, 1826, inviting "all who feel an interest in this important concern," and especially all who were to be members of the approaching convention, to visit the lands on Friday and Saturday, the second and third of June. He added that divine service would be held on the following Sunday, June 4, "either on the proposed lands or in the town of Mount Vernon." Such a service was held on the fourth of June, the Second Sunday after Trinity, probably at the foot of the hill, near the spot where the pumping station now is. The Church papers of the day contained an account of this interesting service.

Sunday, June 4th—at the usual hour of public worship, the people being assembled from different towns, the services of the Church were performed under the spreading trees of the forest, whose valleys were never before made vocal with the prayers and praises of Zion!

It is said that the Bishop preached "to a large and attentive congregation, all seated on the ground." This was, we cannot doubt, the first service of the Episcopal Church, and may, very probably, have been the first Christian service of any sort, ever held on the college lands; and it was held before they were "college lands"—before the convention had authorized their purchase.

The authorization, however, followed within a few days. The convention at Columbus, on the eighth of June, 1826, approved the contract which the Bishop had made, and passed the following resolution:

Resolved, that the Theological Seminary of the Diocese of Ohio and Kenyon College, be, and the same hereby is, forever established on such part of section one, in township six, in range twelve of the United States military land, as may be selected by the trustees of said Seminary and College.

This "section one," known as the South Section, is now College Township, of Knox County; it is two and a half miles square, and contains four thousand acres.

In these proceedings Bishop Chase's Deed of Donation seems to have been forgotten. In that document the Bishop had promised to give his farm at Worthington for the site of his proposed institution, unless the diocesan convention should prefer some other location for the school, and should give, or procure to be given, "a farm equal or superior in value of buildings and conveniences" to that offered by the Bishop. Doubtless it may be said, that in sanctioning the purchase of the Knox County lands the convention manifested a preference for them over the farm at Worthington; but certainly there were no "buildings and conveniences" upon them, and in no sense could it be said that the Convention *gave* these lands, or *procured them to be given*, as the Deed of Donation required. The convention did not give, or procure to be given, one cent of the $18,000 paid for the lands. The English money paid for them.

Bishop Chase's English friends gave their money in order to aid him in establishing his seminary for the education of young men for the ministry, and they never stipulated how it should be used for that end; but certainly it was distinctly specified in the Deed of Donation, in the *Appeal*, and in other documents, that the land and buildings were to be given by Americans—Bishop Chase, or the diocesan convention, or someone else. Thus the English money would be left free to be used for endowments, scholarships, and equipment. Now there was no lack of persons in Ohio willing to give land and buildings for the school. Several towns made offers, and the Bishop's promise of his farm still held good. He said to the convention of 1826, speaking of that promise, "this both myself and family are willing to execute, and carry into full effect," if the contract for the Knox County lands should not be ratified. But his heart was wholly set on those Knox County lands, and upon the great schemes connected with them, of a "domain," and a college; and the convention let him have his way, and left him to get where he could the money to make the purchase. And so it was that England, and not America, gave the land, thus reversing the terms of the Deed of Donation. But this use of the English funds was fully approved by the trustees in London. They saw the Bishop's plans rapidly changing and growing, for he kept them informed by a voluminous correspondence. They had confidence in him, and only wished to help him carry out his "plans of extended usefulness." If those plans took new shapes, they would make no objection, so long as the Bishop, in spending their money, kept in view the main purpose for which it was given.

Bishop Chase was fully aware that in annexing to the theological seminary a college of general learning, open to men who had not the ministry in view, he was departing from the purpose for which his English friends had given their money; and, from the first, he declared that this part of his design was not ultimately to be paid for out of those donations. To the convention of 1826 he said:

It must be noted, that in joining a College to the Seminary, it is an indispensable condition that our funds increase in proportion to the magnitude of the design. To open an institution to the public without an equivalent—I mean an estate or property, equal at least to the fund collected in England, would be as unreasonable as unjust.

This "equivalent," one would suppose, must be secured by obtaining donations in America; but the Bishop had in mind an expedient quite different, for he went on to say:

That this estate—this additional fund worthy of the high destination of our Seminary, might be at your acceptance and disposal in the very act of fixing the site of this interesting institution, has formed a principal feature of my last years's duty. It is presented to you in the proposition of Mr. William Hogg, of Brownsville, to sell us at a reduced price, 8,000 acres of land in Knox Co. on which to fix both the Seminary and College. The sale of one half of this tract, joined with the subscriptions already attained and yet expected, will more than pay for the whole. The remaining 4,000 acres with the Seminary thereon, valuable as it is in *itself*, must and will constitute an equivalent, if not far exceed in value, the whole collections from abroad.

That is to say, the land was to be purchased with the English money, but the North Section was to be sold for more than enough to pay for the whole, so that the purchase money could be replaced, leaving the fund intact, and yet leaving the college in possession of the South Section, of four thousand acres, which would thus cost it nothing. The Bishop was still trusting to a land speculation, and, indeed, not trusting in vain; for the North Section ultimately brought about $22,500 which is not a great deal less than the original $18,000, which was paid for the whole, would have amounted to, had it been lent out on good security.

Bishop Chase foresaw a great, a dazzling, future for the college on the Knox County lands. In a letter to his nephew, the Reverend Intrepid Morse, written in April, 1826, he speaks of it as bidding fair to "polish the minds and manners & save the souls of thousands, perhaps millions." Writing to him again a few weeks later, he says:

If we can obtain it [the Knox County land] there is a broad basis on which to build the superstructure of a great extensive and useful College, and with it promote the interests more effectually of our theological department. It will lift up its head to the admiration of the Christian world. Thousands will give it aid and ten thousands will pray for its success. The living will exert themselves in its favor, and the departing saints will bequeath to it their substance.

FINANCIAL NOTE

HISTORY OF THE ENGLISH FUNDS

ON the eleventh of April, 1825, Lord Kenyon wrote to Bishop Chase, "We have about £6000 for you." That seems to have been the limit of the contributions, for at about that time a period of considerable financial distress began in England, and there was little money to give. The money was in the hands of the English trustees of the fund, Lords Gambier and Kenyon, Doctor Gaskin, and Mr. Henry Hoare. Mr. Wiggin, who had removed to London and opened a bank there, was their financial agent.

The money was to be paid over whenever Bishop Chase should transfer his farm to the board of trustees of the seminary, or when the convention should give, or procure to be given a farm of equal value; and of the due performance of this Henry Clay was to be judge. The delay in settling this matter proved fortunate. On July 14, 1825, Mr. Wiggin wrote to Bishop Chase: "The money was invested in Consols which are about 4 per cent lower than they were and less than cost. I fully expect that they will get up again in less than 6 months, & therefore think it best for you to postpone drawing for the fund till the beginning of next year, if you can get along without doing so."

On March 6, 1826, Bishop Chase entered into his agreement with Mr. Hogg for the purchase of the Knox County lands, on the following terms of payment: "Twenty two hundred and fifty dollars [to] be paid in hand, by way of a draft on R. M. Whitney of Philadelphia," and the remainder of the $18,000 to be paid in three annual installments of $4,000 each, with interest, and a final payment of $3,750 in June, 1830." The agreement bears Mr. Hogg's endorsement that the $2,250 "in hand" had been paid March 7, 1826. How Bishop Chase managed this payment is made plain in a letter from Mr. Wiggin to him, dated August 14, 1826. "It is inconvenient for me to lay [?] out of the $2250 which you took for Mr. Whitney, but I must try to do without it till you draw for the fund, when I expect to be reimbursed. Lord Gambier tried to raise the sum by subscription, but did not succeed."

The English trustees must have bestirred themselves, for already on the sixteenth of April, 1826, Lord Kenyon had informed Bishop Chase that two thousand pounds would be at his disposal for the purchase of lands. Accordingly, on the ninth of June the board of trustees of the seminary appointed Bishop Chase, Henry Clay, and Bezaleel Wells "a committee with full authority to cause to be made a transfer of the funds," and authorized them to reinvest in American stocks. In October the Bishop wrote to Mr. Wiggin, "I intend to go to Washington to see Mr. Clay and consult about the transfer of the fund." In March, 1827, Mr. Wiggin wrote: "The value of £3500 Sterling will be placed in the United States Bank at Philadelphia, before this reaches you. I gave instruction to this effect on receipt of your former letter requesting me to do so. I also purchased some shares in the United States Bank, which I have sent to Messrs Prime, Ward, King and Company to be transferred to the Committee as soon as I am able to state the number that the fund will pay for." This enabled Bishop Chase to complete the payment for the land. In November, 1827, Lord Kenyon wrote to him, "How delighted I am that you have actually paid for your 8000 Acres." The following February the Bishop wrote to his wife from Washington: "I went into Mr. Clay's and transacted the business of investing the remainder of the English fund, which is $7100 and odd dollars. We have authorized Mr. Biddle to use his discretion to invest it in any of the U. S. Bank Stock."

The information is not at hand to show just how much money came from England, and what was done with all that came. Mr. Hogg was paid $18,000 and some interest. Whether there was any discount for the prepayment of the later installments is not known. Bishop Chase was reimbursed out of this fund to the extent of one thousand dollars for his expenditures in going to England. A balance of more than seven thousand was invested in United States bank stock. That accounts for over $26,000. At any rate, the Knox County land was paid for, and there was more than seven thousand dollars left.

CHAPTER VI

THE BEGINNING OF GAMBIER

THE village of Gambier, in Knox County, Ohio, is situated very nearly in latitude 40° 23′ North, and longitude 82° 24′ West. The greater part of it lies upon a promontory—the Hill—of which the boundaries east, south, and west, are, respectively, the valleys of Ransom's Run, the Kokosing River, and Wolf Run, while the northern limit, determined by drainage, lies beyond the Coshocton Road.

Previous to its sale to Kenyon College this region had attracted many "squatters," who, some without any legal right, and some as tenants at will, made their home here. As early as 1812 much of the rich bottom land was under cultivation, with corn almost the only crop. Somewhat below the place where the present mill stands was a little log mill, and beside it a distillery. This was the social center of the neighborhood, and here the men and boys gathered to drink whiskey, race horses, and engage in shooting matches. After a time a larger distillery was built, not far from Ransom's Run, beside the spring on the grounds now owned by Charles Benedict. "Times are altered," said one grateful inhabitant to another, "we have whiskey now as fast as we can drink it." It was said that "every path which led through the bushes pointed as directly towards this distillery as the spokes of a wheel to the hub."

It was not, therefore, into an uninhabited region that Bishop Chase came when he began the work of laying out Gambier and erecting buildings for Kenyon College; and this was fortunate, for, from the first, he was able to get unskilled laborers near at hand. On the ninth of June, 1826, the board of trustees, meeting at Worthington, authorized him to have the land surveyed, sell such parts as were not needed, make whatever improvements he might deem necessary, superintend the laborers, and "perform such other duties as may be directed by the President"—himself—"or the Board of Trustees." Thus the entire development of the lands was left in his hands and to his judgment. Furthermore, the board authorized him to obtain a loan "to enable him to commence the necessary improvements." In his *Reminiscences* he comments with sarcasm upon this authorization to obtain a loan. He found that men would not lend to the college, but would lend to him. "He therefore was driven to rely on his own credit, and get on in his own way."

A few days later Bishop Chase went to take possession of the land, accompanied by his son Dudley, a lad of nine years, and Mr. Archibald Douglas, a man of character and of excellent practical abilities, who had for some time been in his employ at Worthington. This little group of pioneers climbed up the southern side of the promontory. Dudley Chase, writing long after, said:

There met our view a plain of a mile or more, devoid of standing trees but a perfect wilderness of fallen ones, the result of some windstorm which had formerly passed over it, but the undergrowth had so interlaced itself with the fallen timber that it was impossible to move a rod without cutting a path.

On the south end or promontory of this hill [said Bishop Chase, in his *Reminiscences*] (near to which, below, ran the road used by the first settlers) grew some tall oak trees, which evidently had escaped the hurricanes in days of yore. Under the shelter of these, some boards in a light wagon were taken nearly to the top of the hill; there they were dropped, and it was with these the writer's house was built, after the brush was with great difficulty cleared away. Two crotched sticks were driven in to the ground, and on them a transverse pole was placed, and on this pole were placed the boards, inclining to the ground each way. The ends, or gables, to this room, or roof shelter, were but slightly closed by some clap-boards rived on the spot from a fallen tree. The beds to sleep on were thrown on bundles of straw, kept up from the damp ground by a kind of temporary platform, resting on stakes driven deeply into the earth. This was the first habitation on Gambier Hill, and it stood very nearly on the site where now rises the noble edifice of Kenyon College.

On the thirtieth of June the Bishop wrote a letter to his wife, dating it, "Gambier Hill site of Kenyon College."

It will give you great pleasure [he wrote] to be informed that Mr. Douglass, Dudley and myself have enjoyed perfect health since we came hither. As to our progress, we can say nothing but good things —though our hands are so few & everything is in such rude state as to exhibit little besides the incipient footsteps of the Lion-like work we have now undertaken. The Well, you know, was the first thing to be attended to. As soon, therefore, as we could get the *thick bushes* so far cleared away as to enable us to *see* the light of Heaven above and the face of the ground beneath, the men were ordered to begin the herculean task of sinking a well, & finding water on this lofty ground.

What he was undertaking to do, although he did not know it, was to dig down through one hundred and fifty feet or more of rock and reach the gravel bed which now supplies Gambier with pure water. A pump was to raise the water to the surface, and "herculean" indeed must have been the strength of any arm that could operate it. By intermittent work, extended through several years, assisted by a giant auger driven by horsepower, a depth of one hundred and ten feet was finally reached. The work was never carried farther. The hole was filled with stones, and with many timbers, which, as they have decayed in the course of years, have again and again caused a slight depression in the Path a few rods north of the middle door of Old Kenyon.

The Bishop's letter to his wife continued:

If you ask how I get on *without money*, I answer that the Lord helps me. What do you think of his mercy in sending me good Mr. Davis, with a half cheese from his mother, and $25 from his father presented to me out of pure regard to the great & good work which God enables me thus to carry on. Mr. Norton too has sent me some hands (3) for a short time, James Melick came one day, and old Mr. Elliott another. We have built us a tent-cabin, and if we had anyone to cook for us we should live. It is impossible to make the hands find themselves; we must find provision ourselves, or have none to help us. . . . Judge Holmes has been here for 3 days, and is now engaged in surveying the north Section. The streets & roads on this the south section have been laid out as far as can be till *We find Water*.

Water was found, not long after this, in the comparatively shallow well, the opening of which can still be seen a few rods north of the college gates—one of the most venerable monuments on the Hill, and a valuable point of reference in determining the situation of historical spots. This had important consequences, for it undoubtedly fixed the location of Wiggin Street, in the middle of which it is—the proper place for a town well, or pump. It also drew to its neighborhood the large group of temporary buildings which the Bishop soon erected.

The letter closes:

I write by a poor dim hogs lard lamp, which, shining askance on my paper, will hardly permit me to say how faithfully I am your affectionate Husband

P. CHASE.

The work went on through the summer, clearing away the thick bushes, getting out stone from small quarries here and there along the sides of the hill, or elsewhere on the "domain," perhaps excavating for the basement of the middle part of the college building, and making what preparations could be made to carry on the great work with energy as soon as money could be obtained. During this period of hard and discouraging labor, the Bishop found comfort and good cheer in holding a Sunday school, and a church service, every Sunday. Dudley Chase, referring to the spot where the Prayer Cross stands, says:

Having redeemed a limited area out of the wilderness of fallen trees and tangled under and upper growth of young trees, he offered at this spot the sacrifice of prayer and praise according to the Service of the Protestant Episcopal Church and thus began his work for God by calling on his name under the canopy of Heaven. These hills and vales had never heard the sound of the Church going bell but word had been circulated round about the log cabins in the woods, and the children with bare feet & shocks of hair bleached in the sun came through the bye paths, doubtless curious to see and hear something new. A few mothers with babes ventured to come. The first hour was given to a Sunday School of the first comers—then the Bishop's portly form appeared robed in his capacious cassock and began Morning Prayer. . . . A few boards made seats for the front rows, and split rails for the rear. The natives were used to such things and the working men did not mind it.

This was the first Church service on the Hill—though not the first on the college lands—and similar services and Sunday school instructions were continued until the Bishop went east in the fall. In 1827 he organized a parish at Gambier, and called it Harcourt Parish, after Sir Harcourt Lees, an Irish controversial preacher who had contributed to the funds of the institution, and was helping still further to increase them.

In September, 1826, Bishop Chase left Gambier, to attend the General Convention, and to seek financial aid for his great work.

CHAPTER VII

MONEY IS SECURED, AND THE WORK GOES ON RAPIDLY

BISHOP CHASE was suffering severely from swelled and inflamed feet and ankles when he set out for the East. He stopped at Oneida Castle, and tried to induce the Indian chiefs to send some of their boys to the school at Worthington. He visited relatives in New England, and then hastened to Philadelphia, where the General Convention met in November. He found little to cheer him at this convention. He was lame, and in much pain; he received from his brother bishops small sympathy in his effort to build up a seminary and college in the West; he felt that he had no friends. But a friend was raised up in the Reverend Benjamin Allen of Philadelphia, who took him into his own house, kept him there for several weeks, and cared for him. This was not lost time, for, apart from the fact that he was recovering his health, he had many callers, and made many friends for his cause; and with the aid of Mr. Allen and the Reverend Gregory Townsend Bedell, the father of a future Bishop of Ohio, he prepared a small pamphlet, *A Plea for the West*. To this were appended some "Remarks," written by the friendly clergymen, who had become his zealous advocates. They told of what had been done in England.

It would be disgraceful to our country [they said] if, with the example of British benevolence before us to so great an amount as that of $30,000, we should permit this noble design to be paralyzed, for want of sufficient liberality among ourselves to raise the sum of ten thousand dollars, which would bring the whole into immediate and successful operation.

From this time the skies brightened. New friends appeared, and money was subscribed in considerable sums. From Philadelphia Bishop Chase went to New York, where he found himself, as he thought, "under a cloud of prejudice truly appalling." There he printed an *Appeal in behalf of Religion and Learning in Ohio*. He drew a dark picture of the future of the state if schools and colleges were not soon planted, and Christian ministers and schoolmasters sent forth to counteract the increasing illiteracy and immorality. He told of the institution he had founded, and of the generosity of English Churchmen. The funds collected in England had, in great measure, been pledged to pay for the land in Knox County, and now there was the "imperious necessity of obtaining the means to erect the requisite buildings." New Yorkers responded generously to his plea, so that when he departed for New England he felt that he had abundant cause for gratitude. He visited Boston and many other towns of eastern New England, and in each place circulated his pamphlets, made calls, preached sermons, and delivered addresses, as he had opportunity. His reception in New England was hardly less cordial than that which he had experienced in England. In Boston he conducted a campaign that anticipated many of the methods of modern publicity experts and directors of "drives." In Newburyport, Portland, and Gardiner, and some other towns, ladies formed themselves into "Kenyon Circles of Industry," to promote the cause. These seem to have been specialized forms of the familiar sewing society, and they must have sewed diligently, for they were able to send Bishop Chase several hundred dollars. In all, the amount of money secured in the eastern cities during this visit, was about ten thousand dollars.

Meanwhile, Bishop Chase's thoughts were constantly upon the great work that was to be done on Gambier Hill when he returned. He had left a Mr. Warner Terry in charge there, and the following letter will show better than anything else the mind of the Bishop at that time, and his thoughts and plans for the college:

New York 5 Mar., 1827.

To Mr. Warner Terry.

Dear Sir:

The present amount of subscriptions is now about $6,000: It is my intention to proceed on in the course of this week to Boston; thence to return by the way of this place Phila & Baltimore and Washington to Ohio. So long is this journey and in it I have so many things to do that it would not be surprising if I did not get on to the College Ground before the first of May!—Better come thus late & come *full handed* than to hasten on to the spot with my pockets empty. I trust in God, that, before I see you the sum subscribed will have been swelled to $10,000. Hitherto hath the Lord helped most miraculously.—The hearts of men have been opened and they have of their abundance had grace to give most liberally.—Would that God would give *us* grace duly to appreciate the mercies which he is bestowing on us, that our gratitude could in some degree keep pace with his goodness. I hope Dear Mr. Terry *you* think of these things and in the bosom of your dear family look up to the Author of your life and the Giver of all Good things *night*, *noon*, and *morning* for a *blessing* through Jesus Christ our Lord. Do give my love to your wife & beg her from me to read her bible & pray fervently. Remember that you & she are the only persons now on that ground which is destined to be (as is the prayer of thousands & tens of thousands) the seat of *piety* and learning: that if you do not worship God in sincerity and truth you bring a stain on the first page of our history. May God awaken the minds of you both to a due sense of your duty towards God your Maker Redeemer and Sanctifier. That you will do your duty towards the Institution, whose steward you are, I have no doubt. God will give you grace to make a conscience of your ways and to do by us as you will wish you had done when you come to die.

As to the matter of making preparations for the great work which is to go on in building this coming summer, What presses most anxiously on my mind is the *deficiency* in *lime*. You say you have 400 Bushels. What is this quantity in building the College center 100 feet by 44,—a Professor's house, and a Chapel? I tremble at the thought of this incompetency! What can be done? I see no other way than to watch the first fall of the River and seize on the first lime stone that make their appearance from under the water. How immense is the damage which those wicked men did us in stealing the lime stone last summer! What has been done with them? The sooner such men are removed from the premises the better.

Go on making preparations to the utmost of your power. If you can buy good clean stuff of Cherry boards and oak Plank for fifty cents per 100 do it to any extent & keep the teams a halling: and when you have a good quantity build a kiln to season them with hot air; don't risk the contact of the blaze.

Should your quarry of stone prove equal to your expectation get good hands and set them at work: don't fear that you'll have too many on the spot. In short I rely on your exertions—I rely on your choice of good men, for help in this great business. Discountenance all profanity and intemperance. Should these prevail when I come it would grieve me to the heart and I should be inclined to stop the work at once and get others.

Don't be discouraged at my absence. If I am a month or two later remember I come stronger when I do come, & thro' mercy am enabled to get on the faster.

May God be with you & bless you in all your works. This is the constant prayer of

Your faithful friend
PHI'R CHASE

Mr. Warner Terry
Gambier
Site of Kenyon College
Knox County Ohio.

While Bishop Chase was in Philadelphia, confined to his bed by his lameness, his thoughts had turned much upon the impropriety of studying the writings of heathen authors in a Christian school, unless they "should have been rendered subservient to the truths of the gospel." He would not, indeed, "extinguish the lamps of Heathen literature," but he would "outshine them by the splendour of the *Sun of Righteousness*." To effect this end at Kenyon College he could think of no man so well suited as the Reverend Thomas Hartwell Horne of London, the distinguished biblical scholar, whose work on the *Introduction to the Critical Study and Knowledge of the Holy Scriptures* was accepted everywhere in England and America as a standard authority upon its subject. It was he who had written that article in the *British Critic*, which, copied into the *Philadelphia Recorder*, had led Bishop Chase to make his visit to England. The Bishop felt that he must have Doctor Horne at Kenyon College, and he wrote to Lord Kenyon on the subject. Lord Kenyon consulted Mr. G. W. Marriott, who in turn consulted the Bishop of London. These scholarly English gentlemen could not have sympathized with Bishop Chase in his objection to the study of the Latin and Greek authors; but Lord Kenyon simply replied that they were all agreed that Doctor Horne "could be no teacher," and that he could not be induced to leave England and go to Ohio. So the heathen authors have ever remained in Kenyon College, but "rendered subservient," we may hope, "to the truths of the gospel."

Bishop Chase was back in Gambier just in time for the laying of the cornerstone of Kenyon College, on the ninth of June, 1827. The convention of the diocese had been in session at Mount Vernon three days before, and many of the clergy and lay delegates remained over for the great event. The students and teachers of the college came up from Worthington, and there was a general turnout of the countryside. Service was held by the river bank, in the shade of a grove of maples, near where the pumping house now is. The Reverend Intrepid Morse preached a sermon from the text:

Let thy work appear unto thy servants, and thy glory unto their children. And let the beauty of the Lord our God be upon us; and establish thou the work of our hands upon us, yea, the work of our hands establish thou it. Ps. 15: 16 f.

At the conclusion of the sermon the assembly moved up the hill in procession; and when all had arrived at the top,

THIS VIEW OF

KENYON COLLEGE,
Ohio.

Is most affectionately inscribed to the Benefactors therein both in England and America, to whom we owe its endowment
Oxford Decbr 1st 1830

KENYON COLLEGE AS ORIGINALLY DESIGNED

the Bishop offered a prayer. Suitable documents were deposited in the stone, and then, after the recital of certain versicles, the Bishop laid it in the name of the Holy Trinity. The one hundred and eighteenth psalm was read responsively, and the exercises closed with a remarkable prayer for the founders of the institution and their children, and for the students who should dwell in the building. This was its conclusion:

Watch over this institution now founded by thy goodness: bless the youth in this and all future generations who here shall receive their education: preserve them from sin, the greatest of all evils, and from the effects of sin, which are thy wrath and eternal death: let thy fatherly hand, we beseech thee, ever be over them: let thy Holy Spirit ever be with them, and so lead them in the obedience and knowledge of thy word, that in the end they may obtain everlasting life.

Bishop Chase tells in noble words of the tide of emotion that swept through his soul as he laid the cornerstone:

The signal mercies of the past, in rescuing me from so many perils and in overcoming so much opposition, and the countless blessings of the future to the Church of Christ in our dear country, of which this institution must, by the laws of Holy Providence, be the means of producing, in ages yet to come, rushed on my mind, and raised (as the swelling flood raises the ship on its bosom) my whole soul in gratitude to God, the Almighty disposer of events, and the fountain of all mercies. Though surrounded by a very great company of spectators to the eventful scene, the whole seemed to me as the wilderness did to Jacob at Bethel—swallowed up in a deep sense of God's presence, filling all things, connecting earth with heaven; and, in prospect of future blessings, prompting the same expressions which he uttered, when, forgetful of all his earthly troubles and rapt into ecstasy divine, he exclaimed, "Surely the Lord is in this place, this is none other than the house of God, and this the gate of heaven."

Work on the building was pushed as rapidly as possible. A force of masons, stonecutters, carpenters, and other mechanics, was gathered, and unskilled labor was supplied from the vicinage. At that time Ohio flowed with whiskey from innumerable distilleries, and it was almost universally drunk by the inhabitants. The proclivities in this direction of the people who lived near Gambier have already been told of; but Bishop Chase was determined that there should be no whiskey in Gambier. Accordingly, when he first began work on the Hill he issued a notice that the use of liquor was totally prohibited there. This was received with dismay and indignation by the "hands." The Bishop says that they thought "he did not sufficiently understand human nature, and had not appreciated the liberties of his country." They presented to him a petition, asking that they might each have a small glass of liquor three times a day, basing their request upon the common custom of the country, the heat of the sun which they had to endure, and the lack of a constant supply of water. The Bishop sat down with them, and, as he said,

told them his own history, and in so doing, gained their sympathy and enlisted their affections in his behalf. Many of them were in tears, and all arose and went to work without a drop of whiskey.

A great amount of timber was required in building Old Kenyon and the other structures which the Bishop erected. The College has still in its possession the carefully kept "Log Book" in which he recorded the number of logs cut, and the amount of lumber obtained from them. It is an interesting sample of his painstaking, if not very scientific, accountancy. At first a saw pit was in use for getting out the timbers, but this process was too slow and expensive. There was a sawmill on Big Run, where until recently the Hereford Mill stood; but the owner charged what seemed an excessive rate, and the Bishop promptly resolved to have a sawmill of his own. As he forded the river, riding homeward, he selected the place for the dam, and for the intake of the raceway that must extend across the river's great bow. By the end of September the dam was almost finished, but the raceway, nearly one hundred rods long, had been excavated to but a little depth. Then came one of those downpours of rain, continued for several days, which, from time to time, flood all the lowlands to the east and west of Gambier Hill. The Bishop looked forth over the waters, despair in his heart, for he thought that the dam must have been destroyed, and all his labors lost. But when the flood subsided, there was his dam, standing firm, and the water, following the slightly excavated trench, had dug out the raceway for him, and saved him many dollars. Thenceforth the opinion spread among the people of the region that "God was Bishop Chase's friend." A sawmill and a gristmill were soon erected and in operation. "If we had not been blessed with these," said the Bishop, "the College never could have succeeded." The total cost of dam, race, and mills was less than four thousand dollars.

A busy place was Gambier Hill during the years 1827 and 1828. Bishop Chase was making every exertion to prepare quarters for the school, so that it might soon move up from Worthington. Building was going on actively in two places; at the end of the Hill, and a quarter of a mile north, at Wiggin Street, near the well. There must have been a considerable number of quarrymen, stonecutters, and masons at work, for rapid progress was made in building the walls of the college, enormously thick as they were, and near by a small stone dwelling was building, for a professor's house. Other structures, of a temporary character, were put up in this quarter, for the accommodation of the workmen. West of the well, along Wiggin Street, four frame or plank houses were erected, for the use of the students; and beyond them was a hotel, with a barn, coach house, and shops near it. Rudely built stables and granaries, and other buildings connected with the farming and stock raising operations, were scattered about on the lots northeast of the well, and across Wiggin Street from them were the Bishop's log cabin, another cabin, a refectory for the college—to be used also as a schoolhouse and a chapel—and a kitchen. All these buildings, except the two of stone, were hastily and roughly constructed, and as inexpensively as possible, since they were designed to serve but a temporary use—though some of them are in use still; yet they consumed about half of the $10,000 that the Bishop had spent so much time collecting in the East, and they cost the labor of many men. It was an expensive thing to build a college in the wilderness, and people who were opposed to the Bishop's policy did not fail to comment on the waste of money.

When he was in Gambier, Bishop Chase took the active oversight of the whole work. His forces were well organized. Over each department of labor there was a head man. Every evening, says the Bishop,

the clerk appeared with his book, the head carpenter, the head mason, the head teamster, and the head quarrier appeared also, and gave in the work of all who had respectively been under their care that day, and the same was respectively recorded.

The assisting hand of God was evident at every crisis of the work. A large force of men had to be lodged and fed, and the Bishop was faced with a thousand difficulties of housekeeping. On one occasion a number of beds must be supplied.

What could be done? [asked the Bishop, writing to his wife.] God helped me; as I told you I went with the wagon, I don't know how many times, to Mount Vernon, for a new set, and an additional quantity of kitchen and table furniture, and our wants, however numerous, were after a sort supplied. . . . The stone began to fail in quantity on the spot, and no teams could be had but at an enormous expense (knowing I was in great want) to draw them. What could be done and whither could I turn? God opened a door, and through it sent me twelve pair of fine oxen at a very reasonable price.

Domestic help was hard to get.

What could be done!—God helped me: and that always answers for everything else. Two young women came to me from Perry township just in the nick of time.

CHAPTER VIII

APPLICATION TO CONGRESS FOR A SUBSIDY

THE money collected by Bishop Chase in the eastern cities was soon gone. He must have more; and under the pressure of this necessity he took up the project he had long entertained of petitioning Congress to make a donation to the seminary of "wild and unappropriated Lands" to the extent of a township, or 20,000 acres. This he could sell, perhaps, for $40,000, or more. The other colleges in Ohio, at Oxford and at Athens, had received such gifts; why should not Kenyon College be treated with the same generosity? The Bishop knew that he must bring strong influence to bear if he would move Congress to such action, and he therefore sought the aid of the legislature of Ohio, and the Ohio congressmen. To the legislature he presented an address, which bore the date of December 27, 1827. He based his appeal upon the imperative need of schools of higher education in the West. He declared that illiteracy was rapidly increasing among the children of Ohio, outside the cities.

Unless something more be done than has been done for the general diffusion of learning, a *cloud of moral darkness* will soon spread over our community, which nothing short of a miracle will dispel.

The legislature, he said, had made wise provisions for the establishment of public schools, but these had, in great measure, proved fruitless, because so few duly qualified schoolmasters could be found. Ten times as many were needed as the state could then supply. They could not be obtained from the eastern states.

Let us educate these teachers ourselves [he said]. Let us draw from our own soil the moral seed, by which the Western country is to be supplied with the fruits of learning. . . . The best, yea, the only estimable School Teachers, are those who come to their employment with minds uninflated with the vanities which riches seldom fail to inspire. They are taken from the middle and more industrious walks of life. . . . Place the means of educating your School Teachers within the reach of such as these, and the benefit of rearing up Teachers in abundance, to fill your schools, will soon be apparent.

Kenyon College, now commended to your patronage *to this end* is worthy of your regard. Having the good of our country in view in the education of youth, its expenses are reduced beyond all former example, and its government is kept free from every tendency to a sectarian spirit. . . . Never, never since we became a people, have party spirit and sectarian views been laid aside more thoroughly, than in the plans and contributions for Kenyon College. . . . Throughout the Protestant world it has its hundreds, and I might say its thousands, of every denomination, at this time, offering up prayers for its success. The best friends of America, in foreign lands, and the most pious of her citizens at home, would, if they were now present, add theirs to my humble solicitations, that the great objects of Kenyon College fail not for want of *public* and national patronage. . . . Grant us what has been granted to other Colleges, and we pledge ourselves to fill our professorships with good and learned men, and to extend the wings of our Institution so as to shelter thousands, and annually to send forth hundreds of well educated youth, to instruct and ornament the rising generations of our country.

The address went on to beg the legislature to frame a memorial to Congress urging the claims of the College to a liberal donation of land, and to instruct "the Ohio Delegation to urge it on the floor of Congress."

The legislature was moved by this appeal. Ex-governor Morrow drew up a resolution which passed both houses with hardly a dissenting vote.

Resolved, That this General Assembly approve of the object of the application of the Reverend Philander Chase to the Congress of the United States, for a donation of a tract or tracts of land for the support of Kenyon College: And that the Senators and Representatives of this State in the Congress of the United States, be requested to use their exertions in aid and support of the said application.

Armed with this endorsement, Bishop Chase proceeded at

once to Washington, where he arrived on the second day of February, 1828; and there he remained for sixteen anxious weeks, endeavoring to get a bill through Congress, granting the township of land. He had the great advantage that his brother, Dudley Chase, was a member of the Senate, representing the State of Vermont. Senator Chase was untiring in his exertions in behalf of the bill, and succeeded in carrying it through the Senate. The Ohio senators, Benjamin Ruggles and William Henry Harrison, made strong speeches for it, as did Senator Kane of Illinois and Senator Chambers of Maryland. Probably the most influential argument was that of Senator Benton of Missouri, who declared that the Federal Government, owning all the vacant soil in Ohio, was "an absentee landlord in the worst sense of the word," paying no taxes and bearing no share of the public burdens: it was, therefore, morally bound to contribute to the improvement of that state, and to give the land for which the legislature asked. The House of Representatives was much occupied with business, and found no time to consider the bill. Week after week Bishop Chase waited, bringing to bear what influence he could. He wrote letters to members of the House, in which he gave loose rein to his rhetorical propensities, speaking of Kenyon College as the "child of the necessities of the Western world; born in affliction and nurtured in tears; . . . the darling of thousands in the present, and the hope of millions yet to come; . . . destined, it is believed, to preserve untold multitudes of our Western people from returning to pagan darkness." He said, "It occupies the whole heart of the writer," and so it did; but the hearts of most of the congressmen were occupied by other things, and on the twenty-fourth of May consideration of the bill was deferred until the next year.

To the Bishop this was a most grievous disappointment, for he saw in this postponement the defeat of his great hope, the only hope that had in it the promise of large financial

aid. And yet, he was not crushed; he turned to other resources. He drew up and printed a pamphlet, *The Star in
the West, or Kenyon College, in the Year of Our Lord*,
1828. "The anguish of disappointed hope, is the cause of the
following publication," it began. He told of his appeals to
the Ohio legislature and to Congress, and their "sad event."

Great will be the embarrassments which it will occasion. **THE
DELAYS AND DISCOURAGEMENTS; THE DISMISSION
OF HANDS, OF LABOURERS AND MECHANICS, THE
CURTAILING OF MANY PLANS SET ON FOOT TO BRING
THE COLLEGE INTO IMMEDIATE AND EXTENSIVE
OPERATION,** all of which must of necessity follow from this disappointment, produce a deep state of mental depression: from which
there is no escape with life but in **RENEWED EFFORT.** . . .
Who is not a friend to an institution which brings useful knowledge
so effectually and extensively within the reach of the poor, as none
other institution has heretofore done? Never before on any other
plan have the expenses of a public education been brought within the
compass of $70. Never before has the light of science beamed thus
on the cottages of the poor.
Who would not give to expedite the completion of a college erected
in the woods, at great personal sacrifices, and for such benevolent
purposes?
A SMALL SUM ONLY *is asked of* every friend of every name
and class. . . . Whoever reads this is, therefore, most respectfully
and earnestly entreated *immediately* to enclose **ONE DOLLAR,** in
aid of the present struggles of Kenyon College, in a letter addressed
to, **P. CHASE, P.M. GAMBIER, KNOX CO. OHIO, OR P.
CHASE, P.M. CARE OF LEONARD KIP, ESQ., NEW YORK
CITY.**

In conclusion he begged all who ever knew him—his relatives, his former pupils, those to whom he had in many places
ministered, his friends, and even his enemies—to "give
something, *even a trifle*, to this his last attempt at public
charity."
Having regard to the number of persons that responded
to it, this appeal proved one of the most successful that

Bishop Chase ever put forth. Letters poured into the Gambier post office, most of them bringing small sums of money, the offerings of the poor, but some of them with larger amounts; so with this, and what he could borrow, the Bishop was able to keep the work going. "Like Elijah in the wilderness," he said, "all my daily wants have been supplied by the hand of mercy."

With the Bishop's return a period of great activity began on Gambier Hill, for the school was to be brought up from Worthington that summer, and all must be made ready for its reception. Old Kenyon must be got under roof before winter, if possible.

To accomplish this most desirable of all efforts [said Bishop Chase in his address to the convention of 1828] we have concentrated all our forces, and put forth every effort. The day has seldom dawned, but it has found our numerous labourers and mechanics at their posts; our mills have run both night and day, and our long train of teams of more than fifty cattle and horses, have never ceased their strenuous exertions in bringing to our lofty Hill both stone and timber. . . . For the accommodation of our students at their removal from Worthington hither, we have, (besides several dwellings for our numerous workhands,) erected four houses, two stories high, thirty six feet in length, by twenty two in width. The comfort they have afforded, and the means they have proved of concentrating our endeavours and cherishing a small number of students with whom to commence our great and extensive college, fully justifies the expense laid out upon them.

The expense was $626 each, which was not very heavy, considering that these buildings are still standing, some on their original spots, and some elsewhere, and have served many good purposes now for nearly a century; but the "comfort" they afforded was greater in the estimation of the Bishop than in that of their first occupants.

CHAPTER IX

THE FIRST YEARS OF THE COLLEGE
AT GAMBIER

THE school moved up from Worthington in June, 1828, and quartered itself for more than a year in the temporary buildings on Wiggin Street. It was a very uncomfortable winter those boys spent in the thin-walled, unplastered houses, and they may have reflected that the "unexampled cheapness" of their education was not without its drawbacks. Heman Dyer, who came to Kenyon College in April, 1829, tells us that, upon his arrival, Professor Sparrow accompanied him to one of those houses. As they approached it, they

saw a pair of feet and legs sticking out some distance through a crack in the boards. On reaching this room we found the legs belonged to a young man by the name of Weatherby, who was lying on the floor studying his lesson. Dr. Sparrow asked him what he was lying in that position for? He answered, "I am trying to get my feet warm in the sun."

Mr. Dyer was given a room in which there was no furniture. He was resourceful, and made two "horses" and laid on them a "green oak slab, fresh from the sawmill." This slab, which had the property of warping into many incalculable curves, was his bed for six weeks. Then he was given a better bed. In time he acquired also a chair, a stove, a tin washbasin, a pitcher, and a cup. This was probably the standard equipment.

In these houses there were some schoolrooms and classrooms, in which the work of the college and grammar school went on. East of where the gates now are was the plank building which provided a dining-room, and close by was the kitchen. Over this department, as over all the domestic concerns of the institution, Mrs. Chase presided in a competent and kindly way. This dining-room was also the chapel, and the place for all the larger gatherings. A few feet south of it were the two rough log cabins in which Bishop Chase and Mr. Sparrow lived. On the spot where is now the Commons building was the college store, a log house with a frame addition, in which was a stock of goods, imported from Philadelphia, in the variety of which as listed in an early inventory, appear to have been all the necessaries of life, and some of its vanities.

On the ninth of September, 1829, the diocesan convention met at Gambier, in the great room on the south side of the college basement. It was with justifiable pride that Bishop Chase was able to speak of what had been done, and exhibit it.

One hundred and ten feet of a College as you see this to be, four stories high, forty-four feet wide, of massive stone, surmounted with a roof and steeple 75 feet high, for strength and beauty seldom equalled, has been completed. . . . Take the printed account of our expenditures in your hand, and go from this the basement story of our building, through all the intermediate strong and well finished rooms and passages till your eye meets the roof, with its massive and thickly clustering timbers and its well supported and lofty steeple, and then judge if half the usual cost be noticed. What reason this for congratulation, that we gave not our building to contractors greedy of money however unconsecrated by the hand of charity.

Already the college had begun to send forth its graduates.

Our number of students [he continued] is now nearly ninety, six of whom this commencement receive their degrees of A.B. besides several, who in the intermediate time have been qualified as teachers, now so much wanted in our common schools. When I reflect on the facts of which I am now speaking, and compare the present state of things with the past, the language of amazement becomes involuntary. What hath God done! Who but He hath wrought this mighty work!

On the afternoon of the same day occurred the first com-

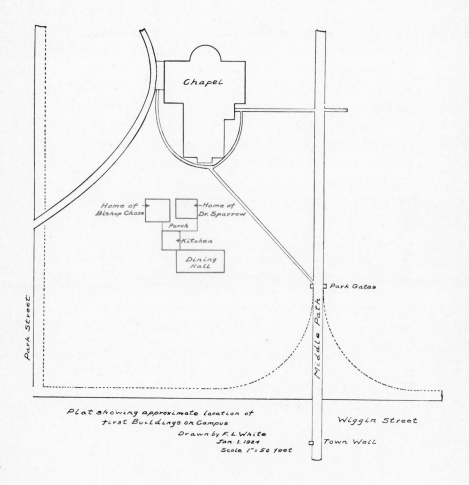

Chapel

Home of →
Bishop Chase

← Home of
Dr. Sparrow

Porch

← Kitchen

Dining
Hall

□ Park Gates

Park Street

Middle Path

Plat showing approximate location of
first Buildings on Campus

Drawn by F. L. White
Jan. 1, 1924
Scale 1" = 50 feet

Wiggin Street

□ Town Well

WHERE GAMBIER BEGAN

mencement of Kenyon College. The exercises took place in the same room in which the convention had met that morning. This is the programme:

College Commencement.

Procession

1. Musick.
2. Prayer.
3. Historical Sketch.—The Sacred Theban Band.   G. Denison
4. Dissertation.—The Origin of Language.   J. B. Chase
5. Musick.
6. Oration.—Vice the Destruction of Free Government.   A. Blake
7. Oration.—History.   S. Chase
8. Musick.
9. Oration.—Permanency of Republican Institutions. P. C. Freeman
10. Oration.—Impossibility of Universal Atheism.   B. B. Sayre
11. Degrees Conferred.
12. Musick.
13. Benediction by the Bishop.

A correspondent supplied the *Ohio State Journal* with the following account:

Kenyon College. The first commencement at Kenyon College took place on Wednesday the 9th ult.—being the day appointed for the annual meeting of the Convention of the Protestant Episcopal Church for the diocese of Ohio. At 3 o'clock P.M. a procession composed of Students, the members of the Convention, the Trustees of the Theological Seminary, the Professors and the President of the Institution, proceeded to the great Hall of the College which had been prepared for the occasion, where the exercises of the day were conducted.

The presence of the Convention, and a large assemblage of citizens and strangers, together with the edifice in which the ceremony took place, the cornerstone of which had been laid but a little more than two years before, and which by the blessing of Heaven upon the almost unaided exertions of one man, had become a lofty and magnificent structure, rendered the exercises of the day more than usually solemn and impressive.

Soon after this commencement day many of the students —both grammar school and college pupils—were transferred from the frame buildings on Wiggin Street to rooms in the college, and the plank dining-hall was supplanted by the large basement room in Kenyon, for which a stone kitchen was built just in the rear of the college. The Bishop and his family, leaving the log cabin, took up their residence in the basement of the West Division. Henry L. Richards, though of the class of 1838, was a grammar school pupil in 1830. In later life he contributed many interesting reminiscences to the *Gambier Weekly Argus*. He roomed at first in Kenyon. "We slept," he said, "in three-story frame bunks, three in a bunk, one above another, with 'wooden sacking' and loose straw mattresses." It is probable that the building was never wholly finished within, and never made very comfortable, until the presidency of Major Douglass, which began in 1841.

From various sources have come down to us reports of incidents in the life of those early days, from which one gathers that students in that age did not differ greatly from those of later times. There was the same disposition to surround Freshmen with restrictions, the same willingness to administer to them discomforts and molestations. Stories are told of pigs put into their beds, of water poured over them while they were sleeping, of formidable sham faculty meetings which they were compelled to face. Tutors residing in the dormitories, or exercising supervision over the dining-room at mealtime, were subject to grievous annoyance. Unpopular grammar school teachers were made unhappy, and were even driven away. The story is famous, how Edwin M. Stanton stole Bishop Chase's favorite horse, Cincinnatus, out of the stable, and rode him many miles one evening to visit a young lady, and how the wrath of the Bishop was dissipated by the engaging frankness with which the future Secretary of War confessed his crime.

Henry Caswall, who came directly from England to Gambier in 1828 and graduated in theology in 1831, and whose wife was a niece of Bishop Chase, tells us, in his *America and the American Church*, many interesting facts concerning the Kenyon students of those days. The young men, he says, had

imbibed republicanism with their earliest ideas, and were by no means inclined to submit to the bare exercise of power in any shape. Yet they were not a disorderly body. They were largely endowed with that capacity for self-government which is so prominent a feature of the American character. And it was through this channel that the influence of the Bishop or of the Professors, was usually brought to bear upon them. Thus, for example, it was decided that an extensive garden should be formed, partly for ornament, but principally to supply the common table with vegetables. Accordingly a few of the more influential students were called together, and the advantage of forming a "Horticultural Society" was represented to them. The idea proved acceptable; most of the students united in a voluntary association for the professed object; they cleared away the trees and bushes, ploughed up the soil with a powerful team of oxen, laid out paths and beds, and in a very short time a useful and productive garden was added to the establishment. Another association was in like manner formed for the cultivation of Sacred Music, and another for temperance.

Further particulars of this Horticultural Society have come to us from Doctor McElroy, who was a tutor in the college at that time. The broad avenue extending from the well down to the college had been outlined by a low rail fence on either side. This the Horticultural Society removed. They carried the rails from the eastern side and built the western higher, so as to provide a better protection for the young orchard which the Bishop had planted there. Then on the eastern side they built another fence of boards, five feet high, doubtless to protect their garden. Professor Sparrow was the leader in these fencing operations. They also set out some hard maples along the sides of the street, and it is probable that some of them yet remain, venerable evidences of the society's beneficent activity.

From the very first, religion had been the chief concern at Gambier. We have seen how Bishop Chase held a Sunday school and a service every Sunday in the summer of 1826, on the site of the Prayer Cross. Later, services were sometimes held in the blacksmith shop, which afterwards became the college store; then in the old dining-hall, near the well. The great hall in the basement of the college was also used for this purpose. The Bishop was rector of the parish. When he was at Gambier he preached; when he was away one of the professors would take his place. A barrel organ which played a considerable number of hymn tunes had been sent from England, the gift of sundry ladies there; and this for a time rendered a precarious aid to the singing.

Bishop Chase intended that Gambier should be a center from which religious light should stream into all the region about; and such it was in his days, and long after. With his encouragement and participation a Bible Society was formed, and in vacation time students rode all over the county, but especially over the eastern half, distributing Bibles and tracts, and depending for lodgings and meals upon the never-failing hospitality of the log cabins. Very notable work was done by the students in maintaining Sunday schools in the villages and woods. At one time as many as seventeen of these schools were regularly held, at distances of from two to twelve or more miles from Gambier. Mrs. Chase supplied the young missionaries with an early breakfast, and they tramped off, singly or in pairs, through the woods; or those who went to the farthest stations rode horseback. The Bishop exercised as close a supervision over this work as he was able, and some of the professors took an active part in it.

The clerical members of the faculty were of the Evangelical party in the Church, which believed in revivals and promoted them. Bishop Chase, as an old-fashioned High Churchman, was rather dubious about these strange means of grace, and did not participate in them; yet he never dis-

couraged them. The students instituted weekly prayer meetings, held on Sunday evenings. An older student would lead
in the General Confession, the Lord's Prayer, and a few
collects, and then, after a hymn, would read a passage of
Scripture, upon which he would deliver a short address.
Then followed hymns and extemporary prayers. Most of the
students attended the meetings, and much good was done.
Religion took hold. Mr. Caswall, who, as a strict Churchman, was not very friendly towards these meetings, confesses
that they exercised a very beneficial influence.

It is certain [he says] that at this period cases of discipline were
rare, that among the younger boys as well as the elder students, bad
language, quarreling and bullying, were almost unknown, and that a
state of public opinion had grown up in the institution, which, though
unhappily not strictly ecclesiastical, was favorable on the whole to
the growth of Christian character.

Mr. Caswall further notices the serviceable kindness of the
students to each other.

If any of their number was afflicted with illness, he was carefully
nursed by his companions, and if he died, it was by them that his body
was laid out, placed in the coffin, carried to the grave, and decently
interred.

A writer who contributed some reminiscences of this time
to the *Western Episcopalian* in 1860, says of these young
men that, notwithstanding the discomforts to which they
were subjected,

A happier, more orderly and industrious class of students, we venture
to say, will not be seen again in Kenyon. To this the example of its
venerated head and founder, ever foremost in self-sacrifice, contributed in no slight degree.

CHAPTER X

LABORS, ANXIETIES, AND TRIBULATIONS

NEVER was there a busier man than Bishop Chase during the years 1828, 1829, and 1830. He carried on a great correspondence, and rose customarily at three o'clock in the morning to write letters. He superintended the extensive farming and dairying operations of the college. In 1830 there were one hundred and twenty-five acres in corn, and one hundred and twenty in wheat, and besides there were fields of rye and oats. Seven hundred acres were fenced with 76,325 rails which the college had caused to be split. There were extensive pastures, sown with timothy and clover, for the feeding of the cattle. There were fifty oxen and many cows.

Our great object [said the Bishop] has been to convert our fine lands into a great *stock-farm*, which, after being duly prepared, should afford us an abundance of milk, butter, and cheese and viands.

He expected to have, in time, two thousand acres in pasture, sufficient for a thousand cattle, "affording milk and meat for five hundred students, on cheaper terms than the world ever saw." There were the sawmill and the gristmill, without which, the Bishop said, "the college never could have succeeded." There were the quarrying and the lumbering. There were carpenter shops, and blacksmith shops, and shoemakers' shops, and printing shops, and the college store. There was the "house for strangers," or hotel, and there was the whole *ménage* of the college, and of the workmen. One is reminded of some great monastery in the Middle Ages, planted in a remote spot, with its farms, its dairies, its mills, its workshops, its guest house, its domestic establishment, its scholars, its laboring brethren, and its autocratic abbot.

Bishop Chase took the oversight of all that went on, riding about the fields, clambering about the rising buildings; and every evening gathering the head men, hearing their reports, and giving his orders. He was postmaster, rector of the village parish, and principal preacher, president of the temperance society, the Bible Society, the Sunday School Society, and whatever other societies there were. None of these duties and offices did he neglect. And beside all this, he was Bishop of the Protestant Episcopal Church in Ohio, a great missionary field, which he felt he could, for the present, serve better by building up the institutions at Gambier than by constantly riding through the woods and visiting parishes. No man could long carry such a load as this, even if he were free from all outside worries; but during these years Bishop Chase was unceasingly harassed by many great anxieties and vexations, from which he struggled in vain to free himself.

The first anxiety, which he had always with him, came from the lack of money. The English fund paid for the land and left something over; but there was the great cost of the buildings. Upon such of these as were to be permanent he did not spare expense. If the cost of the central part of Kenyon was, as he said, about $14,000, it would certainly not have cost less than $50,000 to erect the whole building according to the magnificent design which Charles Bulfinch, the most eminent American architect of his time, had contributed. If the foundation of Rosse Chapel cost about $3,000, as he said, then the whole building, with tower and deep chancel, as he planned it, would have cost ten thousand. So his permanent buildings involved an expense of about $60,000, and the temporary buildings about five thousand. Altogether, not less than $65,000 had to be provided in order to carry out the building projects to which he had committed himself. Experience had taught him that it would be impossible to collect any such sum, or even half of it, from interested friends in this country. There were three main resources to which he looked.

The first resource was the sale of the four thousand acres of the North Section. The Bishop had hoped to sell this land for more than enough to pay for itself and the South Section too. For a number of months before he made the purchase, he was writing to English friends, seeking to find someone to buy this section; but none of them felt able to put money into wild land in America. In 1829, when the need of money was very pressing, Bishop Chase planned, and had surveyed and recorded, a village, which he named Cornish, in the North Section, on Schenk's Creek, about three miles from Gambier. Here were plotted streets, a market place, reservations for a church and schoolhouse, numerous in-lots and out-lots, all seeming very attractive in the plans and prospectus, and the Bishop hoped to find many purchasers. To that end, mainly, he made a journey to Philadelphia. But no one wanted to buy, and so the plan came to nothing.

The second resource to which the Bishop looked for money was the Congress. His failure to obtain the township of land in 1828 had not left him without hope that he might have success a year later. Accordingly, in December, 1829, he again journeyed over the mountains with this in view. Mrs. Chase had warned him to put no trust in politicians, and he had not been long in Washington before he began to fear that she was right. He had come, indeed, at an unfortunate time; the mind of Congress was preoccupied. On the twenty-ninth of December Senator Foote introduced his fateful resolution on the sale of the public lands, which led to the most celebrated debate that Congress has ever known, that which bears the name of the chief protagonists, Webster and Hayne. Week after week it continued, and small chance had the cause of Kenyon College to be heard amidst the clashings of Massachusetts and South Carolina, and the continuous roll of great oratory. The Bishop wrote bitterly to his wife that his bill was completely at rest "during the famous contention of Messrs Hayne and Webster as to who has been the Best Friend to the Western States." If they would give him his township of land he would do more good to the West than both of them together. At the end of March, completely worn out, he committed to his brother, Senator Dudley Chase, what small hopes still remained of a successful issue, and set out for home. At Cumberland his stagecoach was overturned, and he was very painfully and seriously injured. It was a month before he could continue his journey, and he whiled away his time writing many letters. To his brother Dudley he wrote, urging that the bill be pushed. "The thoughts of a defeat," he said, "are to me *like death*. They haunt me, are raw head of bloody bones to me." The bill did not pass; and some who knew Bishop Chase said that he never recovered the buoyantly hopeful spirit which had been his before.

The third resource was England and Ireland. At times the Bishop thought of crossing the ocean again, and renewing his quest for aid; but he was very reluctant to do this, and just then a remarkable agent appeared, and offered himself for this service, and was accepted.

This brings us to the second of those anxieties and vexations that weighed down Bishop Chase in the year 1828 and thereafter. In the spring of 1827, while he was in Boston, he received letters from several of his English friends, telling of a certain George Montgomery West, who, at their advice, was coming to America to unfold to him the particulars of a most promising scheme to procure large sums of money for the college. The story of this man would fill many interesting pages in the annals of rascality, but must be told very briefly here. He was a young Irishman, vain, self-asserting, without principle, yet with a manner that won for him the friendship and confidence of almost everyone he met. He was gifted with a meretricious sort of eloquence which many admired. Having arrived in America, he assured Bishop Chase of his ability to secure in Ireland and England great contributions to his funds, and also to gather a large colony of thrifty, Protestant Irish families, to purchase the lands of the North Section, and come and settle upon them. These plans had the strong approval of Lord Kenyon, Mr. Marriott, and other English friends, who wrote heartily endorsing Mr. West, and also suggesting that he be ordained to the ministry, and that, if possible, some academic degree be conferred upon him, in order that he might more effectively represent the Bishop and the college, in whose name he proposed to solicit money for the cause. Bishop Chase took their word for West's character, qualifications, and ability, and, after obtaining the approval of Bishops Griswold and Brownell, ordained him deacon and priest. West was also made a Master of Arts; and his diploma, the first ever given by Kenyon College, is still in existence, and perfectly valid; yet his name has never appeared on any official list of alumni. Thus outfitted for his mission, and further embellished with the empty title of "Chaplain to the Bishop of Ohio," he returned to England and Ireland, and began to solicit money, especially for the erection of Rosse Chapel, of which he afterwards asserted that Bishop Chase had promised to make him rector. He also said that the Bishop had promised to use his influence to secure for him the succession to the episcopate of Ohio. The Bishop never made him promises of this sort, and yet, in the loose and effusive way of talking in which he sometimes indulged, he may have said something which this young man, consumed as he was with vanity, took as implying such promises; and this incited him to make the utmost exertions. In Ireland he got the names of an astonishing number of Church dignitaries upon his subscription paper, and the pledges and offerings amounted altogether to about $4,000; but this sum dwindled considerably when he deducted his expenses and also paid a man to make collection of the subscriptions. He seems to have transmitted, in all, about $2,500 to America. In England he spent two years, professing all the time that he was securing, or was about to secure, great sums of money, yet never getting much. His schemes for sending out a colony proved futile. Serious charges that he was dishonest were laid before Mr. Marriott by Methodist ministers who had formerly been associated with West in Ireland and England; but Mr. Marriott did not believe the charges, and published several pamphlets in his defence. Meanwhile, West was writing letters to Bishop Chase in a disrespectful tone, declaring that he "did not hold himself officially responsible to him," and demanding to be informed definitely whether he was to be rector of Harcourt Parish, and what provision would be made for his support; to which the Bishop replied, through Mr. Marriott, that if he returned to Ohio he would fare as well as the other clergymen there. In fact, the Bishop would have preferred that West should stay in England, since he had begun to lose confidence in him. Very serious charges against the man's character were circulating about among the American clergy, based on definite reports of rascalities of which he had been guilty in Canada and Nova Scotia several years before. Bishop Chase did what he felt he could to defend West against them, but evidently he half believed that they were true. He could not throw West overboard without offending Mr. Marriott, who had so thoroughly committed himself to West's defence; and he still hoped that some of his stories about great amounts of money soon to be given by anonymous donors might be true; for he was grievously in need of money, and had mortgaged his farm at Worthington, and borrowed heavily from his friends, in order to keep the work going on at Gambier.

In the summer of 1830 West came back to America, evidently determined to force Bishop Chase to make him rector of Harcourt Parish, or give him some equally conspicuous place, with a view to his obtaining the episcopate of Ohio when the Bishop should die—an event which he thought might soon occur. He stopped in New York and called upon several gentlemen who had subscribed money for the endowment of the Milnor professorship in the Theological Seminary, and warned them to be cautious about giving money to Bishop Chase, since he was extravagant in his expenditures, kept no exact accounts, and never knew where his money went. These gentlemen believed West, and commissioned him to investigate Bishop Chase's financial transactions and report to them. Armed with this commission, by means of which he expected to blackmail the Bishop and gain from him what he wanted, he appeared in Gambier; but he failed of his object, for Bishop Chase could not be intimidated. In his recklessness West overplayed his part, making charges against the Bishop which were preposterous and brought discredit upon himself. However he sent to New York evil reports which had the effect of cutting off every hope of money from that source.* Early in the year 1831 Bishop Chase published a pamphlet entitled, *Bishop Chase's Defence against the Slanders of the Rev. G. M. West*, in which he completely vindicated himself, and cited evidence which showed that for many years West had been a rascal, a liar, and a thief. Still the Bishop knew that public confidence, having once been shaken, can only with difficulty be restored; and he trembled for the future of the college which now so greatly needed friends and money. In this pamphlet he exposed to the world all the distress of his heart.

If the public mind has become alienated from me, by reason of unfounded and unworthy insinuations, . . . then, indeed, I have done; my labor is ended; my day of toil for Kenyon College is over,

* The Milnor Fund never came to Ohio, but still remains in the hands of the vestry of St. George's Church, New York, which pays interest upon it to the seminary. This circumstance may be regarded as a monument to Mr. West.

and the night of rest is come. The busy scenes upon Gambier Hill; the works of faith, love and piety for the benefit of Kenyon College, are cut short; the little army of students, their country's hope, and the Church's joy, are gone, and in their places reign silence and despair. Our fine domain, the last retreat of virtue, in her endeavors to educate youth, in seclusion from the vices of the world, forfeited for debts, and sold piece-meal by the unfeeling creditors; our buildings turned into scenes of intemperance; and our college a heap of rubbish.

He would make a last appeal to the bishops of the Church to come to the relief of the college; he would call upon all Christian people to lend their aid. Let the State of Ohio be mindful of its duty and its advantage. It was Kenyon College that had made Ohio famous.

If there is an object, which has attracted the attention of the Christian world to Ohio, it is that of Kenyon College. If there is one thing which, more than any other, has caused the name of Ohio to spread far and wide, so as to attract the wealthy and industrious to her bosom, it is the name of this Benevolent Institution.

Next he appealed to the whole United States.

Europe holds America responsible for the safe keeping, the prosperity or adversity of this Institution. Whatever America may have done, to attract the attention of Europe, the subject of Kenyon College has seldom failed to add the feelings of tenderness to those of respect, and to mingle the sweets of christian charity in the cup of national intercourse.

Finally, extending his entreaty to all Christendom, he begged everyone to send

some token however small, as a hearty "God speed" to our cause— some means whereby, before I die, I may be enabled to finish *"the work which God hath given me to do."* . . . I shall henceforth *remain at home* and, taking my stand on the spot allotted for my grave, and in view of the great day beyond it, that soon awaits me, humbly, yet firmly, assert my integrity for the past, and implore aid for the future.

These agitated words betray not only the depth of Bishop

Chase's feeling, and his apprehension of danger to the college, but also the unsteady condition of his nerves. No man could endure unshaken all that he had borne and passed through. From the day he landed in England, eight years before, his labors and anxieties had been incessant; but within the last year the failure of his application to Congress, which had been "like death" to him, the accident at Cumberland from which for weeks he suffered severe pain, the final disappointment of his hope against hope that Mr. West would bring him money from England with which to go on with the work, and finally the wicked treachery of this man, undermining his credit even here in America—all this was more than he, or any other man, could bear with unshaken nerves. From this time forward, so long as Bishop Chase appears as an actor in the history of Kenyon College, we must regard him as a man with nerves on edge, susceptible to every cause of irritation, however trivial; one for whose words and actions every allowance should have been made; but who found, alas! even among those most closely associated with him, little sympathy, little consideration.

CHAPTER XI

BISHOP CHASE RESIGNS

WE come now to the third of those vexations and distresses that came to Bishop Chase in connection with the college; and this one was conclusive; it drove him from Gambier and from Ohio. It originated in dissatisfactions, misunderstandings, differences, and distrusts that arose between him and the professors in Kenyon College. These disagreements resulted from the manner in which he exercised his office of college president, and this manner was due, partly to his theory of that office, and partly to his disposition, naturally masterful, and now exacerbated by the tremendous labors, burdens, and pains he had endured. The weary Titan was staggering under his load, and came into collision with the more or less innocent bystanders. Bishop Chase never could believe that any way was so good as his way, or that those who opposed him did so from motives entirely pure; and now that he was worn down, and nervously set on edge, he could have small patience with anyone who criticised him or withstood his will.

In his contest with the faculty and the board of trustees Bishop Chase had much more at stake than anyone else, and a much stronger claim to sympathetic regard. The institution for control of which the struggle went on was absolutely his child; he was its "onlie begetter." The original thought of it was his, and so were all the expansions and modifications of that thought. He, in the face of bitter opposition, and with scarcely any encouragement, had gone to England, and there, a stranger, had turned distrust into confidence and enthusiastic support, and had returned with far more money than he had expected to get. Almost every dollar raised in this country, he had raised at the expense of hard, wearing, uncongenial labor. Every bit of the constructive work on Gambier Hill he had planned and supervised and found the money to pay for. He, almost alone, had solved the problems of the work and borne its vexations. Twice he had spent months of weariness and heart-breaking suspense in Washington, vainly endeavoring to obtain a gift of land which would have enabled him to complete the building of the college, which now stood a fragment with less than one-third of its proposed capacity realized. In all this no member of the faculty had helped him, and no member of the board of trustees. Perhaps this was, in a measure, due to his own fault; but the fact remains that he had done it all alone. And on him alone rested the responsibility of meeting the great and pressing demands for money, not only to advance the work but even to keep the institution alive from day to day. This difficult task had been made far more difficult—almost hopeless—by the distrust in his capacity, and even in his honesty, which Mr. West had created in the minds of many persons of influence.

Bishop Chase was a unique man, of the heroic order, with some traits that greatly hindered his success, yet prodigious in his labors and sacrifices for the welfare of men. Never was there a man more unselfish, or more wholly devoted to the service of God and of mankind; but to those who lived close beside him, whose comfort was dependent on his providence, and whose every exercise of independent action was likely to be checked by his intervention—to such persons the defects of his disposition were more evident and momentous than the high virtues of his character. In his office as chief steward Bishop Chase assigned to the members of the faculty the places where they must live, and gave direction where and what they should eat. Now it is a fact of human nature that when someone controls your whole living he is sure to provoke disparaging comment, no matter how considerate he may be; but Bishop Chase was not considerate. Professors and their families were often very uncomfortable under the rude conditions of housing and boarding at Gambier in those early days, yet the Bishop paid little attention to their complaints, observing briefly that they fared as well as did he and his family; which was perfectly true, yet did not reconcile or console. Such things, trivial though they may be from a philosophical point of view, nevertheless seem very important to those who suffer from them; and when the members of a small, isolated community discuss with each other their unhappy experiences, they never minimize the slights and discomforts and injustices to which they feel themselves subjected. There were in Gambier all the requisite conditions for a domestic outbreak, and the warmth thus generated helped to keep the pot of discontent seething; but it was not this flame that finally made the pot boil over.

The institution at Gambier during all the years that Bishop Chase was there was a college and a grammar school, with but a very small and seldom-mentioned theological annex. In his *Defence against the Slanders of the Rev. G. M. West*, written in February, 1831, Bishop Chase used the name *Kenyon College* nearly fifty times, and the term *College* more than one hundred and thirty times, while the term *Seminary* appears but twice, and the term *Theological Seminary* not at all, except twice in a quoted passage.* Reading this large and able pamphlet, a stranger would never dream that theological education was an important purpose of the institution at Gambier. To an extent far greater than he was aware of, Bishop Chase had ceased to be interested in his original purpose of educating ministers of the Episcopal Church. He exerted himself but little to obtain such students. His thoughts had turned in another direction. It was of this other purpose alone that he spoke in his appeals to

---

* This is exclusive of the Appendix, which is chiefly made up of citations from newspaper articles, and other documents.

the Ohio legislature and to Congress; and even in his appeals
to the public in general, such as his *Plea for the West*, in
1826, and his *Star in the West*, in 1828, he scarcely mentioned the theological seminary. In fact, the professors were
professors in a college, not in a theological seminary. True,
Mr. Sparrow spent a little of his time in directing the
studies of the two or three men who, at any one time, were
reading for Holy Orders; but even he was spoken of by
Bishop Chase as "a Professor of Divinity in Kenyon College." The faculty regarded itself as a college faculty, and
expected to have the large share in the management of the
internal affairs of the institution which was, at that time,
customarily accorded to college faculties in America. They
conceded that a theological seminary might very properly be
under the almost complete control of a bishop; but they
said that it was "contrary to the spirit of our age and country" that a *college* should be subject to the "positive and
absolute authority" of a bishop, or of any other man.

Bishop Chase viewed the matter very differently. To him
the "spirit of our age and country" was far from admirable.
He prided himself in the fact that the Church in which he
was a bishop was *primitive;* whereas the modern spirit rejected or chaffed at episcopacy, and even when it retained it,
sought to limit its powers. Bishop Chase magnified the
powers of a bishop; and he believed that he might, and must,
under certain conditions, exercise those powers in the college. By the constitution, as amended in 1826, the school
was placed "under the immediate charge and superinten-
dance of the Bishop of the Diocese, for the time being, as
President of the institution." Why require that a man, in
order to be president, must be one who has episcopal powers,
if you are going to deny to him as president the exercise of
those powers? So the Bishop reasoned. He held that in a
Church college a bishop who is president has the power to
oversee and direct the whole. In this view he was not alto-

gether singular among bishops; his successor in the office held it as firmly as he, and acted upon it much more vigorously and successfully. But Bishop Chase did not put it in just that way; he said that his was the authority of a *father*. To the assertion that Kenyon College should be governed as other colleges were governed, he replied

Kenyon College is like other Colleges in some respects, and unlike all in many other respects. One fundamental principle in which it differs from all others is, that the whole Institution is Patriarchal. Like Abraham on the plain of Mamre it hath pitched its tent under the trees of Gambier hill, it hath its flocks and its herds, and its different families of Teachers, Scholars, Mechanics and Labourers; all united under one head, pursuing one common interest and receiving their maintenance and food from one common source, the funds and farms of the College. This Patriarchal establishment must, it is obvious, have a Father, & that Father must be clothed with authority to seek and effect the common good. Deprive him of this, and the family must come to ruin. Guard his power against *abuses*, but for the common interest preserve it entire.

This guard against abuses was, he said, the board of trustees, which could "meet whenever they please and investigate all subjects of complaint." But when it came to the test he would not yield even to the board of trustees, as we shall see, but made his appeal to the bishops of the Episcopal Church, who, by the constitution of the seminary, had visitatorial authority in its affairs.

Bishop Chase had gathered an excellent faculty at Gambier. Professors Sparrow, Kendrick, Fitch, and Denison, with George P. Williams and Heman Dyer in the grammar schools, constituted a body of teachers that would have been a strength and ornament to any college in the land. They were devoted to their work, and to what they conceived to be the interests of the institution they served. Could Bishop Chase have held the confidence of these young men, could he have inspired them with the splendid ideals that flamed in his own breast, could he, in short, have been to them an admired and trusted leader, they would have borne and sacrificed anything for the sake of bringing to pass the things that he desired. But he had in him scant capacity for leadership. His was, rather, the spirit of a master, a director, and he was displeased with anyone who did not yield to his authority. At such times he could not argue, could not attempt to persuade; but could only disregard those who differed with him, and override them if they opposed.

Bishop Chase had confidence in the members of his faculty as teachers, and did not interfere with their work of instruction; but he trusted them in nothing else, and looked to them for no initiative; and when he thought he saw among them evidences of an independent spirit that would go ahead and plan and act, he was displeased, for he wished that nothing should be done without consulting him; and indeed there was danger that among a lot of young men there might be a lack of mature wisdom in devising and doing new things. Yet the Bishop was often away from Gambier for long periods, and when he was at home he was intensely occupied with the hundred things of which he retained and exercised the oversight; it was therefore impossible for him to attend minutely to the internal affairs of the college, included under the head of discipline. Besides, although he had successfully taught boys in many schools, yet of colleges and the educating of young men he had little experience. His sole acquaintance with a college was with Dartmouth; and what he saw there of the exercise of the presidential office afforded to one of his temperament a very bad model. John Wheelock, who was president when Chase was a student, is said to have been a self-confident, arbitrary man, who would have his own way, and was in conflict with all about him.

The young men in the faculty of Kenyon College knew more about the proper management of a college, and the governance of its students, than their president did. He would have been wise if he had left these matters principally

THE OLD SEVENTY FOUR
EXTERIOR. SCHOOLROOM AND CHAPEL.
FACULTY BENCH

in their hands; but he was unwilling to do so. A contest broke out at this point, exasperated by all the other causes of discontent. For a history of the particulars of this controversy we are confined almost exclusively to Professor Sparrow's statements in his pamphlet, *A Reply to the Charges and Accusations of the Rt. Rev. Philander Chase, D.D.* Professor Sparrow seems to have had a fair share of the irritability and prejudice that ordinarily are found in good men, but his truthfulness and accuracy in stating what occurred cannot be questioned. He tells us that, in the winter of 1829-1830, when Bishop Chase was for several months in Washington, the professors "thought it necessary to hold faculty meetings." But when he returned they discovered that their "measures did not meet his approbation, and that of the authority of the faculty meeting he was very jealous." Although he might tolerate the meetings while he was away from Gambier, yet when he was at home he felt that it was for him to decide all the matters with which the faculty meeting concerned itself. So far our sympathy must be with the faculty; but Professor Sparrow and the others should not have felt towards Bishop Chase so harshly as they did. A great man whose life and effort are consecrated to a noble purpose, should meet with considerate sympathy when he is struggling in the toils of fate; that is no time for a generous man to take offence even at the most irritating conduct; it is no time to criticise, unless the critic is moved by love and endowed with unusual wisdom. But it must be confessed that at this time the Bishop's behavior put the magnanimity of the professors to severe tests.

Let Professor Sparrow exhibit to us a sample meeting of the faculty, after the Bishop's return from Washington.

On one occasion when a relative of Bishop Chase [—Professor Denison, his nephew, probably—] moved that the compositions of some Students who were about to appear at an approaching exhibition, be put for correction into the hands of the gentleman who taught

Rhetoric, Bishop Chase became highly excited and used language painful to the mover and disrespectful to the other gentleman concerned. The next subject that evening, was the propriety of requiring religious exercises at the exhibitions of the Literary Societies in College. Bishop Chase showing no disposition to conduct the exercises, his relative mentioned before, proposed that they be at liberty to select their own chaplain from the clergymen who would be present from abroad. The very mention of this exceedingly displeased Bishop Chase. Telling us that we "*meant to depose the Bishop*," he took his hat and without further ceremony left the room. We of course adjourned.

It is easy to see that the Bishop felt that these young men wished to displace him in the conduct of these matters. Professor Denison, or whoever it was that made those motions, could have consulted him in advance, and should have done so. Here was the place to exercise that considerateness to which Bishop Chase certainly was entitled. He thought, and he had some reason to think, that the professors felt little regard for him, since during all the weeks that he lay sick and in pain at Cumberland, he had received not a single letter from any of them.

Scenes as absurd and trying as that just related were enacted at almost every meeting of the faculty. Elsewhere also there were unpleasant occurrences; the Bishop would rebuke members of the faculty harshly and in the presence of students, when—very often—he wholly misunderstood the matter with which he was dealing. He made rules for the college and expected the professors and teachers to know of them although he failed to publish them. It was evident that these things could not go on much longer without disrupting the institution; and the Bishop, who at this moment was at the most critical pass of the West affair, united with the members of the faculty in requesting the board of trustees, in September, 1830, to define the powers of the president and other officers, "that we may know when we are in the discharge of duty," and to draw up a code of laws for the uniform government of the students. The board, unequal to the task of drawing up codes offhand, gave to the faculty power to make, by a majority vote, whatever rules and laws were necessary, and by these they were to be governed during the ensuing year. Bishop Chase did not welcome this action of the board, but he acquiesced in it, being at that time hard pressed with matters more important.

At the same meeting of the board, a day or two later, the following resolution was passed:

Resolved, that the President be respectfully requested to present to the Board, at the commencement of their annual meetings, a statement in writing of his transactions during the preceding year, as well as of the particular subjects to which he may deem it necessary to call their attention; in order to enable them to proceed with the business which may come before them with regularity and dispatch.

This resolution might be interpreted as implying a criticism upon the Bishop for failure to keep the board informed of his transactions and plans. It is plain that he so regarded it, for he at once laid before the board his "resignation of his agency and management of financial concerns." It could not but be vexatious to him to be formally asked to give such information to the board which, neither in its corporate capacity, nor by the action of any of its individual members, had lifted a finger to help him bear the crushing financial burdens of the past year. They left him to borrow money for the college where he could, and mortgage his farm, and then requested him to submit to them a statement of his transactions. They lacked, at least, a sense of humor. Professor Sparrow, who was in hearty sympathy with the trustees in this action, says that "they showed a disposition, for the first time, to take the reins of government, in a measure, into their hands." They did; and Bishop Chase was to furnish the horses. Exasperated beyond measure, he bade the mover of the resolution sit down, telling him he had said too much. He remained master of the sorry situation, for the board requested him to continue as agent and financial manager; which he consented to do.

After this things went from bad to worse. When the faculty proposed to act upon the authority conferred on it, and draw up the code defining the duties and power of the president and other officers, Bishop Chase would have nothing to do with it. His objection was that, since the rules were to be adopted by a majority vote, he would have no more weight in adopting them than the youngest instructor in the grammar school. Plainly, he would be overwhelmed; and he refused to be bound by an action of the board which exposed him to so certain a defeat. He demanded a power of veto upon all the acts of the faculty, and declared that if it were not granted him he would "leave the institution." The faculty did not doubt that he would do as he said, and they granted him the veto, expressing the hope that he would exercise it with great forbearance. "Here also I was disappointed," says Professor Sparrow.

From this time Bishop Chase ceased to attend the faculty meetings, but required that a report of the proceedings be sent to him for his approval or rejection. He also ceased to speak to the members of the faculty, unless the occasion were very urgent; if he must communicate with them, it was done through the post office, or by means of a third person. One day Mr. Norman Putnam—recently arrived from New Hampshire, a relative of the Bishop, keeper of the college store, for more than sixty years thereafter a most prominent citizen of Gambier—carried about among the professors a paper, written by Bishop Chase, which he desired them all to sign. It had reference to Mr. West's charges that the Bishop had been extravagant and wasteful in the expenditure of money given to the college, and kept his accounts so unsystematically that nobody could understand them. The paper declared that these charges were untrue. Professor Sparrow refused to sign it, chiefly on the ground that he knew nothing as to how the accounts were kept, and thought it the business of the trustees, not of the faculty, to certify to their correctness. Further, although he most firmly believed that the Bishop did not intend to waste money, still he did not think that he had always put it to the best use. The Bishop's *Defence against the Slanders of the Rev. G. M. West*, published in February, 1831, included, therefore, no endorsement of his conduct from the faculty of Kenyon College.

Letters written by Bishop Chase early in 1831 show that he was convinced that the faculty were determined to drive him from Gambier, if they could; and he thought they might be able to do it. He would not remain there if his authority was to be limited in the manner recently proposed. He felt that he could not count upon the board of trustees, as then constituted, for steadfast support; but a new board was to be chosen by the diocesan convention in the fall, and he hoped that he might secure the election of one upon which he could more confidently depend. In order to accomplish this, he spoke of his differences with the faculty to many persons as he went about the diocese upon his episcopal visitations, and published a circular letter presenting his view of the disagreements. This letter was dated, "Gambier, 14th July, 1831." It was printed upon two sides of a large sheet of paper, and the Bishop signed each copy in his own handwriting. It was in the form of a letter addressed to some unnamed clergyman who had written to him making inquiry regarding affairs at the college. The whole point at issue, he said, was whether he must be governed by the votes of a majority of the faculty. He asked:

Was it intended by the Laws of God as set forth in Holy Scripture, and practiced by our Primitive Church, to reduce the Bishop of any Diocese, especially when presiding ex officio over a literary Institution whose government and welfare are interwoven with the prosperity of the Diocese, to such a condition as this? I think not. . . . There must often be presented questions, which involve not only the prosperity of the Institution, but his Episcopal character, to be decided by the faculty; and could it be intended by any law divine or human, ecclesiastical or secular, to place the Bishop (because a President of that Institution wherein a multitude of Counsellors are necessary for safety,) in a condition in which he must experience such evils; that especially of seeing his professional rights taken from him, and measures pursued which, in his opinion, would be destructive of the best interests of the College; and all this without any power to stop proceedings, even so long and so much as to appeal to the Trustees; except what is involved in a casting vote, in the event of a tie, which would but seldom occur? . . . It has been and is maintained by me that by the expression of the Constitution of our Seminary "The President shall have a general superintendence of the Institution," must be understood that he never suffer any thing to take place in it, much less any measure to be established by rule, which in his opinion shall have a destructive tendency; and that when such appears to be the case by the exercise of any principles or measures, it is his duty to stop proceedings, not by any *unlimited* power but by an appeal to the Trustees for their decision in any important matter involving the rights & privileges of the parties, i.e. of the Teachers as well as myself.

The Bishop then proceeds to set forth those views of the patriarchal government of the college which have already been stated.

To this circular letter a reply was at once issued by the "Professors of Kenyon College"—as such they signed it— addressed to the Bishop, but widely distributed, dated July 25, 1831. It was written by Professor Sparrow. Declining to discuss publicly matters which it was the province of the board of trustees alone to decide, the professors yet pledged themselves to show to the board, should it be demanded, that the authority claimed by Bishop Chase was unnecessary, clogged the operations of college government, and was "contrary to the usage of colleges in general, and to the spirit of our age and country." What he had said about interference with his episcopal office was absurd; his "allusions to patriarchal authority" were "mal à propos and delusive." They said that they had once offered him, for the sake of peace, all the power he claimed, provided he would accept it on the ground of personal consideration and respect; but he would not accept it on such terms, and "threatened an immediate dissolution of the whole establishment." To prevent that evil, they conceded what he demanded, until the next meeting of the board of trustees. It is not probable that many Churchmen to-day would publicly address to their bishop a letter so disrespectful as this. It was, moreover, a challenge to a test before the board of trustees.

The diocesan convention of 1831 met at Gambier on the ninth of September. The Bishop began his address by reminding his hearers of the "triennial election of Trustees of the Theological Seminary of the Protestant Episcopal Church in the Diocese of Ohio." It was three years since that name had been heard in an episcopal address in Ohio. Even the term *seminary*, which is applicable to any kind of school, had been almost entirely abandoned by Bishop Chase. It had occurred but once in the episcopal address of the previous year; but now it is found fourteen times; while the term *college*, which occurred twenty times the year before, is found but once. This change was not accidental. Bishop Chase saw that he could not easily maintain in a college the authority that would be conceded him in a theological seminary; he therefore fell back and intrenched himself behind the original, and legal, title. The address went over the ground with which we are now familiar, advancing no new argument of weight. He insisted that when the trustees gave to the faculty power to make "rules for the Government of the bishop," it granted a power that was unconstitutional, "for in its effect it would involve a principle contrary to the doctrine, discipline, Constitution, and Canons of the General Convention, which the Theological Seminary of the Diocese of Ohio is bound to obey." It was contrary to the discipline of the Episcopal Church that a body constituted as was the faculty of Kenyon College should "establish laws that should regulate the duties and privileges of the ecclesiastical head of the Diocese." It was a "gross anomaly."

Such was Bishop Chase's defence of his course in resisting the authority conferred by the trustees to make rules that might limit or govern his action. The convention of the diocese had established the seminary, and had the best right to express an opinion as to the constitutionality of his proceedings. He desired an investigation of the charges made against him, and he demanded an acquittal, if they found him innocent. Having delivered his address he withdrew from the convention, being in severe pain from a recent accident.

After the Bishop's retirement a committee was appointed to take into consideration "the present difficulties and necessities of Kenyon College." The following day this committee in a preliminary report moved a resolution that the convention "now proceed to the election of a Board of Trustees, who shall report a system of bye-laws for the Government of the Faculty of Kenyon College." The resolution was adopted. The next day the committee made its final report. The troubles in the college, it declared, were due to the failure of the board of trustees to lay down rules for governing the action of the president and faculty.

If this shall be done by the Board, as we trust it will, it is not possible that it should fail to have the effect expected. Although the Right Rev. Bishop, by the Constitution is ex officio President of the College; yet as President, he cannot invoke his episcopal functions, or any powers or authority other than the customary functions of president and principal professor of a theological and literary seminary, aided by such as the Board of trustees by law shall confer on him. . . . The exercise of a little patience by each—the President and the Professors—until the Board have leisure to act upon the subject, is all your committee deem it necessary to recommend to them.

They presented a resolution, which was passed, to the

effect that in the opinion of the convention "the Constitution is the only source from which the powers of the officers, both President, Professors and Trustees, are legitimately to be drawn."

This was a total defeat for Bishop Chase. Henceforth as president he must lay aside his episcopal functions, and exercise only such powers as the constitution and the board of trustees might give him. He, to whom the institution owed its life, and everything that it was, must submit to be overruled by men who had done little or nothing for it. That was the grievous thing—that board of trustees which he had been obliged to have in order to carry out the terms of the Deed of Donation; that board of trustees which, he felt, had been never a help to him or to the seminary, but always a hindrance; that board now had him in its power. He was present when the report was read and adopted. He returned to his place of residence in the basement of Kenyon College and wrote this letter:

To the CLERGY AND LAITY *of the Protestant Episcopal Church of the Diocese of Ohio, assembled in Convention in Gambier on this, the 9th day of September,* 1831.

BRETHREN :—

We have heard this day in a sermon preached by the Rev. Ethan Allen, from God's word, (which I desire him to publish,) that we must *live in peace*, or we cannot be Christians : and that to secure peace, especially that of God's Church, great sacrifices must sometimes be made. Influenced by these principles, I am willing, in order to secure the peace of *God's Church* and that of our *loved Seminary*, in addition to the sacrifices which by the grace of God have been already made, to resign, and I do hereby resign the Episcopate of this Diocese, and with it, what I consider constitutionally identified, the Presidency of the Theological Seminary of the Protestant Episcopal Church of the Diocese of Ohio.

The Convention will make this known to the Trustees, whom I can now no longer meet in my official capacity.

PHILANDER CHASE.

A committee of the convention, and many individuals, called upon him and besought him to withdraw his resignation; but since they assured him that the convention would not recede from the position taken by the report which had been adopted, he refused to alter his resolution.

Gentleman, [he said,] I differ with you and the Convention in principle and fundamentally;—you are doubtless conscientious in your views,—I am in mine.

When the committee reported this unshaken resolution of the Bishop, the convention, with no dissenting vote, accepted the resignation.

Thus terminated the connection of Bishop Chase with the seminary and college that he had founded. The diocesan convention within two hours elected his successor, the Reverend Charles Pettit McIlvaine, of Brooklyn, New York. The celerity with which this election was transacted, and the unanimity of the vote, create the impression that there were leaders on the floor who were prepared for this action and held the convention well in hand. These were the men who had relentlessly forced the Bishop into a position from which he could escape only by what would have been in his eyes a shameful, disloyal surrender, or else by resigning. They understood him but little if they did not know which he would choose.

Two or three days later Bishop Chase rode away to a little valley in Holmes County, where his grandniece, Sarah Russell, owned a tract of land with a ruinous cabin upon it. This cabin he repaired, and then sent for his family; and there they passed the winter and spring. The next summer they removed to a farm in southern Michigan, where they lived until, in 1835, he was elected bishop of the newly formed Diocese of Illinois. That office he held until his death, on the twentieth of September, 1852. Although sixty years old when he began his work in Illinois, he repeated there the heroic missionary labors that had marked his early years in Ohio, and endured again all the hardships he had then known. Once more he founded a college, Jubilee College, near Peoria, and visited England to solicit funds. His social success in that country was not less marked than upon his first visit, though he did not gather so much money. The letters written in his old age glow with the same intensity of feeling that makes his earlier letters so remarkable. Discouragements and disappointments could not cast him down. Always, always, there was something just ahead calling him forward. As age came on it was his

> Still to be strenuous for the bright reward,
> And in the soul admit of no decay,
> Brook no continuance of weak-mindedness.

For him the vision never faded into the light of common day, but the light of common day, common duty, gleamed in visions of new services to be rendered to God and to the Church. His chief visible monument is Kenyon College, whose heart will ever keep for him a place of love.

CHAPTER XII

COLLEGE GROUNDS AND BUILDINGS IN EIGHTEEN HUNDRED AND THIRTY-ONE

IF one would form a picture of what we call the College Park as it was in 1831 when Bishop Chase bade it farewell, he must first erase from his mind almost everything that the name recalls to those who know those grounds as they now are. He must put away the gates and the fence, and every building that he now sees, except the middle part of Old Kenyon; and—most striking change of all—he must forget the Path and the trees. Having thus obliterated all the beauty of the present scene, he must conceive before him, as he takes his stand beside the old well and looks southward, a broad, open space, intended as an avenue, reaching clear through to the college, the walls of which are entirely in sight. This same broad street also reaches northward from the well, running the whole length of the town, north and south, bearing in various portions various names, numerously bestowed, in honor of numerous English friends.

Looking southward, then, from the old well, in the year 1831, the beholder saw a very unattractive street, almost chaotic in its incompleteness, with here and there bushes and stumps still unremoved, wagon tracks wandering along its great width, footpaths ranging about in convenient directions, and not a tree to give beauty and shade, save, halfway down the view, a few oaks which had withstood the prehistoric hurricane. The great oak in front of Rosse Hall is one of those trees. Middle Kenyon, looking very much as it looks now, shut in the view at the south. Behind it, unseen by our beholder, was a stone kitchen.

Along the sides of this street, and extending perhaps half-

GAMBIER, ABOUT 1835

way down towards the college, were fences, built mainly by
the Horticultural Society, of which we have already heard.
On the western side the high rail fence protected the extensive orchard of young apple trees that Bishop Chase had
planted. Here a few aged trees still bring forth a gnarled
and scanty fruit, but excellent in flavor: how far into our
history do their roots extend? The eastern fence was made
of boards, and doubtless it protected the garden of choice
vegetables that the Horticultural Society cultivated, perhaps in the neighborhood of the present library. The top of
this fence served as a walk for the students, in the spring
when the paths—as has been ever their wont—engulfed the
feet in mud. Along both fences were young maples, planted
by this same admirable society. Not many of them survived
the investigating snouts of roving swine, seeking for the
potatoes which, injudiciously, for the enrichment of the soil,
had been buried about the young roots; yet a few of the trees
escaped destruction, and are said to have attained noble
size. None of the park maples can now be certainly identified as of that ancient planting.

Halfway down this sorry street, at the western side, men
would be seen working upon the foundations of Rosse
Chapel, which was to stand on the border of Bexley Square.
This Square was intended to be an imposing feature of the
town; it was an expansion of the street, about three hundred
feet in measurement each way; it must be borne in mind by
those who would understand our ancient geography. Just
where the street entered the Square from the north was a tiny
frame dwelling house, called Cascu, a word made up of the
initial syllables of the names of the two students who built
and occupied it, Caswall and Cusack. The ground at that
spot still bears traces of the building, which survived for
many years, serving one purpose and another. This was the
only house on the western side of the street, south of the
well.

Looking down the eastern side of the street many buildings might be seen, only one of them with any pretension to beauty or permanency. Nearly three hundred feet from the college was an odd little building of stone, with pointed windows on the sides of its second story, like the upper windows of Old Kenyon. This was but a fragment of what was designed to be a rather spacious house, in architectural keeping with the college, and supplying part of the northern side of the great quadrangle of which Kenyon College, with its far-stretching wings, was to furnish the other sides. This piece of a house was assigned to Professor Sparrow as soon as it was habitable. After Bishop Chase left Gambier a small front was built on, of brick; and thus completed, the house served as a dwelling for about eighty-five years. Professors Sparrow and Trimble, and, of the present generation, Professor West, were among its occupants. In the neighborhood of this house were some rough, temporary buildings, which, after not many years, were swept away.

In the middle distance, well to the left, east of Bexley Square, loomed up a frame structure of imposing size and remarkable for the unanimity with which those who beheld it spoke of its homeliness, and those who occupied it testified to its discomforts. This was the "Old Seventy Four," a famous and infamous building in our early history, erected by Bishop Chase as a schoolhouse for the younger pupils of the grammar school.

North of Bexley Square there were no buildings until one approached Wiggin Street. Here, conveniently near the well, was the most ancient group of all, consisting of the first refectory and kitchen, and the log cabins that had been occupied by Bishop Chase and Professor Sparrow. These have already been mentioned several times. They were on the sloping ground that is now the lawn in front of the Church of the Holy Spirit. So vividly is this lawn, with the church, and the gates, and the chain fence, impressed upon our

minds, that it is exceedingly difficult to wipe them all from
our memory, and see nothing but a bare space, with a few
rude buildings in the middle of it. Remember that the street
line ran right through this space, continuous with the line of
the western side of the present post office. These buildings,
of course, were east of that line. Their dimensions and relative positions are known, so that it is possible to draw a plan
of the group which cannot be far from correct; but the exact
location of the group upon the lawn is uncertain. The location as shown on the map in this volume is determined by
descriptions that have come down to us, and by two pictures
that show one of the buildings, and by the probabilities of
the case. As the beholder, standing by the old well in the
year 1831, looked a little to the right of southeast, he saw,
at a distance of perhaps one hundred and fifty feet, a low
plank building forty-eight feet long, east and west, and
twenty-two feet wide. This was the refectory and the
church, when the institution first came to Gambier. It was
conveniently placed for the use of the students when they
occupied the houses on Wiggin Street; but when they moved
into Kenyon, and the Old Seventy Four, it surrendered most
of its early functions to the more easily accessible rooms
provided by those buildings. Yet it was well built, and having been converted into a dwelling house, it survived until
the late fifties. Men are still living who remember it, and at
least two pictures preserve, more or less distinctly, its unattractive features. If our imaginary beholder was curious
to see what was behind this refectory, and for that purpose
walked a little way towards the south, he would perceive
that it made one side of a tiny, shabby quadrangle, the
western side of which was unoccupied. Attached to the south-
eastern corner of the refectory was the log kitchen, eighteen
feet square; and south of this, at a distance of ten feet—Oh,
spot ever to be held in reverence!—was the cabin where
Bishop Chase lived three years, and his wife and children

lived with him two years after they moved up from Worthington. This cabin was of the roughest sort, a typical pioneer "shantee." It faced the south. Mrs. Chase had to take but five or six steps from her back door to reach her kitchen, and this space was filled with an uncovered porch or platform. A few feet west of the Chase cabin was Professor Sparrow's cabin, where he lived with his wife, who was Mrs. Chase's sister. This had been built for a dining-room of the men employed in the work, but within a year it was converted into a dwelling. It was of hewn logs. The space between the cabins was roofed over, and here a stairway led up to sleeping-rooms above, in which at first working men, and later, students, were lodged. All these buildings, except the refectory, were removed at an early date.

Westward from the well, along Wiggin Street, were four wooden houses, two on each side, all of the same dimensions, thirty-eight feet east and west, and twenty feet wide. They were two stories high, and were differently partitioned within. These were built as temporary houses, for the occupancy of students until Kenyon should be ready to receive them. One of them stands to-day, on the spot where it has always stood, on the north side of the street, just at the brow of the hill. This is the oldest house in Gambier, still occupied and standing on its original spot. Time has played various pranks with the other three, of which some account will be given in another part of this book. A little further west, on the south side of Wiggin Street, and twenty or more feet back from the street line stood the hotel, which Bishop Chase called the House for Strangers. Near it, still further from the street, was the great barn, stable, and coach house. Here was the point of arrival and departure of the daily mail coach, owned by the college, and plying between Gambier and Mount Vernon, where it made connections for all the world.

At one other building our beholder must look, the college

store. It stood where the Commons now stands. It was a composite structure, consisting of a log house with a frame addition. The remarkable story of this house will be told later, accompanied with some account of its highly diversified merchandise. Looking to the northeast from the well, one would see in the square now bounded by Chase Avenue and Brooklyn, Acland, and Wiggin Streets, many structures that were needed by the great farm which Bishop Chase had been developing. Here were the granary and threshing floor, enclosures for stacking grain, ox sheds, a stable for cattle, and a house for the dairyman. It is not improbable that some of these are still in existence, but so transformed and translated that they cannot easily be identified.

CHAPTER XIII

BISHOP McILVAINE TAKES HOLD

THE Reverend Charles Pettit McIlvaine was consecrated a bishop for Ohio on the thirty-first day of October, 1832. He was a graduate of Princeton College, and had studied at the Princeton Theological Seminary. Although but thirty-three years of age, he was already widely known as one of the ablest and most eloquent ministers of the Episcopal Church. In his first charge, at Georgetown, D. C., he had attained such celebrity as a preacher that many distinguished statesmen came from Washington to hear him, and he was elected chaplain of the Senate of the United States. John C. Calhoun, Secretary of War, appointed him chaplain of the Military Academy at West Point. There he accomplished the remarkable achievement of bringing about a revival of religion, in doing which he was thought by some of those in authority to have exceeded his mandate. From West Point he passed to the rectorship of St. Ann's Church, Brooklyn, a position of importance and prominence, from which several strong parishes in Boston and New York vainly sought to draw him away. He was, therefore, a clergyman of distinction when he became Bishop of Ohio, and, by virtue of that office, President of the Theological Seminary and Kenyon College. Although he had so promptly been elected by the Ohio convention, yet his consecration was delayed by doubts as to the validity of Bishop Chase's resignation; and a year and a half elapsed before he took up his residence at Gambier.

During this interval the trustees carried on the college as well as they could. The long-talked-of "code of laws" was drawn up and enacted. Professor Sparrow was asked to "exercise the rights and duties of the presidency." A steward was appointed to take charge of all the concerns of the college "other than literary or religious"; but he soon resigned and the office lapsed. The Reverend M. T. C. Wing was elected treasurer of the college. He served also as clerk of the board of trustees, and the minutes of their meetings from September 9, 1831, to July 1, 1862, are for the most part in his handwriting.

The college was without available money to pay running expenses, and was in debt to the extent of $15,000; it was not, however, insolvent, for it had valuable assets in its lands. Twenty thousand dollars, it was said, would "place the Institution on a firm and permanent basis & enable it to realize the fondest expectations of its friends." The lands of the North Section were offered for sale, despite Bishop Chase's protest, and within a few months nearly two thousand acres were sold at an average price of four dollars and a half an acre, bringing to the college about $9,000, a very welcome but quite insufficient sum. The Reverend William Preston, a member of the board of trustees, was sent to New York in the spring of 1832, to procure a loan; but no one would lend to the college. He consulted with Mr. McIlvaine, the bishop-elect, who could only suggest that an application be made to England. Mr. Preston left the business in his hands, but nothing came of it. Creditors became so urgent that in September, 1832, the board authorized the prudential committee to raise $20,000, and, if necessary, "to sell, mortgage, or otherwise dispose of any property of the Institution." This authorization, it will be observed, included power to sell lands in the sacred South Section, and even the buildings. So desperate was the situation.

Then, to the great relief of trustees and faculty, Bishop McIlvaine appeared on the scene. Immediately after his consecration he made a preliminary visit to Ohio, spent a week at Gambier, and met the trustees at Columbus. He was not daunted by the discouraging state of affairs, but, on the contrary, saw a great deal that appeared to him hopeful; and his sympathies and energies were enlisted in behalf of an institution which, if it could be saved and strengthened, would be, he said, "of immense importance." Besides satisfying the creditors, the great need, as he saw it, was for additional building—the completion of Kenyon College, and the erection of houses for the members of the faculty, whose domiciliary discomforts had played so large a part in arousing the spirit of rebellion against Bishop Chase. Bishop McIlvaine had not at first intended to reside at Gambier, but at Cleveland or Cincinnati, leaving the faculty to manage affairs unhampered by his presence; but upon visiting Gambier he yielded to the charms of that alluring village, and to the requirements of the case as he saw them, and decided to live there, and arranged that a house be built for his residence. He believed that a great deal could be made of the theological department, and decided to be its head, while a vice president should preside over the college, relieving the Bishop of all but a nominal control of its internal affairs.

Already, before making this visit to Ohio, Bishop McIlvaine had obtained, chiefly in New York and Brooklyn, subscriptions to pay the salary of an additional theological professor, Doctor Joseph Muenscher; and after his return to the East he presented the cause in most of the larger cities, and obtained $28,520, without a great deal of difficulty. This was to be spent mainly for buildings; to pay off the pressing debts of the college a loan of $15,000 was obtained in New York, which afforded great immediate relief, and great future trouble.

Then began in Gambier an era of active building. Six houses were erected for members of the faculty—the brick house, already begun by Professor Fitch, which long stood where now is the northeastern corner of Hanna Hall; the spacious house of brick which is now the "deanery," whose first occupant was Professor Sparrow; and probably the brick house at the northeastern corner of Gaskin and Brooklyn Streets, known as the "Wing house," because Professor Wing so long occupied it; also the row of three frame houses in the park, of which the middle one, bearing the name of Park Cottage, is still in its original place, while another has been removed to a position near the northwestern corner of the college cemetery, and portions of the third, having passed out of the ownership of the college, have been assembled at the northern end of Ward Street. At the same time the Bishop's house was erected, a beautiful mansion, now known as McIlvaine Hall, on the grounds of Harcourt Place Seminary. The diocese was to pay for this house, but ultimately most of the money came from the college. Thus everyone was provided with an excellent new house, and, so far as that can avail, was made happy.

Meanwhile the wings of the college were rising, built on a scale much diminished from that exhibited in Bulfinch's grand design. Neither was there money enough nor stone enough to complete the vast "H" that had been projected; nor was there any prospect of filling so huge a building with students. Besides, there were defects in the design which would have made such wings impracticable. To compensate in some small degree for the loss of space, rooms were finished off in the gables of each wing, and the beautiful bull's-eye windows were devised to give them light. The East Wing was finished in 1834, and the West Wing in 1836.

Bishop McIlvaine had, from the first, a strong desire to complete Rosse Chapel, of which the foundations and the walls up to the first floor had been built by Bishop Chase. The design was greatly changed. Bishop Chase's tower at the front, and his chancel forty feet deep, were eliminated, the intended "gothic style" was set aside, and the plan was redrawn substantially as we see the building now, with its

twin pillars bearing the Ionic capitals. For lack of money
the chapel was many years in building, and was not consecrated until 1845, although the basement on the south side
had then been long in use, and occasionally the great room
upstairs, though in an unfinished condition.

At the eastern side of the village towards the north, on
what was long known as the Academy grounds, was erected
a large, substantial building of brick, for the use of the
younger students of the grammar school. This building,
named Milnor Hall in honor of the rector of St. George's
Church, New York, was at that time one of the best in the
country for a boys' school, and the young residents of the
Old Seventy Four were glad when they were moved into it,
in the year 1834.

One other building of brick, the fairest of all Bishop
McIlvaine's structures, came several years later, but may be
mentioned now. This is Bexley Hall, built with money
obtained by Bishop McIlvaine in England, in 1835, and
named in honor of Lord Bexley, who had given liberally to
both Bishop Chase and Bishop McIlvaine. Henry Roberts,
a distinguished English architect, prepared and gave the
design. So great was the need of money in Gambier that the
trustees diverted the English fund temporarily to other
purposes, and the cornerstone was not laid until October 23,
1839, and the building received its first occupants in 1843,
and was at length finished in 1858.

Bishop McIlvaine and his family had arrived at Gambier
on the twenty-fourth of July, 1833. He was most cordially
received, the students welcoming him with an illumination
of the college building, the first recorded instance of what
afterwards became, and long continued to be, among Kenyon
students, the favorite demonstration of honor or festivity.
Thenceforth, until 1846, he resided there. At first he mini-
mized his responsibility with regard to the affairs of the col-

BISHOP McILVAINE

lege; afterwards he magnified it. We must observe the effects of both policies, for they were very marked.

It was Bishop McIlvaine's intention when he first came to Ohio, to leave the affairs of the college, so far as possible, in the hands of a vice president, retaining for himself only so much authority as might be necessary in order to secure, he said,

that distinct and entire conformity to the Protestant Episcopal Church of the United States, in doctrine, discipline, worship, and interest, on the assurance of which, its endowments were given, and on the continuance of which its great value depends.

Such were his words to the diocesan convention of 1835. Of the theological seminary he proposed to retain the active headship. All this was complicated with a strong desire that was growing upon him, to get away from Gambier. This desire was felt as early as 1835, and by 1837 he had made arrangements to remove to Cleveland, had secured a house in that city, and was negotiating with the vestry of Trinity Church with reference to becoming their rector. He was unhappy in Gambier. He wrote to a friend in November, 1838: "My situation here is far from being happy or, to me, profitable in point of spirits." He said that, with very few exceptions, he was as isolated as if nobody were near him. He believed that most of the professors and college people would be glad if he left town; and in that he was probably right, for some of the very conditions that led to strife between Bishop Chase and the college faculty were again developing for a contest between the faculty and Bishop McIlvaine. Perhaps he had never succeeded very well in his attempt to "minimize" his connection with the affairs of the college. It would have been hard for him to do so, for his disposition, like that of Bishop Chase, was to direct and dominate in every sphere in which he was responsible; and his responsibilities in the college were great. In all financial difficulties the college looked to him to secure money; and people in general, knowing that he was the president of the college, held him accountable for the way its affairs were managed. So long, at any rate, as he lived in Gambier, he could not let go. Just why he abandoned his purpose of moving to Cleveland is not known. The board of trustees, in March, 1838, passed a resolution declaring that his removal from Gambier would be "highly detrimental to the best interests of the Institution," and requesting him to reside there. One would like to know why the board took this action, for its policy, both before and after that time, was to diminish decidedly the Bishop's power in the college. Perhaps this resolution had weight with him; at any rate, he stayed in Gambier.

The board's policy, just spoken of, may be gathered from its actions in successive years. In November, 1835, after the Bishop had expressed to the diocesan convention his wish to be relieved, so far as possible, of attention to the concerns of the college, the board of trustees declared that

Whereas the President of the Institution having expressed the Conviction that as Diocesan he ought to be wholly engaged in the duties of the Episcopate, And whereas the Board, though highly appreciating the importance of the relation which the Bishop at present sustains to the College, do heartily concur in the conviction above expressed, therefore, Resolved . . . that the Board are ready to make the arrangement desired.

This was conditioned upon the provision by the diocese of a salary for him; for the only salary he received at that time was the one paid him by the college. In those days nothing could surpass the Diocese of Ohio in parsimony; but, stirred by this action of the trustees, it did, for one year, collect and pay to the Bishop fifteen hundred dollars, and he made his plans to leave Gambier; but a period of financial stringency ensued, and again the college was left to pay most of the Bishop's salary.

In November, 1836, the board amended the "code of laws of Kenyon College and the Senior Preparatory Department" by providing that

all duties reserved therein as pertaining to the President be considered as henceforth devolved upon the Vice President, except so far as reference may be had to Theological students & to all matters not referred by law to the Faculty. The President being considered as still having a superintending authority over all departments & as the presiding officer at meetings of the Faculty & all examinations and commencements at which he may be present.

It is evident that "a superintending authority over all departments" may mean very much or very little.

In 1837 the board in one of its resolutions referred, with no expression of regret, to the Bishop's proposed removal to Cleveland. Then, strangely enough, six months later, in March, 1838, it declared, as said above, that such removal would be "highly detrimental to the best interests of the Institution." But certainly, if they wished that he should remain in Gambier, they did not wish that he should exercise much authority there, as their action of September 4, in the same year, shows. Bishop McIlvaine was not present at that meeting, being in attendance upon the General Convention. A committee that had been appointed on the subject of defining the powers of the officers of the college, presented its views of the meaning of several sections of the constitution, and asked the opinion of the board on the same. Among these views was the following:

Your committee infer that the only power intended to be conferred by the Constitution upon the Bishop of the Diocese was to exercise as Pres't a general supervision over the police & instruction of the Seminary. And that all control over the property & territory of the institution remains with the Trustees, to be exercised by them, or their specially appointed agents. And your committee do not believe that the Bishop is in any sense the representative of the Board during its recess, nor that he has the right to do any acts affecting the Institution unless distinctly authorized by law. . . . The matter of organ-

izing the College as distinct from the Seminary with its own **Pres.**
& Professors is one which your com'te believe to be of great impor-
tance & very desirable. And they are of the opinion that the last
Clause of the tenth article of the constitution fully authorizes the
Trustees to proceed at once to such a measure.

The board unanimously concurred in the views of the
committee, and referred the subject back, with instructions
to prepare and report by-laws "consistent with the principles
contained in said Report." This sounds as if, in the opinion
of the board, the Bishop had been overstepping his authority,
not merely as to the internal affairs of the college, but also
especially as to the "property and territory" of the institution and its business affairs.

When Bishop McIlvaine heard of this he was much displeased; and he proceeded to act in a manner very different
from that of Bishop Chase seven years before. To one of his
presbyters he wrote:

Have you ever heard of there being a state of *dissatisfaction &
discord* here, *likely at last to explode?* If so, *what & when & how?*
Have you ever heard me charged with the abuse of power or the use
of *unconstitutional* power?

He considered this action of the trustees an invasion of
his constitutional rights, and he was resolved not to tolerate
it. He called the board together in special meeting, intending
to demand that it rescind its offensive action. "I do not know
what will come of it," he wrote to a friend, "but it will be a
crisis of some sort or other."

The meeting of the board was held on the twenty-second
of November, 1838, at Mount Vernon, in the basement of
the unfinished church. The only available particulars are
found in the minutes kept by the secretary. If one uses a
little imagination as he reads them, he will perceive that the
janitor did not have to make great exertions in order to keep
the room warm. The record proceeds as follows:

The Prest. having stated the particular object of the meeting, it was moved to reconsider the resolution accepting the report of the Committee defining the powers &c, passed at the last meeting of the Board. The discussion which followed was suspended by a motion to adjourn till afternoon, which was passed.

It is plain that the reconsideration was strongly opposed. All the afternoon the discussion went on, with the result that finally it was "voted to reconsider the resolution & to refer the report back to the original committee, increased by Messrs Lane and Dille." The original committee consisted of three Mount Vernon men, C. P. Buckingham, B. S. Brown, and Doctor Ridgely.

The committee of five laymen deliberated all the evening, and the next morning came in and requested to be discharged. Their request was granted, and the board then rescinded the objectionable September resolution, and adopted, as a substitute, the following declaration of opinion:

The immediate charge & superintendence of the Seminary in all its departments of instruction & police, as conferred upon the Pres't by the Constitution, necessarily includes so much power as, and no more than, belongs to the Presidents of other institutions by virtue of their office & in accordance with general usage, exclusive of such special & additional powers as may be conferred on them by specific bye-laws. In regard to all other matters connected with the Seminary, the Pres't has the right of inspection & counsel, & the Prudential Committee, to which is entrusted the care of the financial concerns of the Institution including that of the lands, & buildings & tenants thereon, and of which the Pres't is *ex officio* chairman, cannot carry any matter into final action, if he objects, without the concurrence of the Board of Trustees at its next meeting.

This action of the board was entirely consistent with its action in 1831. It treated Bishop McIlvaine as it had treated Bishop Chase; but whereas Bishop Chase resigned when his powers were thus limited, Bishop McIlvaine refused to accept the action as final, held on to his office, and finally overthrew the board and won all that he had contended for. He brought the matter before the diocesan convention at Steubenville in 1839, in connection with an amendment of the charter which, in accordance with the desire of the board of trustees, had been made by the state legislature. This amendment empowered the trustees of the Theological Seminary of the Protestant Episcopal Church in the Diocese of Ohio to "establish, in connection with said Seminary, a College, and Halls for preparatory education," to have the care of the property of the same, and to appoint a president and professors and other necessary officers for them. The president and professors of the college were to constitute a faculty, and might confer degrees in the arts and sciences, under the name of "the President and Professors of Kenyon College, in the State of Ohio." The president and professors of the theological seminary were to constitute another faculty, and might confer degrees in theology under the name of "the President and Professors of the Theological Seminary of the Diocese of Ohio."

The trustees accepted this act in August, and it came before the convention in September, 1839. It might have been thought that the Bishop would welcome it, just as it stood, for it would have given him that relief from concern about the college for which, in 1835, he had expressed so strong a desire; but he was not now of the same mind, and he declared that, although he still desired the change of the presidency, yet he desired it

only on condition that, in surrendering the Presidency, the Bishop shall receive a substitute of authority quite equivalent for the purposes originally contemplated.

Those purposes, he had said in 1835, were, to secure in every branch of the institution "distinct and entire subservience and conformity" to the "doctrine, discipline, worship, and interest" of the Protestant Episcopal Church. He now asked, and obtained, authority to appoint a committee to consider and report

whether any, and if any, what changes should be made, and under what securities, in the present relation of Kenyon College to the Episcopate and the Theological Seminary of the Diocese.

The committee appointed for this purpose was in entire agreement with the Bishop, and in its report went even beyond anything that he had publicly suggested as to the powers to be conferred upon him. Its report, which proposed three amendments of the constitution, was adopted, after some changes that, on the whole, strengthened rather than weakened it. These three amendments were of great importance. The first amendment excluded from membership in the board of trustees all officers of the seminary or college. Not even the president of the college was to be eligible. Professor Wing had been on the board of trustees since 1831, and Professor Sparrow since 1837; Bishop McIlvaine thought them hostile to him, and certainly Professor Sparrow was in favor of limiting the Bishop's powers in the college, as he had been in 1831.

The second amendment made the Bishop, during the recess of the board, "the Prudential Committee in all secular matters of the institution." This gave him all the powers of an executive committee over the business and property of the institutions. Bishop Chase never exercised greater power than that.

The third amendment directed the board of trustees, as soon as the convention of the diocese should so instruct them, to "annex to the Seminary a College with the necessary preparatory schools," which college should have a separate president and faculty, appointed and removable by the board of trustees, but the president was to be nominated by the Bishop. It was further provided that the Bishop's

Episcopal Supervision and authority be understood as embracing the spiritual interests of the college and its preparatory schools, and that the present property of the said Seminary, whatever use the Trustees may permit the College to make of any part thereof, shall always remain exclusively the property of the Seminary.

Thus was granted to Bishop McIlvaine all the power he asked for, and more. It was not granted without opposition; every motion was contested, and was voted on by orders, but the favoring majorities were large. It is true that the attendance upon this convention was small, only twenty of the fifty-two clergymen being present, and but fifteen of the fifty-seven parishes being represented; but there was a canonical quorum. The Bishop was now practically supreme in all matters of the college, unless the board itself should be hostile to him; and lest that should occur, the convention of the following year, 1840, elected an almost entirely new board, composed of men known to be acceptable to him. Very naturally he was elated at his sweeping victory. Writing to his mother, he said that certain "jealous professors" had given him trouble for three years, and that he brought the matter before the convention, and had it "well settled by the diocese, who have no idea of letting two or three men disturb the peace of their Bishop."

CHAPTER XIV

PRESIDENT DOUGLASS AND THE NEW KENYON COLLEGE

THE board of trustees met at Mount Vernon on the eighth of August, 1840, and proceeded to carry out the directions that the convention had given it. In one moment of time it wiped out the old Kenyon College, that had been in existence for fourteen years—the Kenyon College of Bishop Chase, and Edwin M. Stanton, and Henry Winter Davis, and David Davis, and Stanley Matthews— and created a new one in its place. This piece of legerdemain was accomplished by the following resolution:

[Resolved] that a College under the control and direction of the Trustees of the Theological Seminary of the Protestant Episcopal Church in the Diocese of Ohio, be established at Gambier under the name of Kenyon College, and that the buildings heretofore occupied by an institution of the same name be henceforth set apart for the uses and purposes of Kenyon College as now organized.

The old Kenyon College being thus dissolved, its faculty necessarily dissolved with it; and the board did not see fit to elect any of the old faculty to membership in that of the new college. Indeed, most of the men in the strong faculty of two or three years before had already retired as they had found opportunity to do so. Professor C. W. Fitch had entered the Detroit branch of the University of Michigan. Professor Benjamin F. Bache had returned to the navy, where, after serving in various capacities, he became director of the naval laboratory in New York, an office which he held for eighteen years, retiring in 1871 with the rank of commodore. Professor John Kendrick, who held out to the last and was dropped, entered the faculty of Marietta College in 1840, where he served to the end of his life. George

P. Williams, principal of the Senior Grammar School, became a distinguished professor at the University of Michigan, and Heman Dyer, principal of the Junior Grammar School, served the Church in many positions of importance during a long life. Thomas Odiorne, who had been agent of the college, retired also, and entered upon a successful mercantile career in Cincinnati.

Professor Sparrow, who had been vice president of the institution since 1834, being elected to no position in the new college, retained for a short time his professorship in the theological seminary, but soon resigned and accepted the chair of theology in the seminary at Alexandria, Virginia, which he retained for a third of a century. He was one of the most eminent men and scholars that have adorned the faculty of Kenyon College. He had been with it almost from the day of its birth, had made great sacrifices for it, and had served it most capably and with entire devotion. Yet he had been a thorn in the side, first to Bishop Chase, then to Bishop McIlvaine. With Bishop McIlvaine now seated firmly in the saddle, there was nothing for Professor Sparrow to do but leave Gambier; which he did with sorrow, and in a very quiet and amicable manner. Bishop McIlvaine was glad to have him go, but before long wished that he was back. Twice in after years he was called to the presidency of the college on Bishop McIlvaine's nomination, but he would not return to a position fraught with possibilities so unpleasant.

Professor Wing retained his place in the theological seminary, and was the only survivor of the old group of men who had made the college what it was. Otherwise there was a complete clearing of the boards, and a new faculty came on. There were in all, three professors, not one of whom bore an academic degree. Professor Sandels was a young man, taken out of the seminary before he had completed his course there; Professor Thrall was a good country doctor; Professor Ross, a military man, was a teacher of ability. On the

WILLIAM SPARROW

SAMUEL FULLER

BENJAMIN LOCKE LANG

EDWARD CLOSE BENSON

FOUR ACTING PRESIDENTS

whole, the faculty of the new Kenyon College was below the standard of that of "the institution that had borne that name." The Reverend A. Blake and the Reverend Norman Badger became principals of the Junior Grammar School; two men who were to be long, and most usefully, connected with institutions at Gambier.

One man of distinction the college faculty had, the first man who ever bore the title of president of Kenyon College, David Bates Douglass. He had been an officer and teacher at West Point when Bishop McIlvaine was chaplain there, and a warm friendship had been formed by the two men. Subsequently he left the Military Academy, and engaged in engineering work of a most important character. When Bishop McIlvaine first came to Ohio he planned to have Major Douglass as vice president of Kenyon College, wrote him letters begging him to come, thought that he was coming, and inserted his name in the catalogue. The episcopal address to the convention of 1834 contains the statement that

the apparatus of the department of Nat. Philosophy [of Kenyon College] has been increased by valuable donations from D. B. Douglass Esq. who though affectionately attached to the institution, has been unavoidably prevented from becoming, as was hoped and expected, its Vice President.

The principal article of this gift was an Atwood's machine, to illustrate the law of falling bodies—a somewhat ominous acquisition, under the circumstances of the institution. When, in 1839, under the new constitution a president was to be chosen for the college, Bishop McIlvaine again made a determined effort to secure Major Douglass for the office. It would hardly be possible to devise terms more urgent than those in which he appealed to him to come to Gambier and devote his life to Kenyon College.

In the spring of 1841 Major Douglass came, and at once found much to do. Being a military man and a civil engineer, he was distressed at the rather haphazard way in which many things were done in the college; and during his administration he made great efforts to introduce improvements. But what he found most unendurable was the dilapidated and filthy state of the college building, and the neglected condition of the grounds, in which there were still no established walks and drives, and where woodpiles with their accompaniments of bark and sawdust were prominent features of the view, while everywhere there had accumulated through the years all that diversified litter which men living in college know so well how to disseminate about them. The first task, therefore, at which President Douglass set himself, and the one in which he attained permanent results, was that of reformation.

Old Kenyon was in a lamentable state. Bishop McIlvaine, justifying an expenditure of money upon it, said: "Its condition was a disgrace. Our poverty had too long delayed a remedy. We were either to be ashamed to receive students, or make repairs." President Douglass completely renovated the older part of the building, replastering extensively. He tore out the "three story frame bunks," with their long-settled inhabitants, and introduced bedsteads, washstands, and other articles of furniture known to civilization.

The next task that President Douglass took in hand was that of bringing the unsightly grounds of the college into order and beauty. Many old sheds and shanties were removed; the Old Seventy Four perished unwept; rubbish was cleared away, and woodpiles were removed to inconspicuous places. The wide street designed by Bishop Chase, with its Sutton and Bexley Squares, had never been realized, and President Douglass definitely abandoned the idea. He substituted a plan in which the great avenue extended no further south than Wiggin Street, and access to the college grounds by teams and carriages was provided by drives that entered at the eastern and western sides, sweeping around near the crest of the hill, past the college. From the middle door of Kenyon, straight through the midst of the abandoned avenue, he drove a path ten feet wide, terminating fifteen hundred feet north of the college, apparently just on the rear line of a tier of lots that had been laid out fronting on Wiggin Street. There, at the end of the path—it was seventeen years before it was extended further north—he set up the pillars of the gates, which are among the most familiar objects to everyone who knows Gambier. Heavy wooden gates were hung, of which the iron hinge-pins, and the catch are the only remnants, while the inner sides of the pillars bear the deep marks of the iron weights which for nearly sixty years pounded against them. Between the pillars was planted the central post, destined to become a rock of offence to many generations of Freshmen, because not insurmountable. Three stone steps led down to the lower walk outside. Straight east and west from the gates extended a picket fence. In making the path the earth was removed to the depth of two feet, and a foundation of coarse broken stone was laid down, with finer stone and gravel on top. College students contributed much of the labor. Thus originated the Path, and so well was it made that for eighty years it has required only surface repairs. But good as the Path was, it was not beautiful, for there was not a tree near it; so all along its length, as President Douglass had designed, hard maple trees were planted a few years later by Professor Ross, assisted by students.

To President Douglass we owe the college grounds as we know and love them, the gates and the Path, an abiding memorial of him who first saw them in his imagination, and then made them real. So familiar are they to every living Kenyon man that it is almost impossible to think how the Park looked without them.

Another important and enduring institution at Kenyon College which owes its origin to President Douglass, is the custom of matriculation. The catalogue for 1842 contains this announcement:

Matriculation. No student even after his admission to *residence* is allowed to *matriculate*, until, after a probation of *at least* twenty weeks, he shall have established a personal claim to the confidence of the Faculty; failing in which he is liable to be dismissed.

Matriculation alone establishes the condition of full and accredited membership in the Institution, and renders the student, upon whom it is conferred, a proper candidate for degrees and honours. Should any student after matriculation, abuse the confidence on which that act proceeds, he may be degraded, *i.e.* reduced again to the position of a probationer, and then further disciplined, as the occasion may require.

The requirement that a matriculated student be "degraded" before he could be subjected to serious discipline, and, if he were not dismissed, the necessity of restoring him after he had sustained the discipline and had again become good, proved cumbersome, and must sometimes have produced situations that were a little ridiculous in the quick succession of degradation and rehabilitation. So, in time this was abandoned; but the custom of matriculation has remained, and is another monument to President Douglass.

In 1841, after President Douglass had been about six months in Gambier, Bishop McIlvaine said to the diocesan convention that the new president had infused "great life and vigor" into all the government and instruction of the college and grammar schools; but his administration did not realize its early promise. He had a hard task before him when he assumed the presidency; many of the conditions were inimical to his success. In the first place, he was not in reality president of the college. The constitution, as revised in 1839, excluded him from membership in the board of trustees, and, except when specially invited, he could not be present at its meetings, but must communicate with it, if at all, through Bishop McIlvaine. That in itself marked the inferiority of his position, and rendered it almost impossible that he should carry out any vigorous, independent policy. Probably no strong man, except a soldier who was accustomed to being under authority, would have consented to take such a place. Being, however, also accustomed to exercising authority over those who were under him, he seems not to have had the friendship of any members of the faculties, except that of the other soldier, Professor Ross. Again, just as he began his administration the college fell into desperately narrow financial straits, and all appropriations were cut to the lowest notch; and Bishop McIlvaine, who had to spend time and strength collecting money to keep the institution alive, was naturally indisposed to encourage any expenditure that could possibly be avoided. He subjected every item in the bills to a minute scrutiny, and was outspoken in his criticism of every dollar of outlay that seemed to him to have been avoidable. He cannot be blamed for this, for he knew how difficult it was to get money, and in his position as prudential committee he was mainly responsible for expenditures; but his criticism of Major Douglass in this respect seems undeserved, and unjust.

Again, for some reason or other, the college students took to behaving themselves in an unusually bad manner. The mischief had, indeed, begun before Major Douglass came. The records of faculty meetings in 1838 show students expelled for "outrages committed"; and so necessary did surveillance of the students seem, that it was voted that "each member of the college faculty visit the rooms of the College students once a week." But in 1841 the pages of the faculty record book begin to be stained in a wholly unwonted manner with cases of students dismissed for drinking, and for other yet more grave infractions of decency. And moreover, the habit of rebellion fastened on the students, and twice there were serious contests, resulting in many dismissals.

All this disorder seemed to argue some defect in the discipline of the college. It would be hard to tell where the fault lay, but inevitably the president had to bear a good deal of the blame. It was charged against him that he was unpopular with the students; to which he replied that, so far as this was true, it was to be attributed to his strict enforcement of discipline, and to the influence of certain professors and teachers who were undermining him. The number of students fell off. In 1840 there were fifty-one students in the college; in 1842 this number had increased by six, in 1843 it dropped to forty-one, and in 1844 there were but forty-three. The attendance at the grammar school just about held its own: in 1840 there were forty-seven pupils, in 1844 there were forty-eight. But these figures were much below those of former years. At the time when Bishop McIlvaine overthrew the old faculty, there were seventy-seven college students, a greater number than had ever before been known: and there were one hundred and fifteen grammar school pupils.

It was, of course, disappointing to the Bishop that his new arrangement should work so disastrously, and it was natural, under the circumstances, to cast the blame for the failure upon President Douglass. Relations between the two men who had once been so friendly became strained. On the twenty-eighth of February, 1844, a special meeting of the board of trustees was held in Gambier, on the Bishop's call, to find out what was the matter with the college. Bishop McIlvaine assigned them the quest, but himself took no part in their investigations, and expressed no opinion. They went at their business in a very direct manner, going about the town and asking the members of the faculty and other college people, to tell them where the trouble lay; and nearly everybody said that President Douglass was unpopular, and that this was the principal source of the diminutions and disorders. *Vox populi, vox dei:* that seems to have been the conclusion of the board. Of all these proceedings President

PRESIDENT DOUGLASS

Douglass knew nothing, until Professor Ross called and told him what was going on, and warned him of what would probably happen. President Douglass was greatly surprised. In all his experience in the army he had never known of an investigation carried on in this way, and without any notification to the person investigated. When finally he was offered an opportunity to say what he could in his defence, he refused to say anything, unless in answer to definite charges; and no such charges were presented. He was requested, with much profession of respect and regret, to resign; he would not do so. Nothing therefore remained but to declare the presidency vacant; and that was done.

It was a year and a half before Kenyon College again had a president. The Reverend Samuel Fuller, Milnor professor, was acting president for a short time. In August Bishop McIlvaine nominated Doctor Sparrow, and the nomination was unanimously confirmed by the board, but Doctor Sparrow would not return to Gambier. In March, 1845, the Reverend W. W. Speer of Philadelphia was in the like manner elected, and he too declined. In August of that year the Reverend Sherlock A. Bronson, a member of the board of trustees, who had for some time been in temporary charge of the college, became president.

BIOGRAPHICAL NOTE

DAVID BATES DOUGLASS

BORN at Pompton, N. J., 1790. Graduated at Yale College, 1813. Entered the army, and in the War of 1812, as second lieutenant, commanded a company at the battles of Niagara and Lundy's Lane. Rendered conspicuous service in repairing Fort Erie under fire of the enemy's guns, and was promoted first lieutenant and brevetted captain. From 1819 to 1831 he was a professor at West Point, occupying the chair of civil and military engineering from

1823 onward. In 1831 he resigned from the army and became chief engineer of the Morris canal. Subsequently held a position in University of the City of New York, and designed its principal building. Made surveys and plans for supplying New York City with water, and showed the feasibility of obtaining it from the Croton River. In 1838 laid out Greenwood Cemetery in Brooklyn. Was President of Kenyon College, 1840-1844. After leaving Gambier he laid out cemeteries at Albany and Quebec, and was occupied with important engineering work in Brooklyn. Became professor of mathematics at Hobart College in 1848. Died at Geneva in October, 1849, and was buried in Greenwood Cemetery, at the request of its corporation. His monument, dignified, and of impressive size, bears this inscription:

In Memory Of
David Bates Douglass
Who Departed This Life October 21st 1849.
Aged 59 Years.
This Monument is Erected by the Corporation of the Green-Wood Cemetery to Commemorate the Zealous Services of its First President, Who from the Incorporation of the Cemetery in 1838, until his Resignation in January 1841, Earnestly Devoted his Abilities to Promote its Establishment.

CHAPTER XV

DELIVERANCE FROM FINANCIAL
EMBARRASSMENT

BY becoming the prudential committee of the board of trustees Bishop McIlvaine had gathered into his own hands the entire financial direction of the college and seminary. True, the trustees might intervene, but they would not, and did not. The reasons that seemed to justify, and even to require this control of all pecuniary matters were, first, that the Bishop was the only person who could raise considerable sums of money for the institutions; and second, that the experience of the board with financial agents had been unsatisfactory. Again and again it had happened that full and intelligible reports could not be got from the agents, and that money was spent without authority. The unfortunate agents, succeeding one another rapidly, did the best they could, and must have heard with full understanding that passage of Scripture read in the church that speaks of making bricks without straw; nevertheless, they often annoyed the board with their doings. The Bishop, as prudential committee, living at Gambier, could know what was done, and could keep his hands on the purse strings.

As an example of the straits and expedients to which the college agents were put, even with Bishop McIlvaine in charge, consider the case of E. W. Crittenden, agent. In April, 1842, he writes to a New York lawyer who has been pressing for money due his clients. Mr. Crittenden tells him that the college cannot pay anything immediately; but he has purchased more than three hundred and sixty sheep, and expects to buy as many more, and these, with the natural increase, will amount to more than one thousand the next fall. "The entire product of these sheep," he says, shall go to pay the debt, and he is just sending three hundred and fifty fleeces to New York, and whatever they bring is to go to his importunate correspondent. A few months later Mr. Crittenden wrote to Bishop McIlvaine resigning the agency. He said he had given his word to the New York creditors, trusting that the board would support him. Apparently it had not done so. Moreover, he had been obliged to borrow $200 in Newark, to discharge a pressing debt of honor, and had not been repaid.

It will be remembered that in 1833 Bishop McIlvaine had secured $30,000 for the college and seminary, and had borrowed $15,000 for ten years. With this money, and with the proceeds of the sale of lands in the North Section, debts had been paid and buildings erected. Unfortunately, other buildings and improvements had been needed, and they had cost more money than the trustees could pay, and so a new debt was incurred; and in 1843 the borrowed $15,000 had to be repaid. These debts had required a heavy payment of interest each year. Altogether, in 1842, there was a debt of about $30,000, and creditors were pressing for pay, and there was nothing to pay with, unless the trustees should sell lands in the South Section. These four thousand acres, now constituting College Township, had been sacredly preserved as a moral safeguard to the students; and, although the forest walls had not proved impenetrable by evil, still most of the friends of the college felt that they had protective value. Besides, here was a noble domain, and the hills and valleys about Gambier grip one's heart, and no one, owning them, would willingly let them go. There was a very strong sentiment against selling them; but money must be had, and the land was the only asset that could be turned into money. On the other hand, land was then selling at very low prices. The trustees had ample power to sell, but would not exercise it without the advice and consent of the diocese. A special convention was held in December, 1842, for conference upon this subject. The Bishop, in an address of admirable clearness, laid the matter before the convention, declining to give advice. A committee was appointed to consider the subject of the sale of the land, and made a report that "no prudent man would force his real estate into the market unless compelled to do so, during the present pecuniary embarrassment of all classes. . . . A serious loss would be incurred by the sale of the College lands at this time." The committee therefore advised that the Bishop be requested to make an effort to procure pecuniary aid, by donation or loan, to relieve the institutions; and the convention accepted the advice and made the request.

Bishop McIlvaine had probably expected this action, for there was really nothing else to do under the circumstances; yet it was with a heavy heart that he accepted the task—"as a cross," he said, "that cannot well be laid on any other shoulders." The financial stringency of the times had never been more severe than in this very winter of 1842-1843, and he knew that it would be useless to visit the East just then asking for money; and probably his well-informed friends in business foresaw an improvement in the coming summer, and suggested that he delay his visit until that season. At any rate, he did so delay, and when he arrived in New York already the skies were brightening, and in the autumn business, so long depressed, began to revive, and confidence in the future was restored. This, of course, was highly favorable to the Bishop's mission; and other circumstances, immediately to be spoken of, added their help. The money came in, for the most part, in small sums freely given by men and women of little wealth, who devotedly believed in the cause which Bishop McIlvaine represented. This cause was not solely that of the Gambier institutions, but also that of certain theological views.

The Oxford Movement had already begun to have its effect upon the Episcopal Church in America, and Bishop

McIlvaine was coming into prominence as a leader of those who were opposed to its doctrines and practices. From that time forward to the end of his life he was looked upon, both in America and England, as one of the ablest, most aggressive, champions of the Evangelical Party; and the theological seminary at Gambier came to be regarded as one of its strongholds. This history is not concerned with theological matters, but it is necessary to make it clear that from this time onward for many years Gambier was evangelical. The *Western Episcopalian* once said with pride that the name Gambier was "synonymous with the doctrine of Justification by Faith." This identification was a source of strength. It has been said that Kenyon College suffered from its alliance with the Evangelicals; and it is true that for this cause it lost some friends, some patronage, and possibly some money; but Kenyon College lived, while all the colleges started in the West by those who held other views, died. Kenyon could get money—not much of it, but enough to prevent dissolution—while the others could not. The Episcopal Church has never known a nobler man than Bishop Kemper. He was identified with views which Bishop McIlvaine opposed. His college, which began with splendid hopes, perished for lack of a little money; while that of Bishop McIlvaine lived, because it had access to a more generous clientele. The Evangelicals were good friends of Kenyon while they lasted.

The total sum secured was about $35,000, of which less than six thousand came from Ohio. The Bishop's effort was, for those times, a tremendous one, "heavy, arduous, heart-wearying, and soul-trying," he said; but he freed the institutions from debt. If, in the very midst of his laborious efforts he showed a good deal of irritability in his dealings with President Douglass, this may be excused by those who remember that it is much harder to raise money for a school declining in numbers, than for one that is increasing. And besides, President Douglass was, of necessity, always spending money, and Bishop McIlvaine knew that it would devolve upon himself to provide it. If Bishop McIlvaine seemed ambitious in his demand to have power in the institutions, certainly he was ready also to accept the burdens that came with it, and carry the difficulties to a happy issue.

In 1845 the college was free from pressing indebtedness, the inadequacy of its income was not making any special trouble, affairs were moving smoothly under President Bronson, Rosse Chapel was at last finished and consecrated, and the seminary had taken up its abode in Bexley Hall. There was nothing that would imperatively hold Bishop McIlvaine longer in Gambier. He was never happy there; he felt, with some degree of reason, that he was not liked there; he complained that he was made the scapegoat of all the troubles that developed upon the Hill. He purchased property in Clifton, near Cincinnati, and removed thither in 1846. Thereafter, so long as he lived, Clifton was his home. He delegated to others, or simply *left* to them, the direct management of most of the affairs at Gambier, securing thus that freedom from care which he had so strongly desired in 1835, but had refused to accept in 1838. He remained president of the theological seminary, was often at Bexley Hall, and saw to it that men of sound, evangelical views composed its faculty. He was still the prudential committee of Kenyon College, but at his request the board of trustees in 1846 appointed President Bronson, Professor Wing, Professor Denison, and Mr. Columbus Delano of Mount Vernon to aid him in the discharge of the duties of that office. From that time forward he concerned himself but little with the details of its affairs. Why should he worry about them? They would get on somehow, and probably better than if he attended more closely to them. The demands upon him of evangelical truth, as he understood them, were very great; so, in a measure, he let Gambier go; and that was well both for him and for it.

FINANCIAL NOTE

BISHOP McILVAINE'S address to the special convention of 1842 gives much information regarding financial conditions at the seminary and college.

The institutions had three regular sources of revenue. 1, The income from the lands, in the form of rents, receipts from the sale of produce, and so forth. 2, In the college and grammar schools, tuition fees and other charges. (Theological students made no such payments.) 3, The chair of Divinity in the theological seminary received $510 a year from the Milnor Fund, which was the only endowment fund the institutions possessed. For five years after Bishop McIlvaine's coming to Ohio, subscribers had paid six hundred a year to maintain a professor of Sacred Literature, but those subscriptions had not been renewed, probably because of the hard times.

During the last seven years the college and grammar schools earned, in the way of tuition fees, charges for rooms, and so forth, within $392 of enough to pay all regular expenses; but, owing to the hard times, they had not been able to collect all that they had earned. These bad debts, through the seven years, amounted to $2,500; so that altogether the college and schools had fallen behind $2,892. The theological seminary in the last nine years had failed to meet its expenses out of its endowment and its subscribed fund, by $2,730. Therefore the cost of sustaining the college and preparatory schools for the last seven years, and sustaining the seminary for the last nine years, had exceeded their earnings and incomes from endowments, by $5,622.

Now during the last eleven years the income from the lands, after deducting all expenses, had been $14,350, which was sufficient to pay all the deficiencies of the seminary, college, and schools, and leave $8,000 or $9,000 over. But unfortunately during all that time the institutions had been carrying heavy debts, the interest of which had swallowed up the income from the lands.

These financial difficulties, then, were wholly due to the debts. Bishop McIlvaine tells where the items of indebtedness came from.

1. Remainder of debt from Bishop Chase's time, $10,000
2. Cost of house for Bishop McIlvaine, and repairs, 5,700
3. Bishop's salary and moving expenses, 4,030
4. Building twelve houses and shops for people employed
    by the college—farmers, mechanics, etc., 3,900
5. Clearing and fencing land, 2,250

6. Repairs and improvements made by President Doug-
    lass,   3,225
7. Excess of expenses in college and seminary during
    eleven years, as above,   5,622
                                                                      ─────────
                                                                      $34,727

Since in this report some of the items are for seven years, some for
nine years, and some for eleven, it can be taken only as giving a
general idea of receipts, expenditures, deficits, and debts; nevertheless, it contains much interesting and instructive information, and
leaves no doubt as to where the trouble lay.

CHAPTER XVI

THE COLLEGE UNDER PRESIDENTS BRONSON, SMITH, AND ANDREWS

THE Reverend Sherlock Anson Bronson, who became president of Kenyon College in August, 1845, was a graduate of both the college and the seminary, and had for several years been a member of the board of trustees. He was, therefore, well acquainted with the institution over which he was called to preside. During the five years of his administration the internal affairs of the college were uneventful and moderately prosperous. Membership in the board of trustees, which had been taken from the president of the college in 1840, was restored in 1845. The number of students in the college and grammar schools increased slightly. The members of the faculty were diligent in their work, and harmonious one with another. The students manifested nothing of the rebellious spirit that had characterized their predecessors in the days of President Douglass; yet their mild misdemeanors were visited with severe punishments. A young man in whose room a pack of playing cards was found, and another, who rang the college bell between the hours of eleven and twelve at night, were dismissed from college.

It is only in the history of financial affairs that we find something of interest and importance in this administration. Bishop McIlvaine's great campaign of 1843 was thought to have relieved the institutions of all indebtedness; but this was not true. The inexpert bookkeeping of the college agent had not taken account of all that the college owed; so that it was found later that the entire $34,000 which the Bishop had secured was not enough to pay the debt. Two thousand dollars of this money had been designated by the givers to

PRESIDENT BRONSON

PRESIDENT SMITH

PRESIDENT STONE

PRESIDENT TAPPAN

complete Bexley Hall and Rosse Chapel, and was immediately so expended, but was found insufficient. Thereupon the Bishop, as the prudential committee, authorized the agent to go on with the work. He felt justified in doing this, for the income of the previous year had considerably exceeded the expenses, and it had not yet been discovered that the money he had collected was inadequate even to pay the debts. So it was not long before the institutions were owing nearly $10,000, and had nothing with which to pay. It was a familiar situation, yet not the pleasanter because of that. Then the income began to fall off, and for several years expenditures exceeded the receipts from tuition charges and rents. These rents brought in very little; and occasionally, when the crops failed, the farm lands brought in nothing at all.

The trustees exercised the strictest economy, the rigors of which were experienced chiefly by the members of the faculty, whose salaries were cut to very small amounts, and then were paid at irregular intervals, while these unfortunate men were required to keep in repair the houses they occupied, and pay the taxes upon them. Still the college continued to run deeper into debt, and new sources of expense were constantly developing. The roof of Rosse Chapel was crushed in by a heavy fall of snow, and the roof of Old Kenyon became so leaky as to require reshingling. The legislature of Ohio took this unfortunate time to lay a tax of $500 upon the college real estate. This tax was the last straw. The college could not pay it, and when it had defaulted two years in succession the sheriff sold the lands to pay the taxes, and thereupon the other creditors began to press their claims. Never had Kenyon College been in so desperate a situation. Bishop McIlvaine was not disposed to undertake another campaign for money. What could be done? There was one resource: some of the college land might be sold. In the South Section, were four thousand acres, of which at least three thousand five hundred might be sold, probably at $20 an acre, bringing in $70,000—and this was the minimum estimate. If this were done, the college would still have all the land it needed—five hundred acres—the debts, which amounted to less than $15,000, could be paid in three or four years out of the interest on the $70,000, and the entire principal could be saved and permanently invested. Thus would be created what at that time was considered "a very generous endowment," which would in itself pay all the current expenses. Here was an obvious and very easy solution of all the financial difficulties; and, as it appeared, an ample provision against future difficulties of the same kind.

But, even in these desperate circumstances, there was strong opposition to the sale of the land. Ever since Bishop Chase purchased it, the South Section had been regarded almost as holy ground; and he himself had always declared that to alienate any part of it would be to violate the intention and will of the English donors. When the matter was under discussion in the diocesan convention of 1848, Mr. Charles B. Goddard of Zanesville, in behalf of Bishop Chase, read a protest against the proposed sale, saying that it would be in contravention of conditions upon which the college was founded. The board of trustees had no doubt of its right in law to make the sale, and was convinced that there was no other means by which the college could be saved; yet it was unwilling to act without the approval of the diocesan convention, to which, therefore, in 1848, it appealed for advice. Through this convention and the next the matter was hotly fought, and President Bronson was the leader of the forces that advocated the sale. His argument was that the funds of the college, which were then unprofitably invested in lands, ought to be reinvested in something that would bring a larger income; and that a body of substantial and intelligent landowners would afford a better moral environment and safeguard than would poor, and shifting, and irresponsible people who were content to farm other men's lands, and live in homes rented for a year at a time. President Bronson was a master of clear exposition and forcible reasoning; and both in convention and out of it he so unanswerably demonstrated the necessity of selling the land that those who would not be convinced took great offence, and said harsh and unjust things about him. He was sensitive to this criticism, and in February, 1849, presented to the board of trustees his resignation of the presidency. He was persuaded to withdraw it; but in September, 1850, having seen the triumph of the cause he had so strongly advocated, he again resigned, and this time finally. He must be counted among those who have rendered great services to Kenyon College. Taking the presidency at a time when the institution was distrusted, distracted, and disorderly, he brought it into harmony and good order, and restored confidence in it. He had the courage and the ability to lead in the fight for the selling of the land. His is the credit of having saved the college from most serious loss—perhaps from destruction.

The diocesan convention of 1849 adopted resolutions approving of the sale of the land, and recommending that the proceeds be invested

in some safe, permanent, and productive securities, so that only the interest accruing therefrom shall be used, except so far as the rights and demands of present creditors may require an expenditure of the principal.

In February, 1849, the board of trustees directed that so much of the land be surveyed and sold as might be necessary to satisfy the demands against the institution. The sale went slowly, nevertheless some farms, and a good many village lots, were sold, and more and more as time went on; and by one shift and another the college was able to satisfy, or quiet, its creditors, and meet its running expenses.

One early consequence of the sale was the incorporation of the "Town of Gambier" by an act of the legislature, on March 15, 1850. To the town council power was granted to regulate, or prevent, theatrical and other public exhibitions and shows, and prevent gambling and riotous and disorderly conduct, provided that all ordinances that affected the "good order and government of Kenyon College" should be subject to the approval of the authorities of the institution. The sale of ardent spirits, except upon a physician's prescription, was prohibited. It was noticed that as soon as Gambier had citizens that owned their houses and grounds the appearance of the village was greatly improved.

One of the "shifts" to which the college was put in its need of money was the sale of scholarship scrip—a device pregnant with trouble. In September, 1851, the agent was authorized to offer for sale scrip of four classes. The first class sold at $36, and entitled the holder to two years' tuition, for himself or for anyone he might designate. The fourth class, selling at $200, insured a perpetual scholarship. The second and third classes conferred intermediate benefits. All these were good investments for the purchaser, and bad bargains for the college. This insane expedient was in favor with western colleges at that period. It sometimes brought in a good deal of ready money, and always gave cause for much repentance at leisure. Kenyon College resorted to it several times.

Upon the resignation of President Bronson, Doctor Sparrow was again elected president of the college; but he again declined, and in June, 1851, the Reverend Thomas Mather Smith, who, since 1845, had been Milnor professor of divinity in the theological seminary, and for several months past had performed the duties of president of the college, was elected to that office. He took the position at considerable sacrifice to himself, intending to hold it only until a suitable man could be found; and in the meanwhile he retained his theological professorship. His administration was successful, for the faculty was enlarged and strengthened, and the number of students increased. Financial conditions also improved, more land was sold, and for the first time in its history Kenyon College was really out of debt. The prospect seemed to be hopeful, and President Smith, in November, 1853, felt justified in resigning the position he had reluctantly taken. He retained the Milnor professorship until 1864.

Although the college was now out of debt, yet there was no money in the treasury to warrant an increase in the salaries of the professors, or even to make necessary repairs upon the buildings. The standard salary at Kenyon in 1853 was $600 and a house. The money was paid very irregularly, and generally the house leaked. Ex-president Bronson said,

The labor of men at Gambier whose wages have been kept back . . . will cry to heaven for vengeance upon those who have oppressed the hireling and kept back his wages.

He seems to have had definite persons in mind upon whom this vengeance would be invoked, but we cannot now discern anyone who appears especially guilty. The professors felt that something must be done, and they submitted to the trustees a proposal by which they hoped to get some of the money that was due them. According to this scheme the Park and college buildings and houses were to be given into the care of the faculty, who would choose an agent to receive and hold all fees paid by the students, subject to the order of the faculty. The money was to be applied to pay running expenses and make repairs, and the remainder was to go to pay the salaries of the members of the faculty, so far as they were not otherwise paid. This was a counsel of desperation. The trustees adopted the plan, but it was probably never carried into action. That such a scheme could be proposed and approved shows how hard the situation was; and we are not surprised to learn that Professors Thrall, Denison, and Brooke resigned.

Further evidence of the financial difficulties that were caused by an insufficiency of income is presented in a series of preambles and resolutions offered by Judge Swan at a meeting of the trustees in September, 1853. These were to the effect that, whereas it was inexpedient to spend on current expenses and repairs money received from the sale of the lands, and whereas there was not sufficient income to provide for all necessary expenses, "and whereas Kenyon College is but an appendage of the Theological Seminary, and subordinate in importance," therefore, "Resolved that the college department be, and the same is, temporarily suspended." The trustees voted that the trust funds and the money received from the sale of lands should not be used for current expenses; but they refused to suspend the college. Instead of that, within less than a month, when President Smith resigned, they elected Lorin Andrews president of the college, at a salary of $1,500 and a house. Mr. Andrews accepted the office, and soon came to Gambier. The students gave him a hearty reception, and in his honor illuminated Old Kenyon.

Lorin Andrews, when he became president of the college, was well known throughout Ohio as a most zealous and able promoter of the cause of public school education. He was a successful teacher and school superintendent, and was constantly asked to speak at teachers' institutes and other educational gatherings. His reputation, and the confidence with which he was regarded, at once drew students to Gambier. Already, during the administration of President Smith, the number of students had begun to increase, and President Andrews, in order to fill the college, had only to strengthen an existing tendency. While he was president the attendance at the grammar school diminished, but the college enrollment reached the unprecedented number of one hundred and thirty-seven. There were two hundred and thirteen students at Gambier, in the three departments, when the Civil War broke out.

So great an increase of students required an increase of rooms to contain them, and of recitation rooms and laboratories for their work. The completion of Bexley Hall and the building of Ascension Hall were the response to this demand. The rooms in the western half of Bexley, which had never been finished, were now plastered and made ready to be occupied. Old Kenyon had hitherto been adequate to supplying the college with all the accommodations it needed, —dormitories, classrooms, laboratories, library rooms, society halls,—besides giving rooms at times to most of the grammar school pupils; but now, after shifting the preparatory students back to Milnor Hall, filling Park Cottage to overflowing, and reoccupying the bull's-eye rooms—which had long been given over to rats and rubbish—still it was necessary to find rooms in the village for many college students. Therefore Bishop McIlvaine, who, throughout all his episcopate, was the chief reliance of the college when money was needed, secured from members of the Church of the Ascension in New York City a large part of what was needed to build a new dormitory. Hence the name Ascension Hall. Doctor Gregory T. Bedell, afterwards Bishop of Ohio, was then rector of that parish.

Ascension Hall was planned to meet several needs. The wings were to house students, the lower floor of the middle part was to provide a scientific lecture room and a laboratory, the second and third floors of the middle part were to be occupied by the literary societies, and the tower was to furnish an observatory. The building was very conveniently arranged for the purposes its designers had in view. By the first of January, 1860, the north end was completed, and was occupied by students, the society rooms and the scientific rooms in the central part were in use, and the telescope and transit instrument, given by Mr. Peter Neff, had been installed in the tower. It was expected that the continued increase of students would soon require that the rooms at the south end be finished off.

It was President Andrews' good fortune to see the college attain a comfortable financial position. Debts were paid, buildings were repaired, and the standard salary of a professor was increased to $1,000 and a house. This was due partly to increased tuition fees, and partly to the sale of land, which, although disappointingly slow at first, afterwards quickened. The trustees of the college, for the first time in their existence as a corporation, had money to invest, in considerable sums. Not everyone was satisfied that all their investments were sound. An investigation by a committee of the diocesan convention revealed no serious indiscretion, beyond the purchase of $5,000 worth of stock in the Springfield and Loudonville Railroad, which, as then projected, was to run through Gambier. The college also lent some assistance to another dream railway, the Delaware and Coshocton. It did not matter greatly in what direction a proposed road led, so long as it seemed likely to enable one to get into and out of Gambier on a train of cars.

CHAPTER XVII

BEXLEY HALL, 1833-1861

WE have seen that theological education received but little practical attention while Bishop Chase was in charge of the Theological Seminary of the Protestant Episcopal Church in the Diocese of Ohio. An official statement published by him in May, 1830, says that there is "no especial Theological Department" of the institution. The first published catalogue, that of 1831-1832, bears the title of "Catalogue of the Officers and Students of Kenyon College and Grammar School." It begins its lists, however, with "Theological Students," of whom there were three, not one of them a "son of the soil" of Ohio; all were from the Atlantic States. The second catalogue, published the next year, puts the name "Theological Seminary of the Diocese of Ohio" first on its title-page; but it includes no list of theological students, and says nothing about theological education. Nevertheless, both at Worthington and at Gambier a few men had read theology under the direction of the Bishop and Mr. Sparrow, and had been ordained upon completing their studies. Eight men are known thus to have received theological instruction before the coming of Bishop McIlvaine in 1833.

It was Bishop McIlvaine who organized the seminary and set it going. Addressing the diocesan convention in December, 1842, he said:

Prior to my coming to the Diocese to reside, which was nine years ago last July, there had been no course of study for theological students organized. It is now nine years since a full course in all the usual departments of preparation for candidates for orders in our Church was set up.

One of Bishop McIlvaine's first efforts was to provide a

separate building for the theological department. In November, 1834, he sailed for England, and there he remained until the following June. He was received, he said, "with truly christian and affectionate kindness, hospitality, and cordial coöperation."

After seeking advice and the candid expression of opinion on the part of some of the wisest and best of that Church, as to the propriety and expediency of the effort, I ventured to solicit donations in money for the erection of a new building at the seat of our Theological Seminary, for the accommodation of theological students, and also donations in books for the increase of the library of the same. . . . The propriety of the appeal, and the entire sufficiency of the main ground on which it was placed, were promptly and affectionately acknowledged and responded to. I asked only for as much money as I thought would enable us to erect a good building for about 40 theological students, hoping that when more room should be needed, other means would be provided from other sources for its construction. . . . The funds obtained for the desired and much needed building for theological students amount about to $12,600, all of which are appropriated by the contributors to that specific purpose. I am much indebted to Mr. H. Roberts, an architect in London, and zealous of good works, for the donation of a very commodious and beautiful plan of a building, with separate drawings of every, the minutest part, so that any good mechanic may follow them. In conformity with this the building will be erected, if Providence permit. . . . It is so planned as to furnish every two students a sitting room, or study, of about 17 by 15; and each of them a bed room of about 14 by 8, thus allowing all needful opportunity for privacy in devotion and study. So great has been the kindness of the Rt. Hon. Lord Bexley towards the two Bishops of this Diocese, while sojourners in England; such his interest, from the beginning, in the promotion of the gospel in our western states, by means of the Theological Seminary of Ohio, and such the value of his co-operation in the efforts by which the funds above spoken of were obtained, that when about to take leave of him, on my return, I knew no better way of expressing my sense of his kindness and of our obligation, than by requesting his permission to call the proposed building by his name. Having received his cordial, though modest, assent, the edifice will be denominated Bexley Hall. (*Diocesan Journal*, 1835.)

LORD BEXLEY

Eager though the Bishop was to provide a house for the seminary, yet four years elapsed before work was begun on the building. Light is thrown on the causes of this delay by the following extracts from the minutes of the board of trustees:

(November 9, 1836. Gambier.) Resolved that the President of the Board be requested to write to the Trustees of the Sem. fund in England, to obtain their consent to the appropriation of the Bishop's House to the use of a seminary building, to answer, with suitable additions, in the place of the one proposed to be erected according to the plan received from England.

(September 5, 1837. Columbus. From a report of the Committee on Finance.) It is a source of regret that our English friends and patrons are unwilling to accede to the arrangements proposed at the last meeting of the Board. But as it will be certainly many years before the building of the Theological Seminary can be completed, it is recommended that the house about to be vacated by the removal of the Bishop to Cleveland, be appropriated meanwhile to the accommodation of the Theological Students.

To this recommendation the board agreed. This "Bishop's House" is the present "McIlvaine Hall," which the Bishop then occupied as his residence. He soon abandoned his intention of removing to Cleveland, and so his house was not given over to the theological students. They were left to find rooms wherever they could, some in the East Wing of Kenyon, some in the newly built Milnor Hall, some in Park Cottage. There were not many of them at any time before 1857—ten or twelve in the most prosperous years, and from that varying down to four or five. The average was eight and three-fourths.

The cornerstone of Bexley Hall was at last laid on the twenty-third of October, 1839. This was a great occasion. At three o'clock in the afternoon a large company gathered, including the students of all the departments. There were religious services, the hymn "I love Thy kingdom, Lord," was sung, the stone with its contents of documents and papers was laid, and Bishop McIlvaine delivered a notable address, which contained some errors about the history of the seminary, and some very noble expressions of hope regarding the life and work of the men who should there study. He closed with these memorable words:

> What wonderful changes may not be anticipated before these walls shall have become antiquated! What fulfilments of glorious promises and prophecies! . . . The Lord be gracious to this Seminary, and grant that when the day of Jubilee shall come, and all kindreds and nations shall have heard the trump, and gathered themselves unto the Lord, the labors and prayers of the sons of this institution, for the glorious consummation, may come up for a memorial before God, bearing witness that they stood in their lot, and stayed not their hand from the toil or the danger.

Then the hymn "O Spirit of the living God" was sung, and the Bishop pronounced the benediction.

The spot where Bexley Hall stands is said to have been chosen by Bishop Chase as the site of the theological building which he hoped to erect in the course of time. At any rate, the location in 1833 of Bishop McIlvaine's house and Professor Sparrow's house—now the "deanery,"—so far to the north, makes it somewhat probable that already this site had been selected for the seminary's future home. Here was a clearing, eight or ten acres in extent, made long before Bishop Chase purchased the ground; and here Isaac Dial, of venerable memory in Gambier, had at one time a cornfield; but in 1830 the place was nearly overgrown with young trees. In Knox County the natural second growth of trees on land from which the white oak has been cut off is mainly the black oak; and most of the trees about Bexley Hall are of that inferior species. Lightning, wind, and decay are fast carrying them off.

The building made slow progress, and did not receive its first occupant until the eighteenth day of January, 1844, — when George W. Du Bois moved in. It was even then far

from being finished; there were no outer doors, and in the
hallways loose planks served for floors. At that time, and
for many years thereafter, only the rooms in the eastern half
were plastered and habitable. These were supplied with the
necessary furniture by gifts from Ohio parishes; each room
thus fitted up being named after the parish to whose generosity its occupants were thus indebted. Although the building was of brick, yet from the first it was painted, and in the
same color that it has to-day.

Mr. Du Bois during his years in Gambier—1843-1846—
kept a journal and an expense book, from which may be
gathered much information about the life of a Bexley man
in those years. As one reads it he is impressed with the intense
religious earnestness of the young man; and the same spirit
seems to have characterized the entire seminary. One Sunday morning he walked with Robert H. Williams, a fellow
student, to "Kinderhook"—Howard, near the bridge—to
assist him in his Sunday School. "Our walk," he wrote,
"though the weather was very hot, was very pleasant and
agreeable, for our conversation was of God, of His mercies
and unspeakable goodness." It sounds like passages in Bun-
yan's *Grace Abounding*.

I find Robert an excellent young man; the more I know him, the
more I esteem him. His prayer at the closing of the School this morning was beautiful and excellent. Out of the abundance of his heart
his mouth spoke. Truly I have had to-day joy and peace in believing.

The next day he and Robert met and read the Book of
Jonah and the first chapter of Isaiah, and prayed together;
and frequently thereafter they did the like.

Later Du Bois had a Sunday School of his own, as was the
custom with Bexley men. It was near Schenk's Creek. One
may still see, on the road that follows the creek southward
and eastward from Monroe Mills, the ancient tiny burying
ground at one side of which the log church stood. The spot

is consecrated by the devoted toil of many Bexley students during many years. Here Du Bois labored assiduously with the twenty or more children that came to the school. He visited them, loved them, prayed for them. One Sunday he wrote in his journal: "My walk was very pleasant. I endeavored to draw near to God in secret communion and ejaculatory prayer." The students walked to their schools, unless the distance was very great; and perhaps, thinking how the Master went always on foot in Palestine, it cheered them to "walk, even as He walked." There was a prayer meeting at Bexley Hall every Sunday evening in some student's room, or in the oriel room, which was then the chapel, and much larger than it is now; and frequently other prayer meetings were held. The spiritual life which then throbbed in Bexley Hall was strongly promoted by Bishop McIlvaine, the head of the school, whose example, conversation, and teaching led in that way.

Through all these years the seminary was fulfilling the office for which it was created, and which it has ever since fulfilled, that of supplying the Episcopal Church in Ohio with ministers. For ninety years it has performed this indispensable service, and there have been no better ministers in the state than those that have studied at Bexley Hall. In 1836 Bishop McIlvaine, who had then been but three years in the diocese, spoke to the diocesan convention of the growth of the Church. Ten years before there had been, besides the Bishop, only three officiating Episcopal ministers in the whole state; now there were forty-six. Of these forty-six fourteen were graduates of the seminary, or had pursued theological studies there. In 1846 twenty-five out of the seventy-four Ohio clergymen were from the seminary, and two years later, twenty-seven out of seventy. In 1861 there were thirty-two out of eighty-six. The Episcopal Church in Ohio, therefore, during this period, owed one-third of its clergymen, or more, to Bexley Hall. That Church would have been in sore straits for ministers if it had not been for the men from Gambier; and so it would still be to-day.

In 1842 Bishop McIlvaine told the diocesan convention that the average amount of money received by the seminary was $1,077 a year, "giving salaries at the rate of four hundred and eight dollars to each professor." But since the Bishop gave his own services as teacher without charge, the two theological professors, Wing and Muenscher, had $538.50 each. The endowment of the Milnor professorship brought in $510 a year, and the lands that belonged to the seminary supplied the rest. From those lands about $1,300 a year was received; but $1,000 of this income went to support the college and grammar school.

In 1854 began that rise in the number of theological students which was soon to compel the completion of Bexley Hall, and then—in 1861—was to overflow its utmost capacity. With this increase there naturally came more activity and greater interest. This was shown, among other ways, in the formation of societies. The catalogue of 1854-1855 tells of a Rhetorical Society that held weekly meetings, at which the exercises consisted of extemporaneous sermons or addresses, and a debate. In the same year appears for the first time the Bexley Missionary Society, the object of which was to acquire information about missions, and establish and conduct Sunday schools in the vicinity of Gambier. A year later was announced the opening of a reading-room in which were to be found the principal religious periodicals. All these societies lasted until, in the seventies, the attendance at the seminary dropped away to two or three.

The great increase in the number of theological students between 1857 and 1861 was due mainly to two causes. The first cause was the vigorous and systematic effort put forth to bring men to Bexley Hall. In 1853 the Reverend Erastus A. Strong, a recent graduate of the seminary, was appointed by the Missionary and Education Committee of the Diocese of Ohio its agent to secure funds for the work of the committee; and in this he proved so successful that his office was continued year after year. In 1857 an Education Committee was appointed, separate from the Committee on Missions. It secured the services of Mr. Strong, and, feeling thus assured of an ample income, it announced its intention

to place the acquisition of a thorough education for the ministry within the reach of every young man in our communion who desires it, and possesses the requisite disposition and qualifications.

Mr. Strong for several years traveled widely, especially in Ohio, New York, and Pennsylvania, and induced many young men to go to Gambier and prepare for the ministry— some of them to enter Bexley Hall immediately, and others to go first to the college or grammar school. Mr. Strong was a good agent. In 1861 there were at Gambier seventy-eight young men in some stage of preparation for the ministry. Thirty-nine of them were at Bexley Hall, although not all could find rooms in the building; the others were at the college or preparatory school. More than half these students were from the East, and would return there on the conclusion of their studies. "Nowhere else in our land," said the *Western Episcopalian*, "are so many young men gathered together who are seeking the ministry of the Protestant Episcopal Church."

In 1861 another cause became operative to increase the number of students at Bexley Hall: the theological seminary at Alexandria, Virginia, had been forced to close at the breaking out of the Civil War. Just how many men came to Gambier who would have gone to Alexandria cannot be ascertained; but the enrollment at the seminary rose suddenly from twenty-seven in 1860 to thirty-nine in 1861. Those were the palmy days of Bexley Hall. The attendance was of cosmopolitan character. England, Scotland, Ireland, and Canada supplied names to the roll. Massachusetts, Vermont, Rhode Island, Connecticut, New York, New Jersey, Pennsylvania, Maryland, Virginia, Kentucky, Michigan, and Wisconsin were represented. Eleven of the thirty-nine young men had graduated at Kenyon College, two at Princeton, and one each at Racine, Hobart, Williams, Harvard, Columbia, and New York University. To accommodate the enlarged attendance, the rooms in the western half of Bexley were finished off in 1858, and later there was talk of renting, or perhaps erecting, an additional building.

BIOGRAPHICAL NOTE

LORD BEXLEY

NICHOLAS VANSITTART, son of a former governor of Bengal, was born in London, in 1766. He graduated at Christ Church, Oxford, in 1787, and was admitted to the bar in 1791. Thereafter for more than thirty years he served in one public office and another, becoming chancellor of the exchequer in 1812, which office he held for ten years. In 1823 he was created Baron Bexley, of Bexley in Kent. He was an active member of the Church Missionary Society and other evangelical societies. He died in 1851.

CHAPTER XVIII

COLLEGE AND COLLEGE LIFE, 1831-1861

BISHOP CHASE brought up from Worthington to Gambier in 1828 about fifty students, most of them of grammar school grade. In Gambier the number increased, although not to the extent which the Bishop had expected. In 1831, when he left Gambier, there were fifty-nine students in the college and eighty-two in the grammar school; in all, one hundred and forty-one. Until 1855 there were generally more students in the grammar school than in the college; after 1855 the number in college generally far exceeded that in the school. Just before the revolutionary changes of 1839 the number of college students rose, for one year, to seventy-seven; then, until 1853, the number fell to an average of about forty-six. In 1854 the enrollment increased suddenly from forty-one to sixty-three; and year by year thereafter it climbed, reaching the maximum of one hundred and thirty-seven in 1860-1861. This gain in attendance does not seem to have been due to any cause that affected Ohio colleges generally, for other colleges, such as Western Reserve and Marietta, experienced no marked increase, and the growth of Oberlin at that time was due to special financial inducements offered there; we must therefore attribute the gain chiefly to causes internal to Kenyon College itself. There were two of these causes, closely co-operating. Lorin Andrews, who became president in 1853, went constantly about the state, addressing teachers' institutes and winning the confidence of high school principals, whose influence was great in directing boys in the choice of a college. When he became president there were twenty-four Ohio students in college; in 1861 there were sixty. But the increase in students from outside Ohio was yet more remark-

THE GATES AND CHASE AVENUE, ABOUT 1857

OLD KENYON AND NEIGHBORING HOUSES, ABOUT 1870

able, rising from seventeen in 1853-1854 to seventy-six in 1860-1861. The number of students from the East—that is, New England and the Middle States—rose from eight to thirty-four; the number from the South, including the "border states," rose from seven to twenty; the number from the West—states west and northwest of Ohio—from one to fourteen. The gain from outside Ohio was largely due to a man who is almost forgotten in the college, although his name is in one of the chancel windows of the Church of the Holy Spirit, the Reverend Erastus A. Strong, of whose services as agent of the Education Committee of the Diocese of Ohio mention has already been made. There were in the college and grammar school many postulants whom he had gathered in his extensive travels; and wherever he went he advertised the college and looked up prospective students, even though they did not intend to enter the ministry. Kenyon was further helped by the fact that the Evangelicals in the Church regarded it as safe and sound, while Hobart and Trinity were suspected of leaning towards Rome; hence evangelical rectors guided the feet of their parishioners' sons in the direction of Gambier.

The *Reveille* for 1859 glows with enthusiasm over the growth of the college.

> To say that Kenyon now leads the van of western institutions is but giving utterance to a fact now generally axiomatic. . . . Three of the grand divisions of the globe, together with the isles of the sea, have their representatives enrolled upon the latest catalogue. . . . The young and gallant Chief of the Six Nations has laid aside the paraphernalia of office to dwell for a season amid these quiet retreats. [This was Oronhyatekha, '62.]

Most of the students during the years with which this chapter deals attained, after leaving college, places of honor and usefulness, and there were some who rose to high position and fame. Among the most conspicuous may be named Henry Caswall, '30, prebendary of Salisbury Cathedral,

England; David Davis, '32, justice of the Supreme Court of
the United States, and later United States senator; Edwin
McMasters Stanton, '34, the great Secretary of War; Edwin
Hamilton Davis, '35, distinguished archaeologist; Henry
Winter Davis, '37, orator and statesman; Joseph Pere Bell
Wilmer, '37, Bishop of Louisiana; Ralph Pomeroy Buck-
land, '38, brigadier general and congressman; William
Speer, '40, noted Presbyterian missionary to China; Stanley
Matthews, '40, United States senator and justice of the
Supreme Court of the United States; Rutherford Birchard
Hayes, '42, major general, congressman, Governor of Ohio,
President of the United States; John Sanford Mason, '44,
brigadier general; Sylvester Horton Rosecrans, '45, Bishop
of Columbus; Daniel Sheldon Norton, '46, United States
senator; David Turpie, '48, United States senator; Nelson
Boardman Sweitzer, '50, brigadier general; Francis Hunt
Hurd, '58, a lawyer, congressman and statesman; William
Crane Gray, '59, Bishop of South Florida; Alfred Hum-
phreys Pease, '59, a brilliant pianist of national reputation,
composer of notable instrumental music and of favorite
songs; Alexander Viets Griswold Allen, '62, eminent as a
clergyman, theological professor, and author.

In 1845, when Doctor Bronson became president, the
college faculty was small and weak. Besides the president
there were but two professors, Edward C. Ross and Horace
L. Thrall, who between them covered the field of mathematics and science. A professor of the classical languages was
soon provided, the Reverend Alexander F. Dodd; and when
Professor Ross, an admirable man and teacher, was called to
New York, he was succeeded by one not less admirable, the
Reverend George Denison, who returned to the Kenyon
faculty in 1848, having left it in 1833. He was a nephew of
Bishop Chase. During President Smith's brief administra-
tion the faculty was considerably enlarged and strengthened.
Then it was that the names of John Trimble and Edward C.

Benson first appeared on the faculty list. For a few years the Reverend John T. Brooke taught rhetoric, logic, and moral philosophy in the college, being also a professor in the theological seminary. He was a man of brilliant parts, long familiar with the college through membership on the board of trustees, and devoted to its interests. Under President Andrews was gathered a faculty of very great ability, with more than one member of national and international reputation; of these men more will be said later.

Probably no more fascinating recreation has ever been known than that of attending faculty meetings. Everyone whose privilege it has been to have that experience will appreciate the idyllic words with which one of the secretaries of the Kenyon faculty closes his record of a certain meeting.

Thus ended a delightful session. During its swift passage very little occurred to mar pleasure—everything contributed to enhance the joy of all dwelling within Kenyon's walls, or living near the shadow of its lofty spire.

And yet there were times when differences of opinion would throw little notes of discord into the music. Such was the discussion that arose in the year 1836 over the proper pronunciation of Greek and Latin vowels. In June it was "Voted, That i in Latin be pronounced e; e be pronounced a; ae, a; a, ā long." That seems final; but in July the controversy broke out again, and this time the faculty referred the matter to the board of trustees for settlement. No one could question the entire competency of that tribunal to give conclusive judgment in a subject of this kind; yet within a month—long before the trustees could be assembled in special session—the faculty rescinded this resolution, and in a spirit of recovered self-sufficiency. "Voted, That the Faculty do possess entire control over the pronunciation of the Greek and Latin Languages." Undoubtedly those who wished to refer the matter to the board of trustees were advocates of

the old "English pronunciation." They seem to have been
defeated in this vote, yet Latin continued to be pronounced
on the Kokosing as on the Cam or Isis, or, perhaps, on
Dublin Bay.

During this period, examinations were conducted orally
and in public; and people in general, especially members of
the board of trustees, and clergymen who were suspected of
"keeping up their studies," were invited to attend. These
were solemn occasions. A visitor in 1834 noted how "the
professors performed their duty with unflinching faithful-
ness." In the early years the college examinations were held
in the "philosophical apartment," which was the southwest
room in the third story of the West Wing. The room is not
large, it contained much philosophical apparatus, and was
crowded at examination time. Later the examinations were
held in the basement on the south side of Rosse Chapel. A
contributor to an early *Collegian* has preserved for us a lively
picture of an examination there.

As we observe the pale pillars running through the center, the
paler walls supporting lamps sympathizing in color, the official table
piled with dingy volumes, overshadowed on one side by a stately
pillar, and on the other side surrounded by a semicircle of venerable
scholars inflexible in feature and intent upon the page, the five dull
blackboards, prophetic of trembling, placed at a judicious distance
in front of the learned elders, forming a second semicircle, similar
to those in appearance and general effect; the low deep windows
casting on the sable group (men and boards) the dimmest, wintriest
light ever adulterated in passing from the glorious sun through a
miserable pane of glass; the student advancing to the aforesaid table
with the dingy volumes upon it—a pallid picture of anxiety—the
momentary suspense, broken by the examiner's loud voice announcing the portion to be read; then a faint murmur as of someone reading a dreadful passage to himself which alarms him as he proceeds,
. . . the short, pointed questions of the examiners (at this juncture
everyone present has the ridiculous privilege of being an examiner)
and the equally precise answers of the student; all this was so much
like clock-work and the surrounding atmosphere so restrained and

oppressive, that the scene reminded us of certain historical paintings of the Inquisition.

Written examinations were introduced about 1860, as an addition to the others, and gradually won their way; but it was long before the oral method was entirely silenced. A Committee appointed by the diocesan convention was always in attendance upon the examinations, and almost invariably reported its observations in a highly laudatory tone.

From the beginning of the college down to the end of the period now under consideration every student was required to attend morning and evening prayers daily, and two Church services on Sunday, and any other services that might be appointed for his good. At first the old plank dining-hall at the northern end of the Park served as the chapel, and then the great dining-room in the basement of Old Kenyon; but when the Seventy-Four was finished, its schoolroom became also the chapel, and it continued to serve that purpose until the southern half of the basement of Rosse Chapel was in a condition to be used. A writer in the *Western Episcopalian* has left us a picture of the room in the Seventy-Four which to a dozen Kenyon classes was "the old chapel."

Across one half of the room, which is square, are seats of plain boards for students, ranged compactly, for there was no room to spare. Against the wall behind was the faculty seat. . . . In the center of the other half was a square space railed off for a chancel. A cheap carpet covers the space, and the desk is hung with a faded moreen. . . . The space on either side is filled with citizens, a pew being made on the right for the Bishop's family.

"The faculty seat" was a long bench; and a favorite sport of the students was to steal this seat, or demolish it. Angered beyond measure by one of these outrages, the faculty, in 1835, devised a strange revenge: they resolved that they would "remain standing during prayer time." Four months later this resolution was repealed, having, perhaps, accomplished its purpose.

At various times various rooms have been used temporarily as the chapel. The northeastern room in the basement of the East Wing answered that purpose for a good while. The Harry Stoyle house, which was then the college store, was used as a place of worship on Sundays at one time when the roof of Rosse Chapel had fallen in.

The basement room on the south side of Rosse Chapel was long, narrow, dark, unlovely, and uncomfortable; yet in the minds of many Kenyon men it was a holy place because of its association with some of the most sacred moments of their lives. For here, during about thirty-five years, were held not only daily "chapel" and, not infrequently, the Sunday services, but also, from time to time, prayer meetings and revival meetings, in which many a heart was touched, many a new resolution formed, and many a lifelong consecration sealed.

Kenyon College has known marked periods of great religious interest and earnestness. God grant her yet others! In the thirties, and again just before the Civil War, there were days and weeks together when the chief subject of interest among the students was personal religion. In 1831 there were revivals in many colleges, and Kenyon was a partaker in this blessing. Heman Dyer, in his *Records of an Active Life*, gives an account.

About mid-winter on each occasion [of public worship] a prevailing seriousness manifested itself. This seriousness increased day by day until it attracted attention throughout the institution. By the direction of Bishop Chase and Dr. Sparrow informal meetings were commenced in the different halls of the college buildings; recitation rooms and the rooms of students were used for the purpose. An hour in the evening was fixed on, and without any formal notice it was understood among all the students that any one was at liberty to attend. Some of the older students were requested to take charge of the services. . . . At first but few came, but the number steadily increased, until the room became very much crowded, and the interest was deep and all-pervading. The exercises were very brief and very simple. Prayers, hymns, the Word of God, with a few remarks by the person conducting the service, made up the whole of it. . . . For weeks and weeks these informal meetings were held. . . . A large number of students became decidedly religious, and many turned their attention to the ministry. . . . So great was the interest at one time that all the college exercises were suspended for one or two days.

The good effects of this revival were lasting. Two or three years later the *Gambier Observer* declared that "at no previous period has there been so much piety in college." Nearly fifty students were then intending to enter the ministry. The Reverend Charles E. Douglass, of the class of 1837, wrote fifty years after:

There was, indeed, a strong religious feeling prevalent, especially in my last year, which made discipline easy. The danger then became, in truth, excessive asceticism.

The contentions and upheavals in the college government in the later thirties and early forties were not favorable to a growth in personal piety. Religion declined. Henry Calhoun, of the class of '41, in his Junior year wrote to a friend a letter, which, whether or not it was entirely correct and just, yet presented the students' views of the religious situation at that time. It will be remembered that Bishop McIlvaine had recently overthrown the faculty and board of trustees.

Dr. Sparrow is here, but too mad (and not without reason) to have anything to do with the college. . . . Rest assured I have seen enough of Episcopal power to set me forever against Bishops and Monarchies in the Church. . . . The religious state here is truly deplorable, there are no more than five or six professors of religion in College, and they can hardly be told from non-professors. . . . Kenyon seems to be on its last legs, if it is not down off of them now.

This is the fine pessimism of youth. Mr. Calhoun's experience of "Bishops and Monarchies" led him to enter the ministry of the Presbyterian Church.

Twenty-five years later, in 1857 and 1858, the college

was profoundly moved by the great revival of religion which at that time stirred the whole land. Doctor Francis Wharton contributed to the *Kenyon Book* his reminiscences of "that most eventful period."*

I was in Philadelphia at the time when the religious interest began to manifest itself at Gambier; and I well recollect the deep impression made upon me, on my return, in finding a daily prayer-meeting instituted in that basement room of Rosse Chapel, with which, ungainly and dark, I have so many dear associations. It was Mr. William Brown, then in the Sophomore Class, who first urged the importance of these meetings; and soon, to the few who at first attended, was added the great body of the students, as well as of the residents of the Hill. Few among those who stood together in the meetings came forth other than earnest, devoted men.

The good which this revival did was incalculable. It brought into the ministry men who rendered noble service there; it gave to the Church many devoted laymen.

It was not until the year 1845 that the great upper room of Rosse Chapel was ready for regular use in the Sunday services. The arrangement of this church was similar to that generally found in Episcopal churches at that period. There was no chancel, or recess, but a large area at the western end of the room was railed off; and here, within the enclosure, the Holy Table, the desk, and the pulpit were placed. In front, a little way back from the rail, was the Holy Table. This position, in front of everything else, befitted and emphasized its importance. It was a long, narrow table of black walnut, handsomely made, and is now the Holy Table at the Quarry Chapel. Close behind it, and a step higher up, was the desk where the service and lessons were read. Behind this, and still higher, was the ample pulpit. Behind the pulpit a door led into the narrow vestry. In the gallery at the other end of the room was the choir, which generally con-

* The extract here given is greatly abbreviated. See the *Kenyon Book*, pp. 260-264.

THE CHANCEL OF ROSSE CHAPEL

A KENYON ORCHESTRA OF LONG AGO

sisted of men and women from the village. Bishop Chase's barrel organ, improved by removing the barrels and putting in keys and trackers, was skillfully played, first by Mr. Putnam, then by Doctor Muenscher, and afterwards, with more or less skill, by others. When finally it broke down there ensued a series of melodeons and cabinet organs. The services at Rosse Chapel are said to have been heartily rendered, and certainly the preaching by Bishop McIlvaine and a succession of evangelical divines was eloquent in oratory, and in doctrinal exposition and application was sharper than any two-edged sword.

In accordance with a reservation made when the building was consecrated, commencement exercises were held at Rosse Chapel; and, by an extension of this reservation, other public exercises of the college, if of a serious character, were sometimes held there.

Sunday was strictly observed at Gambier. One Sunday in 1851 two "pleasure carriages" drove through the park. The *Western Episcopalian* reported this as "a new sight in Gambier," such as it hoped never to see again. The thing would not be tolerated. The quiet of a Gambier Sunday could not thus be violated with impunity. Next thing, people would be asking to see the libraries on Sunday!

A succession of writers has left us accounts of some aspects of life at Kenyon College in their days. Henry Caswall, of the class of 1830 in the college and 1831 in the seminary, and Heman Dyer, a student at the college, master of the Junior Grammar School, and a graduate of the seminary in 1834, have already been quoted several times in this history. Henry Winter Davis, '37, tells of an attempt in his day to introduce the custom of wearing Oxford caps and gowns. But, he says, "the effort was abandoned as against the nature of the western man." From time to time this effort has been renewed, always with about the same result.

In October, 1831, Lucius G. Peck, then a Sophomore,

wrote to his "Friend Buckingham," formerly a fellow student:

> Our recitations go on with the usual punctuality and strictness. Prof. Buckingham instructs in Natural Philosophy, etc. No excuse, no shamming, no prompting answers with him; understand the lesson you must, and even then he will roar about the room, flourish up to the blackboard and give dissertations of principles with a vengeance. For a number of nights Tutor Nash has been on the watch till 1 or 2 o'clock, yet the woods have been set on fire in every direction around the college, & have burnt up to the very woodpiles.

George W. Jones, '46, tells in the *Kenyon Book* about Lieutenant Edward Coke Ross, professor of Mathematics, one of the notable men in the Kenyon faculty list. He was a West-Pointer, came to Gambier with President Douglass, and remained until 1848.

> It is of the old Professor I would speak. His tall, grenadier form, wrapped in blue cloak with scarlet lining, was a sight for a picture; and as he measured his steps, "just thirty-three inches, sir," and gave a military salute, with a cheery "good morning" to every passer-by, not a man but that felt prouder for the meeting. . . . The Professor was a candidate for the Colonelcy of an Ohio regiment [in the Mexican War] but lacking political influence was disappointed. . . . The excitement prevalent at the time promoted a feeling of unsettledness on his part, inclining him to a wider and larger field, and he successfully sought an appointment on the staff of the Academy of New York, and died in that city.
>
> Those were primitive days [continues Mr. Jones]. Each student carried water from a well far down the hill, cut his own wood, made his bed, did his own scrubbing and mending, and yet had time for a good deal of amusement. The creek gave good fishing, the woods fine gunning, and many the grand fox run that woke up the boys. Still, the stubborn debater, and intellectual toiler, with his dirty lard lamp, was an important factor in the make-up. . . . "Ponies" were unknown—it was square "heel and toe" or "flunk."

No graduate of Kenyon has left so full an account of the college in his days as has the Reverend Alexander V. G. Allen, of the class of 1862. A long and invaluable letter of his is printed in the *Kenyon Book*. It is an appreciation and a tribute such as has been rendered to few colleges—comparable for substance to Hilaire Belloc's splendid tribute to Balliol:

> Balliol made me, Balliol fed me,
> Whatever I had she gave me again;
> And the best of Balliol loved and led me,
> God be with you, Balliol men.

This letter, which opens to us the heart of Kenyon in the golden days when it beat so high, is given here much condensed, but not otherwise changed.

It was in the year 1859 that I went to Gambier. It was a moment of enthusiasm in which teachers and students shared. Everything spoke of growth and expansion. To me, coming from a distant home, it was like waking up in a new world, where everything I saw commanded my interest, my respect also and admiration.

Dr. Lorin Andrews, who was at the head of the College, impressed us by his manly bearing, his earnestness and vigor. He had been a successful man in life, imparting, I fancy, something of his own buoyancy to his new charge.

For three years I sat under the teaching of Professor Trimble. We read with him the usual Greek and Latin authors, with as much thoroughness as they were read anywhere at that time, so far as my knowledge extends. I think we felt that Professor Trimble was quite competent to have done something for us in the higher walks of classical culture; but he was a sensitive man and perhaps he felt as if it would be casting pearls before those who did not know their value if he went beyond the routine required of him. Under the happier auspices of a system where the interests of teacher and taught are assumed as identical, I think he would have shone as a source of general enthusiasm for the work which he loved.

In Physics or the Natural Sciences we had a teacher of whom we were all proud, knowing him to be the peer of his co-workers in his department—Professor Hamilton L. Smith. He was charged with the scientific spirit, and, for those who showed interest in his work, he was unexcelled as a teacher, gladly devoting extra time and energy to their assistance. As a companion on a geological excursion, he had no equal. It was a good thing for us all to have come under his influence, to know that his reputation went beyond the small sphere in which he lived, even if we could not appreciate the full value of his work.

Professor Lang was admirably suited to the task of drilling, even the slowest and most plodding minds, in the various branches of mathematics. He had one gift, which I think is rare, of exciting in a man, even of humble ability, a certain respect for himself. He knew how to fan the faintest sparks of mathematical capacity till they developed into a respectable flame.

Dr. Francis Wharton was then a layman, devoting himself, gratuitously, to the department of Modern History and English Literature. I gained from him a deep and lasting interest in literature. He was, by constitution, a Humanist of a higher order, with an instinctive perception of the quality and meaning of life, with a deep sympathy for all human manifestations. He was a very interesting man, making all that he touched interesting. From him I gained also my first conception of the picturesque aspects of history, and my first conviction of its value as a psychological revelation of the soul of humanity. The same fascination and sense of the living reality of things he carried into his work as a lay-preacher. I recall the crowds that flocked to the basement hall of Rosse Chapel to listen to his lectures on the Acts of the Apostles. It was no ordinary man who could have drawn students from their rooms, or people from their homes, on those winter evenings, as he did for successive weeks, to such an uncouth, ill-ventilated, badly lighted room.

In one respect, Kenyon College, in my time, was in advance of many similar institutions. For two years we had the advantage at Gambier of studying German as a part of the regular course. I mention with respect and with gratitude for what they did for me, the names of Herr Messner and Herr Grauert.

Such were the men who made college life seem rich in actual gains and rich with future promise. I am confining my remarks to the College, but I cannot refrain, in this connection, from an allusion to the Theological Seminary. There was at least one among its faculty to whom I must refer when expressing my personal indebtedness to the influences of Gambier. Dr. McElhinney created in us a respect for scholarship and for the scholar, of whom he was a pure and beautiful type.

I must bear my testimony to Kenyon as a Church College, and to the beneficial influence it exerted under this aspect. There was a decidedly religious atmosphere in the institution, as though all things tended towards a religious end. But at the same time, religion was never thrust upon us, nor was it over-worked, in such a way as to make us react from its influence. One of the things by which I was most struck on entering the College was the fact that it was officered exclusively by laymen. No clergyman came into any official relationship with us. The faculty in their capacity as laymen conducted prayers in the Chapel, and Professor Wharton gave us most edifying sermons as a lay-preacher; but while they sustained well their religious character, they made no direct effort to enforce religious or church influences. We were almost as much shut out from the direct influence of the clergy as the students of Girard College, in Philadelphia. For the first two years of my residence in Gambier there was no Chaplain,* nor when one was appointed was the effect a beneficial one of his attempt to visit the students in his official capacity. There were those among the students who exerted a stronger religious influence than any Chaplain could have done. The religious life of these men was sedulously cultivated among themselves. Class prayer-meetings—let those sneer at them who will—kept alive the soul of spiritual devotedness. We had no beautiful Chapel in those days, nor did we worship to the sound of the organ. In the basement of Rosse Hall, cold and unsightly and dark, we gathered for morning and evening prayers. But religion was none the less real; it had a certain healthy and manly character which commanded our respect. I do not believe that happier or more healthful surroundings for young men then existed than were to be found in Gambier.

I have spoken of the College as represented by its teachers. Let me add a few words about this College as composed of its students. The number, I think, must have been relatively large who came with a desire to work, among whom were men of a high order of ability. Among the formative influences at Gambier for which I am most grateful was my acquaintance and friendship with these men. It was they who set the standards and by their own achievements stimulated others to pursue them. They were left free to develop themselves according to their kind, no dominant influence from without carried them away from themselves. They grew strong and became potent factors in revealing the art of speech, the graces of style, or the methods of political life. It was something to have known and looked up to them.

As I review the life at Kenyon at this distance of time, it seems

* A chaplain is named in the catalogues for these years.

to me to have furnished in a remarkable degree the conditions necessary for the development of personality. It reminds me in some respects of the small Italian republics in the age of the Renaissance. No great central influence overshadowed us so as to make us feel our insignificance. It was not difficult to take in the range of the required studies, there was healthy and generous rivalry, opportunities were offered for distinction and fame,—fame such as it was, and to us it seemed great. The Literary Societies created a sphere for other capacities than scholarship, while distinction met at once with public recognition. Perhaps we did not measure ourselves accurately with the great world outside of us. There were motives at work in society of which we did not dream. But we were storing up enthusiasm and self-confidence, qualities which might not have grown so easily and naturally had the conditions which surrounded us been different. Gambier intensified its influences and tendencies by its isolation from the world. Those were the days when the railway station was at a distance of five miles and was reached only by daily stage. There were few social opportunities or distractions. Life became simple and homogeneous, and was beautiful in its simplicity. The only thing of importance was the College which existed for us and we for the College. We were learning to study, we were gaining a knowledge of men, and a sense of personality deepened within us, till we were filled with a boundless enthusiasm. As I reflect on all that it was to us, I say again, there could not have been a better home for young men than was Gambier in the years I am describing.

The new life and enthusiasm of the college in President Andrews' day naturally sought new channels in which to flow, and flooded old channels with a fuller stream. It was in many ways a period of transition, a period midway between the cramped and rather narrow interests of former days, and the diffused and less serious interests that were to find recognition in the days to come. The new life was vigorous and not altogether easy to control; and the faculty learned by experience that they had to do with a college spirit that could not always be overawed by edicts and penalties. There were a good many "rebellions." "No less than thrice," said the *Collegian*, "have the gates of the temple of Jupiter Quirinus been opened."

During President Andrews' administration there were many new developments of student life and activity. Athletics, which had been all unorganized before, and but languidly pursued, now became a predominant interest. The first baseball clubs at Kenyon were formed in 1859, and nearly all the students played on one nine or another. Wickets also had some vogue. But athletics was not then the absorbing interest that it was to become later, and intercollegiate games were not yet dreamed of.

In December, 1855, appeared the first issue of the *Reveille* —"Vol. I, No. 1." This is the eldest of Kenyon periodicals, and is said to have been the third publication of the kind in America. It was a small newspaper of four eighteen-by-ten-inch pages; and this continued to be its format for more than ten years, although the size of the page increased a little, and the quality of the paper and presswork improved. At first there were a few crude woodcuts, executed by the pocket-knife of the chief editor, D. D. Benedict, intended mainly to exhibit the symbols of the fraternities; in time the fraternities supplied better blocks. The *Reveille* in its early years was edited by four Seniors, two from each of the literary societies. It appeared twice a year, in December and June. The price was five cents a copy. It was a rather serious publication, was well written, and contained much information about the various organizations that existed in the college. There was always an editorial addressed to the Freshmen, strongly commending virtue and industry to their susceptible young souls.

The *Collegian* first appeared in 1856. It had been projected nearly twenty years before, as a publication of the Philomathesian Society; then the plan was broadened so as to give Nu Pi Kappa a share. But never until this day of growth and enthusiasm was there energy enough to start it. Now the Senior class took it up, through a board of editors.

The *Collegian* in its first years gave the important news of the college, but its main purpose was literary.

We have commenced the publication of a literary Magazine [said the editors] ; obstacles present themselves which, if labor and perseverance can accomplish anything, shall be surmounted. An attempt of this kind was before made, but failed—that last word has been stricken from our dictionary.

Such was the spirit of the college in that day. The prose contents of the magazine were creditable, the poetry was tolerable. As one turns the pages of the old *Collegians* he receives the impression that literature as such was valued by the students, that to produce it was an ambition on the part of many, and that to have a piece published in the college paper was a distinction comparable to that attained nowadays by performing some remarkable exploit in football.

In these years the literary societies attained their acme.* They moved out of their basement rooms in Kenyon and took possession of their beautiful halls in Ascension, for the completion and furnishing of which their alumni had contributed generously. Their increased membership, and the marked ability and earnestness of many of their number, insured good orations and essays and strenuous contests in debate. Yet already some of the causes that were later to bring about their decay had begun to operate. Philo and Nu Pi had always been secret societies; but in 1859 their rules, mottoes, and arcana were divulged, and their meetings were thrown open to the public. This publicity was, very likely, not advantageous to them. Again, many new interests came in and broke down the monopoly which the literary societies had enjoyed. Very effective to this end was the introduction of Greek letter fraternities. The Lambda Chapter of Delta Kappa Epsilon was established in 1852, and after some months of concealment, emerged, and was given recognition

* For the earlier history of these societies see Appendix VIII.

by the faculty in 1853. Theta Delta Chi came the next year, and Alpha Delta Phi in 1858. Psi Upsilon came in 1860. Theta Delta Chi withdrew in 1861, but even so, Kenyon was left with an extraordinary galaxy of strong fraternities, probably unequaled in that day in any small college in the United States. Here was the beginning of new, great, and permanent interests and loyalties which were to increase as the years went by and other fraternities established themselves and bodies of devoted and influential alumni grew up and became a power in their chapters and in the college. Unquestionably the literary societies in American colleges were weakened by the drawing off of interest to the fraternities; but the main causes of their decline are the inrush of athletics and of social functions, and the predominance of scientific studies; and these were beginning to make themselves felt at Kenyon College even in the days when the literary societies were at their height.

Besides the major intercollegiate fraternities there were at Kenyon local societies, and chapters of obscure and short-lived fraternities, which are named in the *Reveille* along with some that probably had little but a name. Not many of them lasted more than two or three years. Psi Omega, a Freshman and Sophomore society, was founded in 1855 and lived ten years—at least, upon the pages of the *Reveille*. In 1858 appeared a "Kokosing Tribe," with the motto, in the Delaware Algonquian language, "N'dahoaleen Aninshilhillsisak," which is said to mean, "I love chickens." Professing so permanent a sentiment of human nature as this, the "Kokosing Tribe" continued in existence for eighteen years. A "Chess Club," and a "Shakesperian Club," were formed in 1858, and in 1861 a "Historical Society," which was annually reported until 1875.

Among the chief honors bestowed upon superior scholarship in American colleges is membership in Phi Beta Kappa. Kenyon's Chapter, the "Beta of Ohio," was instituted in

1858. The "Alpha of Ohio," at Western Reserve College, authorized John W. Andrews, a Kenyon trustee, and Professors Thomas M. Smith and Hamilton L. Smith to form a chapter; and they chose five professors and nine Juniors to be charter members. The student members took part equally with the professors in the exercises of the monthly meetings, which consisted largely of debating and the reading of essays.

Earlier than the fifties there was little singing in American colleges, but then students began to bring back songs from German universities, and these were taken up here. Many of the songs were Latin, as "Integer vitæ," "Lauriger Horatius," and "Gaudeamus"; and some were translated from the German, and retained their native tunes. The *Collegian* said, in 1857, that the students sang a great deal, "but we have no students' songs, or at least none that we can claim as our own." They sang "Gaudeamus," "Lauriger," "Old Dog Tray," "Annie Laurie," and "Bango"—which seems to have been a local variant of "Bingo," and to have had reference to President Andrews' dog. In 1859 Packard and Sturges of the Senior class published a little *Song Book of Kenyon*, which in a measure remedied the defect that the *Collegian* had complained of.

It was inevitable that the fraternities should take up singing, for among young men song is a natural expression of comradeship. In the close association of fraternity life men must sing; therefore songs burst forth telling the glories of "Dear old Zeta Alpha Mu"—or whatever the collection of Greek letters might be—and professing an undying devotion to it and to its sacred teachings. Enthusiasm produced some pretty strong statements, but all were verified in the heart of every loyal son. Most of the tunes were borrowed from the popular songs of the day, and that day was the decade before the Civil War, and the years of the war itself; and, owing to a spirit of strong conservatism, many a tune written long ago to carry some tender sentiment of personal affection, is still heard on the Path, under the maples and the stars, as generation after generation of new devotees pours it forth in praise of the beloved idealization of brotherhood which they find in their fraternities. Thus they have given immortality to such lovely tunes as "Annie Lisle," "Rain upon the roof," "How can I leave thee?" and others as good. Some convivial songs have passed on their tunes, and even their refrains, to this alien day; such as "Sparkling and bright," "Vive la compagnie," and "Drink it down." The Civil War brought forth a number of excellent tunes— "John Brown's body," "Tramp, tramp, tramp," "Tenting on the old camp ground," are examples—and these are still heard on the Path, where the recent Great War has no such memorial.

Kenyon has always been patriotic. Almost from its very beginning the college celebrated the Fourth of July, by appropriate exercises on the part of Philo and Nu Pi, and also in ways less intellectual. Freshman R. B. Hayes writes to his sister a letter descriptive of the celebration in 1839. At four o'clock in the morning, flags were hoisted and bands played. Then prayers, followed by breakfast. At ten o'clock the marshals got the students in line and marched them to the chapel, in the Old Seventy-Four, to the sound of music. Here were prayers, the reading of the Declaration of Independence, and an oration. Then all marched to Mr. Sawer's famous "bakery"—at the house now occupied by Mr. H. K. Doolittle. "We had the best dinner I ever saw," says Freshman Hayes, "and every one of the faculty and all the rest said it was the best they ever saw." After this dinner came many toasts, and an ode. Then all returned to the chapel and listened to "about a dozen speeches from different students." Mr. Hayes says:

I went to bed after having spent the happiest day I ever spent without exception. I believe there is not a student but thinks we had the most happiness here of any place in the United States.

Celebrations more or less of this character occurred year after year.

Patriotism displayed itself in sterner guise when the United States made war upon Mexico. In June, 1846, the students formed a military company, which they called the "Kenyon Guards." They were enrolled as the Fifth Company of the Second Regiment of the Third Brigade of the Ohio Militia. Their uniform consisted of "a glazed cap, blue jeans, roundabout, and white pantaloons." Professor Ross was their commander in chief. They seem to have been diligent in the drill as long as the war lasted. Their records, preserved in a little book, end in June, 1848. It is fortunate that they were not called into service in so discreditable a war as that against Mexico.

CHAPTER XIX

KENYON AND THE CIVIL WAR

ON Friday, the twelfth of April, 1861, the batteries about Charleston opened on Fort Sumter and the Civil War began. The following Monday President Lincoln issued his first call for troops to suppress the rebellion. The response was immediate and tremendous. The North, so long quiescent, uncertain, even submissive, instantly blazed out in wrath at the assault upon the flag, and its tens of thousands rallied to support the government and preserve the Union. The telegraph had hardly flashed the President's call when Lorin Andrews answered it by offering himself to the Governor as a soldier. It is said that he was the first man in Ohio to enlist. He at once raised a company in Knox County, and was ready within a week to set forth for the camp where he and his men were to learn the drill and the duties of soldiers.

The sentiments and behavior of the Kenyon students during the weeks that immediately preceded the war had been what one would expect of college men under such circumstances; feeling ran high, yet was held in control. With the exception of one man, the students from the seceding states left college; there were but nine of them, and they went quietly and were not molested. A few men from Kentucky and Maryland also went home; yet altogether the numerical loss of the college from the withdrawal of southerners was not serious. Most of these men entered the Confederate Army and rendered good service to the cause which they believed was right. Joseph Packard, from Fairfax County, Virginia, of the class of 1860, and a tutor when the war broke out, resigned his position. The faculty did not accept his resignation, but granted him leave of absence and sent Professor

Wharton to tell him of their hope for his speedy return. Mr. Packard fought through the war on the Confederate side, and did not return until fifty years had gone by.

On Sunday, April 21, the services at Rosse Chapel were very impressive. The regularly appointed Scriptures seemed remarkably appropriate—Joel, third chapter, with its stirring call,

Prepare war, wake up the mighty men, let all the men of war draw near; let them come up: beat your plowshares into swords, and your pruninghooks into spears: let the weak say, I am strong.

And the first epistle of St. Peter, chapter two, with its exhortation to honor and obey rulers. Chaplain Clements in his sermon said that men must pray for peace, yet must not forget that liberty, truth, and righteousness are of more importance than quietness. There was a call for quilts and blankets to keep the soldiers warm; and in the afternoon "the quiet of the Sabbath was broken" as almost every citizen scurried along the streets and across the Park, his arms laden with bedclothes. The following day the Stars and Stripes floated from every building and flagstaff, and the whole college and village accompanied President Andrews to Mount Vernon, and cheered and waved farewell as he, with his company of Knox County soldiers, took the train for Newark.

Within a day or two the Seniors sent a petition to the faculty, asking that they be released from further study and be graduated immediately, "so that they might return home and enlist, if necessary, in the United States service." This petition was not granted. The policy of the faculty, which had first been laid down by President Andrews, was to allay excitement, and retain the students in college until such time as it might appear that their services were needed by the government. They did not think that the war would last long. Professor Wharton was given permission to suspend the regular rhetorical exercises,

PRESIDENT ANDREWS

as the great political excitement in the country had a tendency to disturb the studies of the students, and it was necessary on the part of the faculty to relax somewhat the strictness of study.

A military company, the "Kenyon Light Guards," which had been formed before the war, and now included all the students, went through an exacting drill daily.

President Andrews' service in the army was brief. He was appointed colonel of the Fourth Ohio Volunteer Infantry, and was ordered with his regiment to West Virginia. His health was not rugged, and it broke down under the hardships and exposures of military life. In August, 1861, he came back to Gambier to die. The president's house at that time was on the ground where Hanna Hall now stands, close to the college. The students maintained great quietness in all that part of the Park, and refrained even from singing. On Wednesday, September 18, at a quarter past three in the afternoon, the college bell began to toll, slowly striking out the number forty-two—the years of Lorin Andrews' age. Stillness fell upon the college and the town, and on every building the flags dropped to half-mast. At evening prayers Professor Lang, speaking with difficulty because of deep emotion, formally announced to the students the death of their president. On the day of his funeral a very great company of people assembled, filling Rosse Chapel and the grounds about it. Twelve students bore the body—the coffin splendid with the flag—to the chapel and there stood guard over it. The burial service was read by Bishops McIlvaine and Bedell, assisted by other clergymen; and then members of the faculty carried the body to its grave, at the northeast corner of the churchyard, between two great oaks. There they buried him, and sang the "Gloria in Excelsis." In 1866 a monument was erected at the head of the grave, and there, ever since, year after year, the memorial services of the Grand Army of the Republic have been said, and a bugle has sounded "Taps." Kenyon has no memory more precious than that of Lorin Andrews, who brought her out of weakness into strength, inspired her with his high example of manliness and devotion, and, almost with a boy's impulsiveness, rushed into war at the first call, and gave his life for his country.

The company of "Kenyon Light Guards" was enrolled in the Ohio militia, and when, in September, 1862, the Confederate general, Kirby Smith, threatened Cincinnati, the "Light Guards," to the number of forty, went into service. With great enthusiasm they piled into wagons and rode to Mount Vernon, whose inhabitants feasted them and bestowed upon them innumerable cheers; thence by rail to Cincinnati, where kind ladies gave them an excellent dinner, after which the boys spent the night sprawled out on the floor in a great room, and realized something of the hardship of war. The next morning Bishop McIlvaine came to see them, and gave them words of approbation and encouragement. A freight train took them to North Bend, where they went into camp, received guns, and made ready to resist whatever foe might try to cross the river. But Kirby Smith revised his plan and did not come to the Ohio, and so, at the end of two weeks, the "Kenyon Light Guards" were back again in Gambier, having done well whatever was required of them.

Gradually, as the war went on, the number of students decreased. Some went into the war, and some went home and took the places of fathers and brothers who were in the army. Of the one hundred and fifteen students in the Junior, Sophomore, and Freshman classes in 1860-1861, but sixty-nine returned the next year, and the number of Freshmen entering fell from fifty-six to thirty-three. In 1862-1863 there were but seventy-three students in all; the next year seventy-four; the next year, when the war ended, there were sixty-eight—just half the number in 1860-1861.

In 1872 the college published a "roll of students" who

had served in the Civil War on the side of the Union. This roll is, of course, chiefly made up of students who had been in college before 1861. Two graduates of Kenyon's first class, that of 1829, are named—J. B. Chase and Samuel Chase; and most of the succeeding classes are represented in the list, down to and including the class of 1873. The names of Bexley men, even though they were never students in the college, are included, and also the names of grammar school students. In all, there are one hundred and seventy-eight names, eleven of which are of Bexley men who were never in Kenyon College, twenty-one are of grammar school students who did not enter college, and one hundred and forty-six are of Kenyon College men. Seventeen of these men lost their lives in the war, of whom nine were killed in battle or died of wounds, and eight died of exposure, exhaustion, or sickness due to their military service. The number of those who were wounded, but did not die, is not known. In this "roll of students" are given the ranks to which each man attained. Out of the one hundred and seventy-eight, four became major generals, five brigadier generals, fourteen colonels, twelve lieutenant colonels, eleven majors, twenty-five captains, twenty-four first lieutenants, eight second lieutenants, one ensign, sixteen chaplains, thirteen surgeons or assistant surgeons—in all, one hundred and thirty-four commissioned officers. There were nine noncommissioned officers. And over these and all the other officers and soldiers in the army was the great Secretary of War, Edwin M. Stanton, Kenyon '34.

Kenyon's record in the Civil War has been an enduring source of pride to her sons. It set a standard which had its influence in the War with Spain, and in the Great War.

CHAPTER XX

THE COLLEGE UNDER PRESIDENTS SHORT, STONE, AND TAPPAN. 1861-1875

WHEN President Andrews went to the war the board of trustees, declining to accept his resignation of the presidency, gave him indefinite leave of absence, and appointed as acting president Professor Benjamin S. Lang, who for the past year had borne the title of "dean of the college." His administration, which continued for two years, was efficient and uneventful, under the discouraging circumstances of a constantly diminishing enrollment, owing to the war. During this period the college suffered two great losses; the death of Professor Marcus T. C. Wing, and the resignation of Professor Francis Wharton. Professor Wing had been connected with the institutions from their earliest days, had rendered faithful and competent service as professor at Bexley and at the college, had been for many years financial agent of the college, and secretary of the board of trustees. Professor Wharton had held the very wide chair of English literature, history, politics, the Bible, and anything else he cared to teach. He was ordained in 1863 and wished to devote himself to the work of the parochial ministry, in which work he preferred to breathe an atmosphere not so militantly evangelical as that of Gambier. Proficient in many branches of learning, he was eminent as an authority on international law; and during his later years he was solicitor of the Department of State at Washington. He left a memorial of himself in the house he had built—"Sunset Cottage"—on the brow of the hill, overlooking the western valley.

Two clergymen in succession were elected to the presidency of the college, but declined it: Daniel R. Goodwin, provost of the University of Pennsylvania, and M. A. DeWolfe Howe, rector of St. Luke's Church, Philadelphia. The Reverend Henry C. Potter was approached on the subject of becoming president, but gave no encouragement. Having, therefore, failed to get a clergyman, the board of trustees selected a layman, Charles Short, a graduate of Harvard College in 1846, headmaster for six years of the Roxbury Latin School, and then principal of a private classical school in Philadelphia. Mr. Short was a gentleman of fine culture and taste, was one of the foremost classical scholars in our country, and had an extensive acquaintance with Oriental and European languages. The remarkable gifts and acquirements of such a scholar can hardly have found much scope for exercise in the presidency of Kenyon College, as it was at that day, and it is not strange that after holding the office for four years he resigned, and was very soon called to the professorship of Latin at Columbia College, which chair he filled and adorned to the end of his life. He had been a successful president, and, had he remained, the college might have been spared the evils and depressions under which it labored for the next twenty-five years. During his administration the enrollment of students gradually increased, rising from seventy-four to ninety, which exceeded by far the average enrollment before President Andrews' time. It was he who originated the library of the college, procuring several hundred books to make a start, there having been before only the theological library and the libraries of the literary societies. The strong faculty which he found when he came to Gambier held together as long as he remained, and James Kent Stone, a young man of brilliant parts, recently graduated at Harvard, was added to it as professor of Latin. With such a group of scholars in the faculty, all living and working in harmony, and with a steadily increasing enrollment of students, the college seemed in a fair way to regain the prosperity it had enjoyed just before the war. But a spirit of criticism seems to have been abroad in Gambier in 1867, and "Fama" who cut such didos at Carthage began to scamper over the roof of Old Kenyon—always a favorite romping-place of hers. The board of trustees investigated charges made by some people of the town that "defects of a serious character exist in the discipline of Kenyon College." The Kenyon faculty in 1867 was as competent to govern the college, and was probably as alert in doing so, as at any period of the history of the college; and no doubt it would have been better if the board had not undertaken its investigations, for there can hardly be a surer way to make trouble in a college. The committee charged with this business reported that "so far as President Short is regarded as connected with these rumors, no action is required"; as to the other members of the faculty, the need of some action seems to have been implied by this exception of the president, but nothing was said or done. However, Professor Lang and Professor Stone immediately resigned, as did Mr. Newton, the chaplain; and President Short's resignation soon followed. Professor Lang had been twelve years in the faculty. He was a man of strong, admirable character—"an Abraham Lincoln sort of man," it was said —and was a remarkably good teacher of mathematics.

Upon President Short's resignation the trustees at once elected Professor Stone to succeed him. They were confident that he was the right man. He was then about twenty-eight years of age, and had since 1863 been a professor in the college. He had come to Gambier on the invitation of Bishops McIlvaine and Bedell, who recommended him as "a young gentleman of exemplary character, and promising abilities, and fine literary acquirements." He proved to have all these qualities, but also some others of which the bishops did not dream. The students found him interesting, and liked him exceedingly. His administration was marked by a prevalence of good order in the college. As president he was

PRESIDENT SHORT

professor of mental and moral philosophy, subjects that give the teacher a wide field to range over, if he is disposed to do so. In his classroom President Stone began to impart teachings that were novel and surprising at Gambier; and in a sermon preached in the college pulpit, in March, 1868, he further disseminated the strange doctrines. To those who were expert in such observations he appeared to be minimizing some of the venerated cornerstones of Protestant orthodoxy, and to be leaning towards Tractarianism, which had by that time made considerable progress in the Episcopal Church, but had never showed its head at Rosse Chapel. President Stone's published sermons of that period contain nothing very inflammatory, but he cannot have failed to know that there was a great deal of highly combustible material at Gambier, and that a very small spark would set it ablaze. For thirty years Gambier had been solidly evangelical. That was its well-known character throughout the American and English Churches. That had been its boast and its strength. It is not a question whether the president's opinions were right or wrong: he knew that they were not in harmony with the long-established theological position of the institutions, and that when the bishops and the board of trustees elected him president they did so on the supposition that he was in agreement with them in this matter. Undoubtedly he was guided by his conscience in what he did; but it would have saved the college from a great disaster if his conscience had guided him in the opposite direction. The trouble began soon.

Doctor Bronson, ex-president of the college, and at that time a professor at Bexley Hall, was temporarily chaplain of the college, and was by no means the man to keep silent when what he regarded as erroneous and dangerous teachings were spread abroad in that college which he had known and loved almost from the day of its foundation, and had, through many years, served with whole-hearted, self-denying devotion. Under such circumstances nothing could have made him hold his peace. He at once exposed from the college pulpit, where it was his official duty to preach, the errors which he thought were contained in President Stone's sermon. President Stone, it was said, countered by suggesting to students that they might leave the chapel on Sundays, before the preaching began. Doctor McElhinney added to the disturbance by questioning Seniors about President Stone's teachings in class. There was great excitement. The students, though quite ignorant of the theological and ecclesiastical points involved, were delighted to have a rumpus in the college, and were disposed to have a share in it; and, since they liked President Stone very much, they arrayed themselves on his side. Most of the members of the faculty also sympathized with him, or at least, liked his theology—of which they knew but little—better than that which prevailed at Bexley Hall; and they did not approve of the attack that was made upon him. The two bishops took up the matter; and, while reserving for mature consideration the alleged erroneous teachings of the president, they referred to the board of trustees the charges and counter-charges of discourtesy and breach of discipline which those of each party brought against those of the other. The board was composed of men, clerical and lay, who were as fair-minded, and had as good sense as any twelve men in the Church. They were called in special session, and, having gone into committee of the whole, they discussed the subject at great length, and then rose and reported that, in their opinion, no one had intended any wrong; and they passed resolutions counseling peace.

But it is vain to cry "Peace, peace!" when there is no peace. The Seniors asked Bishop McIlvaine to appoint President Stone to preach their baccalaureate sermon. The Bishop at first declined to appoint him; whereupon the Seniors resolved that they would listen to no other preacher. The

Bishop yielded, and President Stone preached the sermon, taking as his text the verse in Jude about the duty of contending earnestly for the faith once delivered to the saints. Now if there were any men in the world who intended to do just that thing, and thought that they did do it, it was the professors in the Bexley faculty, and the evangelical divines that flocked to Gambier at commencement time. Under ordinary circumstances the sermon would have passed with little notice; but the circumstances were not ordinary, and, after all that had happened, there was something of bravado in the selection of such a subject, since the preacher knew that whatever he said would meet with a minute criticism that would detect and emphasize anything that might seem wrong or dangerous. The theologians who heard it understood its tendency, perhaps better than the preacher did; and they found plenty in it that was objectionable. The Seniors, however, found it very edifying. The whole thing seems boyish. The president's attitude and action were those of a boy, not of a mature man with a sober sense of responsibility; it was the boys of the Senior class who had forced Bishop McIlvaine to appoint him preacher; and, as we shall now see, it was a boy, and a very young boy, who brought matters to a crisis.

Upon commencement day the valedictorian, in distributing the customary compliments, spoke of President Stone in high terms, and added that he "was the victim of those who, while professing to be advocates of religious toleration, were unwilling that it should apply to any except those whose opinions agreed with their own." Upon hearing these words the students broke out in wild cheers. That settled President Stone's fate, and he knew it. Within a few days he tendered his resignation, and the board of trustees accepted it.

Mr. Stone went directly from Gambier to the presidency of Hobart College. He held that office one year, and then entered the Roman Catholic Church. It was afterwards clear to him that he had long been tending that way, led by Providence: the Bexley professors had perceived the tendency earlier than he, but had attributed it to a different leader. He had been accompanied to Hobart by Professor Hamilton L. Smith, who had for fourteen years been one of the brightest ornaments of the Kenyon faculty. Several students also went to Hobart, some of whom were soon glad to return to their former college.

The effect of this theological outbreak was calamitous. In comparison with it the injury wrought by the Civil War was slight, for that did not disturb the internal peace and harmony of the institutions, and the diminution of numbers caused by the war was in the way of being remedied by the steadily increasing enrollment. But all hopes were wrecked in 1868, and both seminary and college began to decline, until in 1873 and 1875 there were at Bexley no students at all; and in 1890 there were but thirty-three registered at the college, not all of whom were in attendance at any one time. The grammar school also felt the shock, and fell from forty-nine pupils in 1867-1868 to thirteen in 1875-1876, but after that recovered. The controversy when once set going swept the institutions from side to side. The major theologians engaged in it were admirable men, but were more mindful of their promise to "banish and drive away from the Church all erroneous and strange doctrines" than of that other promise, to "maintain and set forwards quietness, peace, and love, among all Christian people." The man who might have exercised a moderating influence was gone: Doctor Thomas M. Smith had retired from Bexley Hall in 1864, after occupying for eighteen years the chair of systematic divinity, and having, during his last years, been designated as the "dean of the seminary." He was succeeded in his professorship by the Reverend Henry Tullidge, and he in turn by Doctor McElhinney, who also became "dean." Doctor McElhinney had previously occupied several other chairs.

The Reverend L. W. Bancroft was professor of ecclesiastical history, and the Reverend Frederic Gardiner was professor of Biblical literature. All were strong men.

Trouble began at Bexley while yet Doctor Short was president of the college. The first gun in this unhappy war was fired in April, 1867, by Professor Gardiner, who astonished the board of trustees by sending them a number of communications in which he charged Professors Bancroft and McElhinney with teaching unsound doctrine. The minutes of the board do not disclose the nature of the alleged heresies, but the trustees called in all the theological professors and spent much time in examining them. The conclusion was that the charges had not been proved, and that no action was required of the board. Professor Gardiner thereupon resigned; Professor Bancroft had already done so.

After President Stone's resignation had been accepted the board of trustees endeavored to obviate conflicts between college and seminary in the future by providing that thereafter the offices of president of the college and dean of the seminary should be held by the same person. Some trustees were ready to go much further than this. A motion was made, and debated long and seriously, declaring all chairs at Bexley and at the college vacant. A substitute was proposed, to the effect that Doctor McElhinney and Professor Hamilton L. Smith be requested to resign—the ablest two men in Gambier, but irreconcilably and outspokenly opposed regarding President Stone's course. Doctor McElhinney, hearing of what was proposed, sent in his resignation; but, by a vote of six to four, it was not accepted. A month later Professor Smith presented his resignation, and it was not accepted; but after he had gone to Hobart College it was accepted of necessity.

When President Stone resigned, the board of trustees once more invited Doctor Goodwin of Philadelphia to take the presidency of the college, and this time they coupled with it the office of dean of the seminary. He would not be persuaded. In December, 1868, Professor Eli Todd Tappan, then at Ohio University, was elected president of the college, the plan of uniting dean and president in one person being temporarily abandoned. Mr. Tappan was a member of a distinguished family. He had been a lawyer, an editor, and a teacher. At Athens he was professor of mathematics, and he had published a series of mathematical textbooks. He was a member of the state board of school examiners, had been president of the Ohio Teachers' Association, and later was president of the National Educational Society. Thus he was a practical teacher and school man, and had a wide acquaintance among Ohio teachers, which might be expected to help in drawing men to the college.

Great hopes were entertained that under President Tappan Kenyon would be restored to its former strength. At the inauguration of the new president Governor Hayes said, "I do not doubt that you are now entering upon a period of prosperity, of success, not surpassed—I trust I may say not equalled—by any former period in the history of Kenyon College." In 1870 the old-time scenes of commencement day were reënacted. The country people for miles about crowded the Park with their buggies and wagons, and the citizens of Mount Vernon flocked out. The Sandusky band played stirring music, and altogether it was a gala day. No one could doubt that the college was once more on the upward road. One thing that was bound to help was the railway, which had at last reached Gambier. As early as the fall of 1866 there was a freight train, running upon an uncertain schedule—and an uncertain track—and carrying a single passenger car. It was spoken of as an "excruciating convenience." In July, 1872, the road was finished to Mount Vernon. In the fall of 1873 cars ran through from Cleveland to Cincinnati without change. All trains stopped at Gambier, but there were few new students getting off there. The number in the college remained constantly at about fifty; but the grammar school, which, at the close of the Civil War had reported eighty-seven pupils, reported but thirteen in 1873. Milnor Hall had been rented in 1871 to Major Riley, a well-known and useful citizen of Gambier, to be kept as a hotel, and the few students were transferred to Ascension Hall and put in charge of one of the college professors. Frequently articles appeared in the *Standard of the Cross*, or in the *Reveille*, or, later, in the *Kenyon Advance* or the *Argus*, or in some Cleveland or Columbus paper, asking, "What is the matter with Kenyon College?" These articles followed an outline that had gradually become standardized: Kenyon had a splendid faculty, it had noble and ample buildings and grounds, it had a great history—and here would be brought in the names of Stanton, Hayes, and others that had been there in the thirties and forties—it was the only Church college in the West; why, then, did not more students come to it? The answers followed: Episcopalians were to blame for not sending their sons; the alumni were to blame for the same reason; the college was not sufficiently advertised; the course of study was not sufficiently modern. The *Reveille* confessed itself puzzled, saying, in 1874:

When Miami closed we hoped to be gainers. Other colleges in the state received quite a number from that quarter, Kenyon not one. Why so? Some time ago, when it was rumored that Gambier was to have a railroad, we were all overjoyed. Everyone was confident that this connection with the rest of mankind would swell the number of students to a hundred at least. The track was laid; the locomotive shrieked; the cars passed daily filled with people from the great world, but no one for Kenyon. Our next hope was: when the college is separated from the theological seminary, and when the alumni figure in the board of trustees, then will Kenyon assume a new life. The much abused seminary now stands at the head of the avenue in majestic solitude—a cenotaph; the alumni, who were to work such mighty reform now have the power; the antecedent of the conditional proposition is fulfilled, the consequent ————. Where is the fallacy?

The "fallacy" lay chiefly in the omission of some of the important "antecedents." A house divided against itself cannot stand, or, at any rate, cannot attract people to come and live in it; and it seemed as if some kind of fight was always going on at Gambier. The disturbed and disturbing conditions at Bexley Hall alienated many Bexley men, and the good will of Bexley men has always been one of the most valuable assets of the college. The continual beating of theological tom-toms was unattractive to the laity. Disagreements between the college faculty and the board of trustees, and between the faculty and the bishops, were frequent, and the faculty expressed its views very plainly and openly. Again, the financial situation, and the way the board of trustees dealt with it, caused much irritation.

In January, 1872, the board of trustees, and the seminary, and their friends were again thrown into excitement by an effort to remove Professors McElhinney, Bronson, and Morris A. Tyng—the last had come in 1870. These gentlemen had signed a paper approving the refusal of the Reverend Charles E. Cheney of Chicago to submit to a sentence imposed upon him by an ecclesiastical court for his teachings and practices in the matter of baptism. A motion in the board to remove the three professors was laid on the table, but a resolution was passed,

that in the opinion of this Board the Professors of the Seminary should use great caution in appearing before the public as participants in partisan controversies in the Church; and the Trustees regret the necessity of observing that in one or two instances of participation in such controversies in the past year they have seriously embarrassed them, and diminished to some extent (as they have reason to fear) the confidence of the patrons of our Institutions.

But the professors would not permit the board to teach them their duty in such matters; so in March the board passed a resolution declaring that, while appreciating the long services of Doctor Bronson to the Church and to the institutions at Gambier, it regarded his further occupancy of a chair at Bexley Hall as not advantageous to the seminary, and it therefore declared the chair vacant from the first of the following July. This was a lamentable end of long and devoted services to the college; and it was complicated by the fact that the chair had been endowed by Mr. Jay Cooke expressly "to provide a life position of dignity and usefulness for his friend, and the friend of his father and mother, the Rev. Dr. Bronson." It is said that Mr. Cooke proposed to reclaim his gift, and use the money in some other way for his friend's benefit; but Doctor Bronson would do nothing to injure the institution that had so long been dear to him.

Doctor McElhinney's resignation at once followed, and a year later Professor Tyng's chair was pulled out from under him because there was nobody left in the seminary for him to teach. Being now emptied of both students and faculty, Bexley Hall at last enjoyed great peace, and its orthodoxy could not be called in question. But these things had not occurred without causing heated discussion throughout Gambier, and among the alumni and friends of the institutions, with disastrous effects upon the prosperity of the college.

While this was going on, the bishops, who seem for a long time past to have taken no active part in the internal affairs of the college and seminary, began to make themselves felt in various ways that had an unhappy effect. Bishop McIlvaine appointed a daily service for the college at eight o'clock in the morning, and required the theological students also to attend it. The Bexley faculty, which had not been consulted, protested in vain; but the speedy collapse of Bexley solved the difficulty. Bishop Bedell also fell out with the college faculty because of what he regarded as an invasion of the dignity of the episcopal office as represented in himself and Bishop McIlvaine. It may be remembered that on commencement day, 1868, the valedictorian had spoken of President Stone as the victim of those who believed in religious toleration only for their own opinions. Bishops McIlvaine and Bedell understood that these words were intended to apply to them. The speaker being called to account denied that he so intended them, but would not apologize, further than to say that he regretted that he had been misunderstood. Therefore three years later, in 1871, when he applied to the faculty for the degree of Master of Arts, to which, under the rules of that time, he was entitled, the board of trustees directed the faculty to withhold the degree. This, and all subsequent actions of the trustees in this matter were undoubtedly dictated by Bishop Bedell, although he may have had the willing support of some members of the board. The faculty replied that it would always "hear with becoming respect" any statement the board might make regarding the fitness of any person upon whom it was proposed to confer a degree, and would give such statement due weight in making up their decision; but they reminded the board

that the laws of the State confer upon the President and Professors of Kenyon College the power to confer degrees in the Arts and Sciences; that this power carries with it the responsibility for either allowing or refusing a degree, which responsibility is exclusively upon us, since no other body has any legal power to direct or control us in this work.

In the case under discussion the valedictorian had tendered a statement which the faculty considered sufficient; they therefore voted him the degree. The board of trustees then requested the faculty to reconsider its vote. The faculty voted to postpone giving the degree; but six weeks later, the young man having repeated his statement of regret that his words had been misconstrued, the faculty, with unanimous consent, gave him the diploma. The board of trustees made no protest, but Bishop Bedell was never satisfied. In 1873 a motion was made in the board of trustees to appoint a "Board of Honors" to which should be referred "all nominations to honorary degrees," and that no such degree should be conferred without the consent of that board. This would not have applied to the degree conferred upon the valedictorian, for that was not "honorary," but was given "in course." Such a board of honors was subsequently appointed, but this was plainly an invasion of the rights conferred on the faculties by the act of incorporation. It was dropped in 1910, having long been inoperative. This pother over the degree was not a helpful advertisement of the college.

One effect of the Civil War had been to reduce the income of the college, while at the same time the cost of living was increased. The exertions of Bishop Bedell, and his characteristic generosity, saved the faculty from a reduction of salaries at the very time when they were petitioning for an increase. In 1867 the salary of a full professor was fixed at thirteen hundred dollars and a house, and there it long remained. No sooner had the war ended than the college and seminary began to receive gifts, due in most instances to the solicitation, or influence, of Bishop McIlvaine or Bishop Bedell. The givers admired them personally, and approved of their theological position. Nearly all these gifts were made during President Short's administration, and seem to show approval of him. The theological upheaval of 1868 and the following years put an end to this flow of generosity. Upon the death of Professor Wing, Mr. Mardenbro White, who had long been connected with the college in one capacity and another, was appointed agent and treasurer. These offices he held for nearly twenty years, and administered them so well that he is named in the *Memorial* among the chief founders of the institutions.

In June, 1868, the committee on finance expressed to the board of trustees its belief that "the financial prospects of

the institution are brighter than ever before," and that continued exercise of strict economy would soon bring the day
when the current expenses would be met by the current
income. In 1873, however, the same committee considered
the financial situation precarious, and propounded, in substance, the following dilemma: If we do not contract expenditures the institutions must die; but if we do contract expenditures the institutions cannot live. So far as Bexley
Hall was concerned, the board chose the latter horn of the
dilemma, discharged the only remaining professor, and
closed the school. Yet it did not do this with an entirely good
conscience, but still sought some device by which the seminary might be revived at small expense, and under conditions that would insure peace. Someone—in all probability
Bishop Bedell—thought out a plan, and accordingly the
board resolved

that the President of the Board be authorized to enter into communi-
cation with some eminent clergyman of our Church, in this country
or abroad, and to offer him the sole charge of instruction of students
of theology in our seminary, at a salary not exceeding three thousand
dollars . . . for a definite series of years, or indefinitely, as he may
deem best; the said instructor to be competent to appoint, at the
expense of the Board, a teacher of sacred languages and an instructor
of pastoral theology at the expense of the Board.

This was more easily said than done, and it is not known that
Bishop Bedell ever approached any eminent clergyman with
that proposition; certainly the seminary was never thus put
in commission.

The lack of available money was in large measure due to
the honest and businesslike determination of the board to
stop using trust funds to meet current expenses. The finance
committee declared that $80,000 of "enhanced value real-
ized in sales of portions of the original domain have been
sunk in floating the expenses of the college which were in
excess of legitimate income." The policy of the board was

now one of strict economy, cutting down expenses to the lowest point. Against this policy the faculty of the college protested in a remarkable letter written in January, 1872, addressed to the board, and signed by the president and every professor but one.

The college [says this letter] languishes now for want of greater expenditures and more teachers. You propose to make it do with less. Your proposed future action as to salaries and work, connected with the want of any act to increase the endowment, is a declaration that the Trustees have not the means to make a College of high rank, that they have abandoned the hope, and that henceforth the course of Kenyon is downward. . . . We protest against this suicidal policy. . . . We therefore most respectfully ask the Trustees to resolve that immediate efforts shall be made to add Two Hundred Thousand Dollars to the Endowment of Kenyon College.

The trustees had become somewhat accustomed to being talked to in this way by the faculty. They seem to have borne it patiently, but they made no great effort to raise the money. President Tappan issued a circular asking for gifts, and the literary societies sent out appeals and tried to secure $30,000 each, to endow Philomathesian and Nu Pi Kappa professorships. The fountain of public generosity responded but feebly.

It was in the early days of President Tappan's administration that the Church of the Holy Spirit was built. In 1866 the Reverend John Cotton Smith, son of Ex-president Thomas M. Smith, a graduate of Bexley Hall, Bishop Bedell's successor as rector of the Church of the Ascension in New York, proposed in the name of that church to erect a chapel for the college, as a tribute of affection for the Bishop. The cornerstone was laid at commencement time in 1869, and the completed church was consecrated on Ascension Day, 1871. The Church of the Ascension paid the contractor's price, $32,000, but the furnishing and ornamenting of the building cost more than $10,000 in addition to this, far the greater part of which was borne by Bishop and Mrs. Bedell. It was, indeed, their church, planned wholly according to their ideas, and built under their supervision. They devoted to it not money alone, but constant thought and attention. The features wherein this church differs from most others are due to them, and each means something. Externally the church is lovely; and it is effectively placed, the ground falling off in front of it, and the wide lawn stretching to the street.

The chime of nine bells, the clock, and the machinery to strike the quarter-hours were placed in the tower in 1879. They were purchased by means of a subscription, chiefly of small sums, contributed by nearly three hundred persons, through the agency and laborious efforts of Mr. R. S. French, for many years a merchant in the village, whose name, said Bishop Bedell, "will never be dissevered from the Chimes and Clock of Gambier." The largest bell—it weighs nearly a ton—was given in memory of Charles Morris McCook, whose story is one of the treasures of Kenyon. When the Civil War broke out he was a boy in the grammar school, preparing to enter college. Belonging to the family of "fighting McCooks," he enlisted, and was in the battle of Bull Run. Surrounded by Confederate soldiers, and ordered to surrender, he said, "I will never surrender to a rebel," and was shot down and killed. The clock and the bells have been part of the life of the college and of Gambier ever since they were placed in the Abbott Brown tower of the church. Before the citizens had grown accustomed to the striking of the quarter-hours some of them found it impossible to sleep at night. A great war was fought over this, lawyers were employed, injunctions sought; then a compromise by which the ringing of the bells was omitted in the night time—and then all the objectors got used to the bells, or had removed from town.

In the year 1874 the Diocese of Ohio was divided into the

two Dioceses of *Ohio* and *Southern Ohio*. The line crosses
the state nearly in the middle, and Knox County is in the
Diocese of Ohio. For a number of years it had been seen that
a division would sooner or later be made, and it was evident
that it would necessitate a considerable change in the constitution of "The Theological Seminary of the Protestant
Episcopal Church in the Diocese of Ohio"—which, since
1824, had been the legal designation of the institutions at
Gambier. It was the part of wisdom to make these changes
in advance, that they might be ready and familiar when they
should be needed; and this was one of the reasons why, in the
year 1871, the board of trustees began a revision of the constitution. Another reason was the desire that there should
be in the board representatives of the alumni of both the
seminary and the college, elected by them. In addition to
these main purposes there were several other changes which
it was desirable to make while the work of revision was
going on. These were designed to legalize for the academic
department the name *Kenyon College*, and make the board
of trustees in part self-perpetuating. Discussion of proposed
amendments occupied several sessions of the board, and at
last resulted in a new constitution which became effective in
1872, and embodied all the proposed changes. The bishop
of the diocese in which the seminary was situated was to be
president of the board. The seminary was to be "under the
immediate charge and superintendence of the Bishop who
may be President of the Board, and during the recess of the
Board he shall be the Prudential Committee in all secular
matters of said Seminary." When Southern Ohio elected a
bishop be became *ex officio* a member of the board, but the
presidency of the board, and the office of prudential committee, remained in the hands of Bishop Bedell.

In the year 1873, on the twelfth day of March, Bishop
McIlvaine died at Florence, where he had gone in search of
health. His death called forth many tributes to his memory,

and in them all he was recognized as a great man and a great bishop. As his body passed through England it rested four days in the chapel of St. Faith, at Westminster Abbey, and was then borne to the steps of the presbytery in the vast church, where the service for the dead was said by Dean Stanley, and the psalms and hymns were sung by the great choir. He was buried at Spring Grove Cemetery, in Cincinnati.

The debt of Kenyon College to Bishop McIlvaine is very great. It was his, as Bishop Bedell said, "to receive the elements of an Institution of religion and learning, and to give them permanent shape and coherence." The Founders' Memorial says the mere truth when it calls him the "second founder of these institutions," and says that his "decision of character and self-devoted labors saved them at two distinct crises of difficulty." Without his efforts in securing money they must have perished. The evidences of his faith and works in their behalf are seen in Gambier upon every side. Before he came there was no regular course of theological study; he organized the seminary, built Bexley Hall for its use, and for many years performed arduous duties as an instructor of classes. He built Ascension Hall, Milnor Hall, and the main part of Rosse Chapel. Of these labors and services something has been told in this book. His action in 1839, when, through his hold on the diocesan convention, he overthrew both trustees and faculty, and made himself master of the college, was ill-advised and harmful; but he saw his error, and acknowledged it by twice seeking to recall Doctor Sparrow whom he had driven away. After his unhappy experience in dealing with President Douglass, he wisely removed from Gambier, and thereafter exercised in but a moderate degree, and mainly in a beneficial manner, the authority which the constitution conferred upon him. Bishop McIlvaine placed upon the institutions at Gambier a decidedly evangelical stamp, and this gave them for many years a loyal and generous constituency. The large sums of money that he obtained for them in 1833 and 1842, the gifts that enabled him to build Ascension Hall, the large contribution of George Peabody, were all given out of admiration for Bishop McIlvaine, and in acknowledgment of his eminent services to the evangelical cause, of which he was the foremost leader in America. It must have been a grievous thing to him in his old age to witness the collapse of the theological seminary and the decline of the college, because of differences over doctrines which, his life long, he had preached and upheld with all his power; but he was a man of faith, an undiscourageable man, and cannot have doubted that the prayers and labors which for forty years he had made in behalf of the schools at Gambier would yet find their due answer and reward. This has increasingly come to pass; and Bishop McIlvaine must hold in the honor and affection of Bexley and Kenyon a place second only to that of the heroic Bishop Chase.

In June, 1874, President Tappan resigned his office. He had held it seven years, exhibiting therein a durability exceeding that of any of his predecessors except Lorin Andrews. With the attendance at college fallen off during his administration from seventy to fifty, and still falling, and that at the grammar school reduced to twelve or fifteen, he may well have desired release from an undertaking that must have seemed hopeless. Fortunately, the college was able to retain him upon its faculty, of which he remained a valuable member until the year 1887, when he resigned and became Commissioner of Common Schools for Ohio. He died in 1888. The college faculty, in their resolutions upon his death, declared him to have been "one of the best of men, intelligent, brave, unselfish, true, a strong thinker, an accomplished scholar, a cultivated Christian gentleman."

FINANCIAL NOTE

THE following gifts were received in 1865 and 1866. In 1865 Mrs. C. L. Spencer gave $5,000 to complete the endowment of the Lorillard and Wolfe professorship, which thereafter bore the name of Spencer and Wolfe. The same year Mrs. R. B. Bowler of Cincinnati gave to certain trustees land valued by her at $25,000, to endow the Bowler professorship of natural philosophy, in memory of her husband, who in his lifetime had generously contributed money to purchase physical apparatus for the college. These trustees sold the land for more than $51,000. Of this amount about $31,000 was set apart to pay the salary of the Bowler professor, and the remainder as a fund for the purchase of apparatus and books for his department.

In 1866 the philanthropist George Peabody, in order to mark his high regard for Bishop McIlvaine, gave $25,000 to endow a chair of mathematics and civil engineering. Mr. Jay Cooke gave $30,000 to endow a professorship at Bexley Hall, to bear the name of his father, Eleutheros Cooke. He expressed the desire that his friend, the Reverend Doctor S. A. Bronson, should hold that professorship "so long as he retains in fair measure his strength and vigor." Mr. Cooke in 1888 cancelled the condition which limited the use of the fund to theological instruction. In 1867 Mrs. Sarah Lewis of Cincinnati left nearly $10,000 to the seminary, which was used towards completing the endowment of the Milnor professorship, thenceforth known by the name of "Milnor and Lewis."

CHAPTER XXI

THE COLLEGE UNDER PRESIDENTS BODINE AND STERLING. 1876-1897

UPON the resignation of Doctor Tappan the board of trustees took up once more the familiar task of finding a president for the college, who was now to be also dean of the seminary. Following their usual procedure at such times, they aimed at several shining marks, but failed to land any of them—if the figure may swerve so far. The Reverend John Cotton Smith, of the Church of the Ascension, New York, rejected the combined offices with which went a salary of $2,500 and a house. The Reverend Phillips Brooks, of Trinity Church, Boston, declined them, although to him a salary of $5,000 was offered. Other clergymen also, of hardly less eminence, were called, but would not come. For a year Professor Edward C. Benson served as acting president, and kept things going well. Meanwhile there was in Gambier a young man who for some time had been making himself useful in college and seminary, and had exhibited many of the qualities of a good president. The Reverend William Budd Bodine, a Princeton College man, graduated from Bexley Hall in 1864. In 1871 Bishop McIlvaine nominated him for chaplain of the college, that office having been vacant since Doctor Bronson's tenancy of it. With this chaplaincy was combined the rectorship of Harcourt Parish. In 1873 and the following year, when Bexley Hall was closed, Mr. Bodine added to his ministerial duties those of the librarian of the seminary. When, in 1875-1876 Bexley so far revived as to have one student, Mr. Bodine took on the work of educating him, and was, for a time, the entire teaching faculty of the seminary. Notwithstanding all these occupations he found time and inclination to travel about, seeking money and students for the college, and was duly appointed agent for this purpose. In all these capacities he showed himself an efficient worker, devoted to the interests of the institutions. He was a man of dignity and force of character, and had unusual power as a preacher. It is therefore not strange that in December, 1876, when it had been demonstrated that great men from afar could not be induced to come to Gambier, Mr. Bodine was elected president of the college and dean of the seminary. At that time there were forty-six students in the college, five at Bexley, and in the grammar school thirteen. It required a hopeful spirit, a brave heart, and a considerable degree of self-confidence, to undertake the saving of an institution that had sunken so low, and seemed still to be sinking; but all these qualities Mr. Bodine possessed.

Having found a man at last who was willing to take office, the board of trustees made the most of its good fortune. Not only was he to be president and dean; they also made him professor of mental and moral philosophy in the college, professor of ecclesiastical history and homiletics in the seminary, chaplain of the college, and special agent to travel abroad soliciting gifts and attracting students. The rectorship of Harcourt Parish he resigned to the Reverend Flemming James, D.D., who had just come to Bexley Hall as professor of Biblical literature; and the fidelity of this man in his pastoral labors over the widely extended parish is still remembered by many who love him and revere his memory.

The financial situation was not altogether encouraging, nor yet hopeless. By closing Bexley Hall and Milnor Hall, and renting Milnor for use as a hotel, the accumulated deficit, which had been about $5,000 in 1870, had been reduced to less than one thousand; but now it was decided to reopen both institutions, and an additional endowment was needed. Above all, economy must be strictly observed, and the exercise of this grace was laid rather heavily upon the faculty.

PRESIDENT BODINE

PRESIDENT STERLING

MARDENBRO WHITE

MARCUS T. C. WING

The rules for students and faculty were revised and made more stringent. Moreover, the professors were required to keep their houses in good repair, must teach at least fourteen hours a week, were denied the cherished privilege of "pasturage for one cow," and were informed that they were "expected to attend the daily service of Evening Prayer." There is a limit to human endurance, even in college professors; and these enactments seem to have approached that limit closely. The cry of the faculty came up to the ears of the board of trustees, and the board consented to invite the faculty to meet with it for consultation. The minutes tell us that the professors "improved the opportunity extended to them in expressing their views and feelings in regard to matters and things in general, and the new statutes in particular." They must have made an impression on the board, for not only were the new statutes extensively revised within the next year, but the salaries were raised to $1,400, with the following encouragement added, "until the annual income justifies an increase." The board, however, "reserved the power to designate duties other than those specially belonging to the chair of any professor to be performed by him"—but not to exceed eighteen hours a week.

During the early years of Doctor Bodine's administration his enthusiasm and energy imparted themselves in large degree to all who were connected with the college. There was a general feeling that better times were at hand, and that Kenyon was at last about to move onward to that high place which she was entitled to occupy. Senator Stanley Matthews said that he discovered at Gambier "the spirit of a new life which will make buildings where forests only grew." The *Gambier Argus* was confident that a new era had arrived. In 1878 the enrollment of the college began to rise, reaching, after some fluctuations, sixty-seven in 1884, which was higher than it had been at any time since the disastrous year of President Stone. In this respect the college was back about where it had been in the early thirties. Beyond that point it would not advance. All that President Bodine could do, all that Bishop Bedell could devise, could not draw men to Kenyon; on the contrary, the numbers declined rather steadily to thirty-three in 1890, when President Bodine resigned. The question, "What is the matter with Kenyon?" had become inveterate.

Bishop Bedell was full of resources and indefatigable in his efforts to advertise the college, enlarge its constituency, and increase its funds. In 1880 he and Mrs. Bedell gave $5,000 to found a lectureship at Gambier on the evidences of natural and revealed religion, or on the relation of science and religion. All Saints' Day was to be observed especially as Founders' Day, to commemorate the founders of the institutions, and the lectures—known as "Bedell Lectures"— were to be delivered every other year on that day; and on the same day the matriculation of new students was to occur as a public ceremony. It was hoped that by securing eminent men to lecture, many people might be attracted to Gambier to hear them; and this hope was in a measure realized in the early years of the endowment. The Founders' Memorial, which was prepared by Bishop Bedell, and has been read every year, is dignified and impressive with its sonorous roll of great names, and its recital of services rendered.

The constitution had, from the very first, provided that all the members of the House of Bishops, individually, or any two or more of them together, should be "visitants" of the seminary—including the college—to take care that nothing should be taught or done contrary to the doctrines or laws of the Church. Of this provision no bishop had ever availed himself, or had shown any inclination to do so; but Bishop Bedell believed that something could be done with it, to the advantage of Kenyon and Bexley. In January, 1880, six bishops assembled at Gambier in answer to his invitation. The Bishops of Western New York, Pittsburgh,

West Virginia, and Michigan came from Cleveland in a special car supplied by a member of the board of trustees. The Bishops of Kentucky and Southern Ohio arrived from the south. Carriages conveyed them up the Hill, and the chime of bells rang out greetings. They attended the matriculation ceremonies and addressed the students. There was a general reception at Kokosing. The bishops saw the buildings, the grounds, the faculties, and the students. They were impressed, and said that they "recognized the seminary at Gambier as no local institution, but rather as a precious inheritance and possession of the whole Church." Bishop Bedell explained to them, and sought to impress upon them, the fact that they were by the constitution of the seminary, "visitants"; and by that name they were, for several years, put down in the catalogue. The next year two or three of them made a second visit, but nothing of importance was done. Indeed, there was nothing they could do as "visitants," unless some heresy should spring up at Gambier. Meanwhile, in 1881, the constitution had been so amended that the Dioceses of Pittsburgh, West Virginia, Kentucky, Indiana, and Michigan might each elect two members of the board of trustees, one clerical and one lay. This they did in 1882, and for four years thereafter; but in 1887 Indiana ceased to be represented, and two years later West Virginia failed to elect trustees. Few of the trustees from outside Ohio took much interest in their office, and little advantage came to Kenyon or Bexley from having them on the board.

For a few years fortune gave to Kenyon a unique means of advertisement, of which she made all possible use. Rutherford Birchard Hayes, of the class of 1842, after making an excellent record in the army, and attaining the rank of major general, was twice sent to Congress, and three times elected governor of Ohio. His third campaign, made in 1875, was on a hard money platform, and he was confronted with a very strong opposition. There was high interest at Gambier in this campaign, and the students celebrated the election of Hayes in a demonstrative manner, and sent him a telegram of congratulation, to which he made a reply in words that Kenyon has never forgotten:

I hope you will all have reason to remember Old Kenyon with as much satisfaction as I do. I have no more cherished recollections than those which are associated with college life. Except the four years spent in the Union army, no other period of life is to be compared with it.

The next summer he was nominated by the Republicans for the presidency of the United States, and in the fall he was elected.

From the time of his third nomination as governor to the time of his death, in 1893, Hayes was a great Kenyon figure. Within a week after his nomination for the presidency he attended the commencement exercises of his college. A special train of seven coaches came from Columbus, crowded with passengers. Cannon banged, bands played, a flagpole was set up in front of Old Kenyon. The country people turned out and thronged the Park, leaving their horses picketed in the groves below. Reporters from all the important newspapers were present, and sent out accounts that made Kenyon known to the ends of the earth. This was good advertising, and the number of students fell off by only three the next year. On commencement day in 1880 President Hayes arrived on the Hill attended by Chief Justice Waite, Senator Stanley Matthews, and other prominent persons. A battery from the Columbus barracks fired presidential salutes, the crowds flocked in, and it was a great day. Again the next year he was present at commencement, accompanied by a number of eminent men, including two Cincinnati editors who repaid in effective publicity the attentions shown them. In 1882 he came, and at other times. He attended the funeral of Bishop Bedell, in March, 1892; and at commencement that year he made his last visit to the college he loved so well. Two rooms in Old Kenyon are associated with him, which he is known to have occupied: the southwest room of the third floor of the West Division, and the front bull's-eye room of the East Wing, now marked with a bronze tablet.

In the effort to build up Kenyon College the revival of the grammar school seemed to be one of the most necessary undertakings. Milnor Hall had been rented for use as a hotel and summer resort, the old hotel having fallen upon evil days. In 1876, when the college again came into control of the building, the grammar school was reopened at Milnor Hall, with J. P. Nelson as principal. In 1879 the school was handed over to a board of regents, consisting of President Bodine, Professor Rust of the college, and Professor Bates of Bexley Hall, who at once took steps to improve it. A good school might be expected to supply many students to the college. Milnor Hall was thoroughly repaired, and the best possible educational and domestic arrangements were provided. The response was immediate. The enrollment sprang from twenty-four to seventy-six the first year. To accommodate the increased number of pupils Delano Hall was built in 1880, through the generosity of Mr. Columbus Delano of Mount Vernon. In 1881 the board of regents was increased by the addition of Mr. Harry N. Hills, a graduate of Kenyon in 1877, and already recognized as a young man of great energy and large ideas. In 1885 President Bodine and Doctor Bates sold their interests in the school to the other regents, and Doctor Rust resigned his professorship in the college that he might give all his attention to this work. Military drill and discipline had been introduced, and the name of the school was changed to the Kenyon Military Academy. Old Milnor Hall burned down in 1889, but was at once replaced by a much better and larger building bearing the same name. Mr. Hills traveled incessantly in the interest of the school, and the regents advertised widely, so that the name of the Kenyon Military Academy was known by thousands who had never heard of Kenyon College. In 1891, when there were but forty-three students in the college there were one hundred and thirty-four in the academy, a number surpassed only in 1836.

It had been supposed that the college would grow with the growth of the preparatory department; but from 1884 onward, while the academy was going up and up, the college was going down and down. The growth of the school showed that large numbers of young men could be drawn to Gambier: why could they not be drawn into the college? To that question there were various answers; but before we listen to them our attention must be directed to two other schools in Gambier, one of them closing an honorable life in 1885, the other springing up in place of it.

In the year 1852 the Reverend Alfred Blake, a graduate of the college in 1829 and of the seminary in 1837, and from 1840 to 1845 one of the principals of the grammar school, had purchased Harcourt Place, the former home of Bishop McIlvaine, with its extensive grounds. Here he and Mrs. Blake opened a family school for boys, the original Harcourt Place School. The grammar school of the college was then in a languishing state, and was carried on in the East Wing of Old Kenyon. Doctor Blake's school supplied a much more desirable home for boys; and parents who could afford to pay $250 a year preferred it to the grammar school, where the entire expense was but $100. Harcourt Place School throve and soon had as many pupils as it could take. The boys slept in a large dormitory in the attic, and the present "Yellow House" near by provided schoolrooms. In 1877 Doctor Blake died. He was a man of strong character, a born schoolmaster, an active and leading man in the community and the Church. The school continued under other masters, with about fifty pupils, until 1885, when the regents, Rust and

Hills, not wishing to have a rival school close beside theirs, bought the property. Their first thought was to use it for a school for young boys, but they abandoned that plan and had the ground divided into lots which they tried to sell; but there were no purchasers. They then offered the entire property to the college for $8,000, to be used for a Church school for girls. It was a good offer, but the college had no money to spend in that way, and Bishop Bedell was opposed to having a girls' school in Gambier. The regents, after a time, persuaded the Bishop to withdraw his objections, and they themselves, in 1887, established Harcourt Place Seminary, a school of high grade for girls. They built the two brick structures, "Lewis Hall" and "Delano Hall," and connected them with the McIlvaine house by bridges. The limitations of this book forbid us to follow the history of that school—a history of earnest, consecrated effort on the part of those who have had it in charge, and of growth in knowledge and in the graces of character on the part of many of its pupils. It has been a beautiful school in its ideals, and rich in what it has accomplished. It has added greatly to the pleasure of life in Gambier, and has supplied to the more ambitious girls of the village an opportunity to acquire as "day pupils" a thorough secondary education, to form helpful friendships with girls from many parts of the state and country, and to fit themselves to enter any college for women.

Surely now Kenyon College could not fail to grow, with all that it had within itself to offer, and with the remarkable growth of the preparatory school, besides the attraction which the girls' school added to Gambier. On the contrary, it went steadily downward in numbers. Who, or what, was to blame? Some blamed the management and policy of the Military Academy. They maintained that the school was not sending to the college as many men as it might send if the regents were sincerely interested in building the college up. Figures seem to lend some support to this contention. During President Tappan's administration nearly one-fourth of the boys in the grammar school entered Kenyon College. While President Bodine and Professor Bates were on the board of regents a little more than one-sixth of their boys entered Kenyon. When they withdrew from the board, and left the school wholly to the other regents, only about one in fourteen of the academy boys became a Kenyon Freshman. The Military Academy was a far better school than the old grammar school, but relatively it was not nearly so good a feeder to the college: and even absolutely it was but slightly better than the old school, for it sent fewer than seven boys a year to the college on the average, while the old school in President Tappan's time sent six. To the question, "What is the matter with Kenyon College?" many replied, "It does not receive proper support from the Military Academy."

President Bodine's answer to this question was quite different from that. He said, "The great present need of Gambier is unity of plan and purpose—'working at cross purposes' has been the bane of the Institution for sixty years." In the beginning the Bishop of Ohio had been *ex-officio* head and president of the one institution which included theological seminary, college, and grammar school. In 1839, the constitution having been changed, he ceased to be president of the college, but continued as president of the seminary, while the college had its separate president. So it was until 1891. But during all those years the Bishop was able to exercise, and at times did exercise, great authority over the college, as well as over the seminary. We have seen how President Douglass, when he ceased to be satisfactory to the Bishop, was summarily dismissed from his office. Every succeeding president knew that the power of the Bishop must be taken into account. It was undefined, and often quiescent for considerable periods; yet it was there, and no president

BISHOP BEDELL

could be certain what he could do and what he could not. For this reason President Bronson had found his position uncomfortable; and from several sources have come reports that even President Andrews had the same experience. The position of the Bishop also was in this respect a difficult one; for his relationship to the college was such, and its dependence upon him to get it out of financial difficulties was such, that he must often have felt himself obliged to direct its policy; and yet he too was uncertain just what power he had. President Bodine was greatly annoyed, as was the entire faculty, when on one occasion Bishop Bedell, without consulting them, changed the hour of daily college prayers, and on another occasion forbade a dance for which the faculty had given permission. His right to do these things was very questionable, and, with regard to the dances, the faculty replied that they were compelled to "withhold the prompt compliance with the will of the President of the Board which under ordinary circumstances they would be most happy to give." But the Bishop maintained that college prayers, and dances on an Ember Day in Lent—for such this dance was— came within the domain of spiritual interests, over which he had control.

President Bodine believed that the president of the college should be president of the seminary too—one man president of both. The necessity for this was impressed upon him by the peculiar condition in which the seminary was during his presidency. For most of that time it was barely alive, and now and then the breath left it. If for a year or two it revived, it soon fell back again. Undoubtedly President Bodine was interested in the college much more than in the seminary. He was laboring night and day to build up the college, but felt little responsibility for building up the seminary. When there were but a few students at Bexley certain of the professors, drawing their salaries from seminary funds, were assigned work in the college; and there were those who thought that President Bodine would like to have them occupied there exclusively. It might be said in extenuation that Bexley was far better supplied with funds than was the college. The principal chairs at Bexley were endowed, while at the college there were no endowments for the chairs of Latin, Greek, and modern languages, and only a partial endowment for English. There were no regularly constituted chairs of history or political science, but these subjects were assigned to one professor and another. To Doctor James, who taught exclusively at Bexley Hall, and had its interests much at heart, it seemed that the funds of the seminary had been unwarrantably diverted from the purpose for which they had been given. There was a sharp discussion of this question between him and the president, which the reader may find all fairly set forth in the *Kenyon Book*. It was carried on without bitterness, yet earnestly, and President Bodine must have been the more convinced by this that divided counsels were the curse of Gambier, and that all the institutions there ought to be under one head, and be, indeed, one institution, as originally they were. To this one institution he would give the name Kenyon College, and the college should be one branch of it, and the seminary another.

To bringing about these changes Doctor Bodine devoted his efforts during the later years of his presidency. He proposed a series of amendments of the constitution, providing not only for the changes indicated above, but for others also which would deprive the Bishop of most of his authority in the institution. The exclusive power to nominate the president of the college was to be taken from the Bishop; he was no longer to be the "prudential committee," having charge of all temporal affairs during the recess of the board of trustees; he was no longer to be president of the theological seminary. The bishops of the several dioceses in Ohio were to share equal relationships to the board of trustees, and alternately hold office as president of the board for one year.

These were revolutionary changes. They restored the unity of the institutions under one head, as in the beginning, but they set limitations upon episcopal authority therein such as neither Bishop Chase nor Bishop McIlvaine would ever have tolerated. It is not probable that Bishop Bedell would have assented quietly to them had he not been in broken health during the years while the amended constitution made its slow way through the board of trustees and the diocesan conventions. Before it was finally ratified he had resigned his episcopal jurisdiction, and was patiently awaiting the hour that should release him from all earthly responsibility. To plan and carry through these amendments of the constitution was President Bodine's great work, for which, more than for anything else, he will be remembered; yet there were also other achievements that must be recorded.

The need of money to increase the general endowment fund was not met, but for special purposes there were welcome gifts. In 1881 President Bodine obtained from Mr. Columbus Delano $10,000 to build an additional hall for the Military Academy. He received from Mrs. Ezra Bliss the money to erect Hubbard Hall in memory of her brother, George Hubbard. Mr. John W. Andrews established three scholarships, and Mrs. Alfred Blake established three in memory of her husband. Mr. Henry B. Curtis, of Mount Vernon, Ohio, a lifelong friend of the college, gave the sum of $15,000, to be lent to students in small amounts, at a very low rate of interest. This has proved one of the most useful gifts that Kenyon ever received, since by these Curtis scholarship loans many young men have been enabled to remain in college; and so well has the fund been managed that it now amounts to $32,000. President Bodine said that altogether he had procured for the college about $100,000. It was undoubtedly he who induced the Reverend Archibald M. Morrisson and Mr. Jay Cooke, who respectively had endowed the Griswold and the Eleutheros Cooke professorships in the seminary, to grant such release of the conditions attached to the funds as would enable the board of trustees to assign work in the college to the occupants of those chairs.

While Doctor Bodine was president two halls were erected for the Military Academy, Delano Hall in 1881, and in 1889 the new Milnor Hall, which replaced the old one that had burned down. In this hall the college invested $10,000 of its permanent funds. Hubbard Hall, first intended as a gymnasium, a cornerstone for which was laid in 1881 a little south of Ascension Hall, was finally built in 1885 as a library on the spot now occupied by the Alumni Library. The college now had all the buildings it wanted. Bishop Bedell said in 1885, "We have every building at Gambier that we shall need for fifty years." Every building erected through the efforts of President Bodine has been destroyed by fire. In 1883 Old Kenyon and Ascension were declared by a committee of the board of trustees to be in a "condition of marked dilapidation." To make the necessary repairs would cost $10,000. Only $1,200 could be granted, and the repairs must have been inadequate.

The entire stretch of land along the south side of Wiggin Street, west of the gates, as far as Ward Street, had been sold in the fifties and was occupied by buildings. In 1876 the college began to buy this land back, and in the course of about thirty years repossessed it all. The first purchase was of the hotel, which had fallen into bad repute and was considered a menace to the morals of the students. After receiving thorough repairs it was leased to L. P. Kilbourne, a former student, who is said to have "kept a first class house." East of the hotel was the original "Scott's store." This was a composite building, made up of one of Bishop Chase's four temporary houses, to which had been annexed, about 1860, a building that had stood in the southeast corner of the present Psi Upsilon lot, and had been occupied by Captain Brown, who kept a billiard "parlor" and an "oyster palace."

The college in 1881 bought the combined buildings of Mr. Scott, who then moved across the street where the A. G. Scott store now is. The old Chase building was removed to the academy grounds, where to-day it is part of a stable; and the portion that had originally been Captain Brown's was moved to a spot just north of the present "deanery," and there, in 1885, it was greatly enlarged, and became a professor's house. Old houses are never wasted in Gambier. Nearly every ancient frame building that was ever in the village is still in existence somewhere, much disguised, perhaps, but still useful—excepting those that have burned down. Even some of the oldest log houses, antedating the college, having been moved to other lots, and clapboarded without and plastered within, are still occupied.

In 1890 Doctor Bodine resigned the presidency of the college, "to take effect when the pending constitutional changes are finally acted on." Bishop Bedell had already resigned—in 1889—and Bishop Leonard had succeeded him. Similar changes had occurred in the Diocese of Southern Ohio, to which Bishop Vincent had come in 1889 as coadjutor, and, although not full diocesan until 1904, yet from the first had performed nearly all the episcopal functions, owing to the incapacity of Bishop Jaggar. So there were new men, young and vigorous, at the head of the Episcopal Church in the two Ohio dioceses, and the new constitution was certain to be enacted soon, making great changes in the interrelationship of the institutions at Gambier, and substituting for the authority of one bishop the strong influence of two who were *ex-officio* members of the board of trustees and alternately its president. Doctor Bodine had lived through the last fourteen years of the old régime, had struggled with its difficulties, had carried its heavy burdens, and had at last secured such changes in the fundamental laws as, it seemed to him, provided the only effectual solution of those problems of control that had vexed the institutions for sixty

years. He had not built up the college in numbers; it was
never so small as when he resigned; but he believed that he
had laid the foundation of future prosperity, if only there
were found capable builders to labor upon its walls. While
he was president he received many calls to large churches,
but he would not be drawn away from the work to which he
had set his hand. When this work was finished he was free.
He soon became rector of the Church of the Saviour in
Philadelphia, in which office he remained until his death,
which occurred in 1907. That church, while he was its rector,
grew to be one of the largest and strongest in the city, owing
in part to his executive ability, but chiefly—so his bishop
thought—because of the spiritual quality of his influence,
exerted through his preaching and his pastoral ministrations.

Doctor Bodine was succeeded by Doctor Theodore Sterling, for one year as "president pro tem.," but thereafter as
president. Doctor Sterling had come to the college in 1867
from the Cleveland Central High School as professor of
mathematics, and the next year had become Bowler professor
of natural philosophy and chemistry; and this chair he retained until the close of his presidency. He was the first man
to be president of "Kenyon College," as including all the
institutions at Gambier, and it is to be observed that he was
a layman. On the whole, lay presidents had been rather more
successful at Gambier than clerical presidents; yet it seemed
incongruous that a layman, a doctor of medicine, should be
at the head of a theological school; and the immediacy of his
contact with the seminary was alleviated by the appointment, in 1891, of the Reverend Doctor Hosea Williams
Jones to be "dean of the faculty"; that is to say, to preside
over the meetings of the theological faculty in the absence
of the president, to exercise an undefined care over the building, to enforce the disciplinary rules of the faculty, to assign
rooms to students, and to be librarian. He had no voice in the
election and dismissal of professors. Doctor Jones was a

graduate of the seminary in 1870, and had been professor of ecclesiastical history since 1884. He was a man of great social attractiveness, had unusual command of language and discrimination in its use, was much sought for as a preacher and speaker, and lent to his office as dean a distinction which it did not of itself possess. He had a philosophical grasp of history, and was an able teacher in his department.

President Sterling, though he sometimes presided at its faculty meetings, did not give much attention to the theological seminary. He did not need to do so. In 1889, the year when Bishop Leonard and Bishop Vincent came to Ohio, there were but six students at Bexley Hall. The next year there were twenty-two, and the numbers averaged twenty a year for the next twelve years. What brought these men to Gambier is indicated by their provenience. In 1890 fifteen men were from the Diocese of Ohio, five from Southern Ohio, two from other dioceses. In 1891 fourteen were from Ohio, eight from Southern Ohio, two from other dioceses. For the ten years following 1889 there were every year, on an average, almost eleven and a half men from Ohio, six men from Southern Ohio, and a little more than two from other states. These were very much larger numbers for Ohio than had ever before been known. In 1862, the year when Bexley Hall overflowed with thirty-nine students, only seven of them were from the state of Ohio, and of these only two from the territory now within the Diocese of Ohio. The new bishops were very active in securing candidates for the ministry. They found in Bexley Hall a good place at hand for training these men, and they used it. But much of the strength of Bexley Hall had been diverted to the other end of the Hill, and had to be called back. In 1889 every theological professor but one was teaching at the college; from 1892 onward the theological professors, except one, were employed exclusively at Bexley Hall, where they had enough to do.

If numbers increased at the seminary, they mounted yet more rapidly at the college. No sooner had Doctor Sterling taken on the functions of president than he began a campaign to gather students. At his suggestion the board of trustees offered free tuition and room rent to one student from each county in Ohio. It was hoped that eighty-eight men would grasp this opportunity. Several students of the college were sent out as agents to bring other men in. There was much advertising. All these were legitimate methods of seeking increase; but other methods also were employed which did not meet with universal approval. Men were admitted to college who were but poorly prepared. Students might make up in college almost any number of entrance requirements. Doctor Sterling justified this as a temporary expedient. He told how, when he studied medicine, one of his professors used to say, "When a doctor is called in to treat a serious case, his first duty is to obviate the tendency to dissolution." Doctor Sterling thought this advice very pertinent to the situation at Kenyon College. When he came to the presidency the attendance had for six years been falling steadily, and had reached the low record number, nominally thirty-three, actually less than thirty. Dissolution was imminent, and almost any method seemed to be justified which would obviate that tendency. There was a quick response to the stimulants that were applied. In three years the attendance rose to ninety-one. So far as numbers were concerned, things were now back where they had been twenty-five years before, when President Stone checked the rising tendency. The faculty also was increased and strengthened by the addition of a number of young men, chiefly to take the places of the Bexley professors that had been withdrawn. In the catalogue for 1890-1891 appears for the first time the name of Leslie H. Ingham, who at first taught Greek, and afterwards chemistry. The next year introduced to Kenyon Charles F. Brusie, professor of English, and in

BISHOP LEONARD

1892 came William N. Guthrie, professor of modern languages, and William F. Peirce, professor of mental and moral philosophy and instructor in history and economics. A little later came Henry T. West and John G. Ames. Doctor Sterling chose young men, and experience showed that he chose good ones.

Still, all was not well. The regents of the Military Academy complained that President Sterling was taking boys even out of their third form and admitting them to college, and was thus making it difficult for them to hold their pupils. President Sterling on his part complained that the regents were advising boys not to go to Kenyon College, and thus were injuring the institution. The trustees grew weary of these dissensions. Again, a good many of the new students could not do the work required by the college; they failed in class work and in examinations. After 1893 the attendance at college fell away, dropping to sixty-five in 1896. It looked as if the decline would continue. The tendency to dissolution had temporarily been obviated, and perhaps no methods except those that President Sterling employed could have accomplished that; but the patient's recovery was still doubtful, and it seemed to the board of trustees that another physician should be called in. Doctor Sterling's only desire in this matter was for the prosperity of the college: he resigned in November, 1895.

The board of trustees, having canvassed many names, elected as president Professor Flavel S. Luther, of Trinity College, who had been headmaster at the grammar school twelve years before, and then for one year professor of mathematics in the college. Professor Luther considered the call, but at length declined it. The choice of the trustees then fell upon Professor William Foster Peirce, of the college, who, since he came to Kenyon in 1892, had proved to be an able teacher, had shown remarkable interest in the college and a readiness to be helpful in any possible way, and had gained great favor among the students by encouraging their athletic sports and taking part in them. He had impressed the trustees as a very capable young man, likely to succeed. They elected him, and he accepted the office.

CHAPTER XXII

COLLEGE AND COLLEGE LIFE, 1862-1896

THE years from 1862 to 1896 constitute a fairly distinct period in the history of Kenyon College, beginning and ending with a time of transition, the Civil War and the presidency of Doctor Sterling. The Civil War interrupted the rapid growth of the college, and there followed what was, on the whole, a period of declension and weakness, lasting more than twenty-five years. The short presidency of Doctor Sterling was marked by the coming into effect of a new constitution, radically different from the old; by the entrance of two new, strong, and active bishops into intimate relationship with the institutions at Gambier; and by the appearance in the college faculty of a number of young and enthusiastic professors. Doctor Sterling himself, though somewhat advanced in years, was young in spirit, untrammeled by excessive conservatism, and determined to accomplish something for the college. Only two professors held over from the old faculty, and they were as responsive as anyone to the idea that Kenyon was now going to grow and do things worthy of her history and opportunities. Doctor Sterling was just the man to give the initial shove. He saw the need, he had the courage. He put his shoulder to the wheel and things began to move; then he gave way to a younger man. His presidency, therefore, was another period of transition.

A plotted line indicating the variations in attendance at the college from the sixties to the nineties shows a peak at each end, and between them a depression of varying depth. As one peruses the record of these thirty years, "depression" seems to be a good description of them. Superficially viewed, this seems to have been an unhappy time. Men were contending and sometimes wrangling; unpleasant stories, and untrue, were whispered about; the pinch of poverty was felt, and there was no sure sign of better times. But not everything gets into the record; and it is the best things that are most likely to be unmentioned. There were in Gambier during those thirty years men and women of the highest character, educated, interesting, generous of heart; and some of them were charming. Gambier has never known a finer, more intellectual society. The intercourse of these persons, one with another, must have been cheerful and elevating.

At the head of this society were Bishop and Mrs. Bedell. These thirty years are the period of Bishop Bedell's predominance in Gambier; and if ever a man loved Gambier and all that therein is, it was he. The Bedells were highly cultivated persons, accustomed to the ways of the most polite and generous people. In their own home, entertaining guests, dispensing hospitality, they were delightful. When first they came to Gambier, in 1859, they lived at "Park Cottage," which they improved and beautified. It is still one of the most admirable houses in Gambier to-day, just to look at from the front. In 1864 they built their lovely home, "Kokosing," which the Bishop formally blessed and dedicated on the eleventh of August of that year. There they lived for almost twenty-five years, and it was their delight to entertain college people, village people, and students, in simple, but very agreeable, fashion.

Bishop Bedell was a lover of beauty, and in most things his taste was excellent. In large, out-of-doors things it never failed. When he came to Gambier the Path, beginning at Old Kenyon, ended at the gates, or, perhaps, at the old well. In 1860 he extended it to Bexley Hall, and planted the trees along it. He bore almost all the expense of making, and of subsequently keeping up, this "Bishop's Walk," as he named it, and earnestly desired that it should be called. It would be well if his wish should be observed. By an agreement between the board of trustees and the trustees of the township the college cares for the Walk and keeps it in order. The Church of the Holy Spirit was to Bishop Bedell as the apple of his eye. Long before he built it he had it in mind and already loved it, and must have chosen its exact site; for when "Kokosing" was built, although that was several years before the church, he had a small oval window made, through which he might some day look and see the spire, framed as in a picture. To Bishop Bedell's good taste we owe the restoration to our stream of its Indian name, "Kokosing," or the "Place of Owls." This had been anglicized in early times into "Owl Creek," by which it is popularly called to-day. Bishop Chase imposed upon it the name "Vernon River," now happily forgotten.

During his years of office President Short was so fortunate as to be associated in the faculty with Professors Trimble, Lang, and Hamilton Smith, who held over from the preceding period. In the Latin chair was the youthful James Kent Stone. This was a very able faculty, and they lived together in happiness and mutual respect. President Short occupied "Sunset Cottage," then by far the most beautiful house in Gambier, except "Kokosing." Professor Trimble continued to live in the little brick and stone house east of the Path, near Old Kenyon, but built him a house on Acland Street. Professor Smith occupied the house in the Park near Rosse Chapel. A little to the east and south of this was the observatory through whose unfolding roof he looked forth at the stars. This was old "Cascu" of Bishop Chase's time, enlarged and made variously useful. The unevenness of the ground still shows where it stood. Professor Stone was in "Park Cottage," and Professor Lang in the house that now stands between "Sunset Cottage" and the cemetery, but then was where "Cromwell Cottage" is. Living harmoniously so near together, working together, these scholarly gentlemen and their families must have enjoyed life in Gambier. President Short remembered it as a place where he had been happy.

In 1867 came Professor Theodore Sterling, who succeeded President Short in the occupancy of "Sunset Cottage," lived there nineteen years, and then moved to the brick house that stood where Hanna Hall now is. His last years were spent in the "Wing House," at the corner of Chase Avenue and Brooklyn Street, and there he died in 1912. Doctor Sterling was a Connecticut man, was educated at Hobart College, studied medicine at the Western Reserve Medical College in Cleveland, practiced for a while, and then became a teacher. He was as genuine a man as ever lived, outspoken, active, progressive, abreast of the times, kindly, dignified without formality. When the infirmities of age came upon him he bore them in a brave and Christian spirit, so that one felt that here was a man who, through Christ, had won the victory.

No name was associated with Kenyon College for so long a period as that of Edward Close Benson. He came to Gambier in 1846 from Illinois, encouraged by Bishop Chase. He graduated in 1849, was tutor in the college for two years while he studied at Bexley Hall, from which he graduated in 1853. He taught in Doctor Blake's school for many years. He entered the faculty of Kenyon College in 1867 as professor of Latin, and retained that chair until his retirement in 1898, remaining emeritus professor until his death in 1902. He occupied the house west of Bexley Hall, and later the house near Rosse Hall. Professors Benson and Sterling were contemporaries through their years in the faculty, and in many respects were not unlike. Professor Benson was a man decisive and forthright. One always "knew where to find him." He was generous of time and money, even to extravagance. In his early days he was deemed a severe man, and students feared him; but in his later years he was loved and intensely admired by almost every man that studied under him. He was a great teacher, and if he could not impart Latin to you, then nobody could. He and Doctor Sterling were with Kenyon College through its long period of depression, and lived to see it once more arise and shine.

With President Tappan came the Reverend George A. Strong, to be professor of English literature and history, succeeding Francis Wharton after a long interval of time, and not unworthy to succeed him. Professor Strong graduated from Kenyon in 1850. He was a cultivated and delightful man, and during his residence there, "Park Cottage" was a center of social life. He wrote "Dear Kenyon, Mother dear," which, until twenty years ago, was the great Kenyon song. Doctor Strong was the first clergyman of prominence in Gambier since Bishop Chase's time who was not of the out-and-out evangelical stamp; although Doctor Wharton was not intellectually a genuine Evangelical. Broad Churchmanship, after the sort of Phillips Brooks, was coming in, and we must count Professor Strong, Doctor Bates, and President Bodine as of that belief and temperament. The body of militant professors at Bexley Hall had been dispersed, and there was no watchman on the tower when this notable change was occurring.

Professor Strong was followed, both in his chair and his residence, by Professor George S. C. Southworth, another charming man, the very type of urbanity and sympathetic cheerfulness. He was full of humor. When he was a student at Yale College his classmates had voted him the "wooden spoon," as their most popular man; and he kept the great rosewood spoon on the wall of his study as a proud trophy. Such a man is a treasure in any society, and he was a treasure in Gambier; and in his classes he maintained the high level of interest which had become a tradition of the English chair at Gambier.

In 1883 came Russell S. Devol, whose services to the college extended over more than a quarter of a century, in two periods, separated by an interval of seven years, from 1896 to 1903. He held at first the professorship of mathematics, and afterwards was college treasurer and professor of history. He was a man of the utmost fidelity and kindliness, and was held in honor not only in the college, but by the people of the village who again and again elected him to local offices.

Mention has been made only of men who held their professorships for a considerable time, and made for themselves permanent places in the history of the college. Others who taught for a shorter time were not unworthy associates of these. We are familiar with President Garfield's specifications for a good college—a young man on one end of a log, with Mark Hopkins on the other. Garfield was a Williams man. Kenyon, even in its lowest estate, was much better than the best of logs, and the youth who sat at one end of it could find in these men at the other end those gifts of personality, character, wisdom, learning, and ability to teach, which are associated with the name of the famous president of Williams College. A college that has such a faculty is a good college, be it large or small, rich or poor.

The history of Bexley Hall during this period has been sufficiently told in the preceding narrative. Its plotted line descends from the peak of 1861 into a lowland, and twice disappears below the horizon. Then in 1890 it rises to a long table-land of from sixteen to twenty years. The causes of these variations have already been shown. Bexley Hall had some strong men in this period. Nine of them became bishops: John Mills Kendrick, '64, New Mexico and Arizona; David Hummel Greer, '66, New York; Henry Damerel Aves, '83, Mexico; William Montgomery Brown, '83, Arkansas; Charles David Williams, '84, Michigan; John Charles Sage, '91, Salina; Joseph S. Motoda, '93, Kyoto; Ernest Vincent Shayler, '96, Nebraska; Robert Le Roy Harris, '99, Marquette. Three other men, graduates of Kenyon College in

'73 and '74, when Bexley Hall was closed, became bishops: John Hazen White, '72, Northern Indiana; Lewis William Burton, '73, Lexington; Francis Key Brooke, '74, Oklahoma. The catalogue for 1882-1883 shows a Senior class of five men at Bexley Hall; three of the five became bishops: Aves, Brown, and Williams. This is the record percentage at Bexley, thus far. But to provide bishops is only a small part of the work of a theological school; and, except when it was closed, Bexley Hall through all these years, as throughout its entire history, was sending into the ministry well-equipped men, some of whom have filled prominent places, east and west, while others, in the main rank and file, have done a work quite as good and as necessary. To Ohio Bexley has been indispensable. Taking up at random a clergy list of the Diocese of Ohio from about the middle of this period, we find among the seventy-one clergymen enrolled in 1881, twenty-five Bexley men—a few more than the customary one-third. And yet from that time onward for ten years, Bexley Hall was neglected, and allowed almost to perish.

The life of Kenyon students was much less monotonous and placid in this period than in earlier times when debating and fishing supplied the chief excitements. New interests had begun to stir even before the Civil War. Some of them were checked and retarded by the war, and by the subsequent depression of the college, but all of them had sprung into vigorous life again before 1896.

In this period athletics, and intercollegiate athletics in particular, became an absorbing interest, and Kenyon, with her small number of students, established for herself a place among the foremost Ohio colleges. There were few kinds of athletic sport common at that time in American colleges which were not attempted at Gambier. More than once there were boxing classes; in 1889 there was a polo team that played three games against a Mount Vernon team, and won two of them; Lacrosse was tried; hare and hounds raced over the county. Boating was at times very popular, and deserves special mention.

In 1865 the *Reveille* listed four boat clubs, constituting the "Kenyon Flotilla." Each club had its uniform and its colors. The boats were of various sorts—six oared gigs, wherries for sculling, and a cedar shell longer than the river is wide. Interest having lagged, there was a revival in 1877, when the "Kokosing Boat Club" was founded. To this revival Mr. Kilbourne, the hotel keeper, contributed by buying several skiffs and renting them out. He advertised boating as one of the attractions of his house. But the Kokosing is a poor stream for boats; the canoe is the craft for use there. In the later eighties canoeing became very popular. The most famous achievements of this sort were two trips with homemade canoes, from Gambier to Cincinnati. The first trip was made by three men, in 1886; the second, by four, in 1890. In each case the five hundred miles were covered in nineteen days, and the adventurers had a glorious time roughing it along the way.

In 1883 two clubs were playing tennis on the lawn in front of Ascension Hall. In 1890 a "Tennis Association" laid out courts northeast of the college, and Bexley had its courts also. Tennis was a popular game, and from time to time there were individuals and teams capable of contending with the best.

Baseball has been played at Kenyon ever since 1859 at least, but its great vogue was after the war. Most of the early games were between rival class nines. In the seventies Kenyon and Western Reserve, then at Hudson, used to interchange annual games. The field at the foot of the hill was laid off in the spring of 1876, and liberal provision was made for the game by purchasing a dozen bats and balls of Peck and Snyder. Masks, gloves, and defensive armor were then

THE GATES THE PATH, LOOKING SOUTH

CORNER OF WIGGIN STREET THE HOTEL
AND CHASE AVENUE

GAMBIER PICTURES TAKEN ABOUT 1865

unknown. All through the eighties baseball was the great sport at Kenyon, and the college nine won many games. Its dearest enemy was Adelbert, or Western Reserve, and next were Wooster and Ohio Wesleyan; and against these it played an even game. Then came Denison, Ohio State, and Buchtel. Oberlin was too far away to be scheduled in the early days, but later the whole state was within range. In the nineties strong teams had been developed in many of the colleges, and Kenyon won fewer victories. In 1896 the *Collegian* said that the history of baseball at Kenyon had for the last few years been "an almost continuous line of defeats." "Kenyon," it said, "never had a picked team in the true sense of the word. It has rather been made up of ten or twelve players, the only men in college who could even make a fair showing." In fact, most of the interest that Kenyon had once taken in baseball had by that time been transferred to football, in which her teams were making a remarkable record.

We read of football at Kenyon as early as 1850. At that time it had already been played for a number of years, and had its devotees. The game was very unlike that which is played to-day. A round ball, which must never be touched by the hands, was kicked back and forth, and every man tried to kick it as often as he could, avoiding being bumped over by some opponent's shoulder. It was like the modern Association game, with most of the science and team-play left out. At one time the Path near Ascension Hall was the field, two pairs of trees being the goals. It was a rough game, the faculty frowned upon it, and it died out before 1860; but it was revived later, for in 1874 the *Reveille* enrolled the "Kenyon Foot Ball Club" in its list of organizations, and this club continued on the list for several years. It was still the old-fashioned kind of football. In 1879 the *Kenyon Advance* asked, "Why have we no organized football club?" There were many scrub games, it said, but there was no regular club. In October, 1881, the history of organized football at Kenyon began. The students gathered in mass meeting, formed a football association, elected officers, and took up a collection to purchase a ball. A "university eleven" was chosen, and this association and its eleven appeared now and then in the *Reveille* in succeeding years. This arousing of interest came with the increased number of students that marked the middle years of Doctor Bodine's presidency; it declined as the attendance declined. But when the attendance at the college was at its very lowest, interest in football revived. Mr. W. H. Foley, '91, and Mr. C. F. Brusie, an instructor at the Military Academy, had played the game at other colleges, and they took it up at Gambier. Under their enthusiastic leadership a team, composed in considerable part of boys from the academy, was got together and instructed in the rudiments of the game; and on the first of November, 1890, Kenyon played at Granville its first intercollegiate game of modern football. The score was, Denison 14, Kenyon 0. The *Collegian* attributed the defeat to "lack of team play, and inability to fall on the ball." The Granville men treated their visitors hospitably, and though the Kenyon team was disappointed, still there was no discouragement. They had a feeling that they would soon be able to play football. Two weeks later they were defeated by Wooster, with a score of 30 to 2; but they were encouraged by the fact that they were able to score at all. On Thanksgiving Day Kenyon played O. S. U. at Columbus and won the game, 18 to 10; and the next week when Denison returned their visit, Kenyon won, 22 to 8. Kenyon was immensely heartened by the record of its first year at football, and it at once took a prominent place among the colleges of the Ohio Intercollegiate Athletic Association. In 1891 the most notable game was at Cleveland, with Western Reserve. People came out to see this game. More than one thousand tickets were sold for the grand stand, and carriages, dogcarts, and tallyhos were drawn up all along the sides of the field. The score was, Western Reserve 42, Kenyon 6. In 1892 Kenyon won every game until the last, when Ohio State defeated her, 26 to 10. The next year Kenyon defeated Ohio State twice. Thus fairly started in her career on the football field, she maintained during the remainder of this period a position higher than would have been supposed possible; but this history cannot be related here. Kenyon's early record was indeed creditable and even remarkable; but her victories, especially in 1890 and 1891, were not so astonishing as they appear, for the football team was not composed entirely of men drawn from the college, but Bexley Hall and the Military Academy, in which there was an enrollment of more than one hundred, supplied many of the players. This was at that time entirely legitimate.

It was in 1880 that track athletics began to command decided interest at Kenyon. In that year "Kenyon Day" was celebrated for the first time, and athletic sports held a prominent place in its programmes. Year after year these "Kenyon Day" contests were carried on, but they were entirely between Kenyon men. Ohio intercollegiate track field days began to be held in the nineties, and Kenyon sent representatives, but was generally outclassed by her chief opponents, Denison, Ohio State, and Western Reserve. In 1895 Ohio State held a field day to which Kenyon sent a team of five men, who won first position in four events, second in three, and third in four. At subsequent meets that year she did well, and established several records for Ohio. An evidence of the interest thus created was the construction in 1896 of the cinder quarter-mile track around the ball grounds.

Kenyon students gave few plays, if any, before the Civil War, though there is mention of some "colloquies." The lapse of the *Collegian* in 1860, followed by a long dearth of information on such subjects, makes it difficult to trace the early history of dramatics in the college. A notice has been preserved of a play, "The Loan of a Lover," to be given on the eighth of February, 1876. Then ensues a long blank, until, in November, 1885, a small poster was printed, announcing "Tom Cobb, or Fortune's Toy! a Comedy in Three Acts." This play was given by students, assisted by several young ladies of the village. In 1886, at commencement time, there was a play, entitled "The Adventure Club." The *Standard of the Cross* spoke of it discreetly as a "dialogue." In 1888 the "Kenyon Dramatic Company" was formed, and presented plays at Philo Hall, generally assisted by Gambier young ladies, but sometimes giving the female parts to men. Old-fashioned farces and light comedies made up most of the programmes. It was not until near the close of this period that dramatics began really to flourish at Kenyon.

In music there was much interest during the sixties, if one may judge by the number of musical organizations listed in the *Reveilles* of those years. A surer indication, perhaps, was the publication in 1866 of *Songs of Kenyon. Published by the Class of '67*. It was a small paper-covered book, of words alone, but the tunes were indicated. "We have endeavored to supply what has long been a desideratum in our little world of Kenyon," say the editors; and yet the book was not a great advance upon *Student Songs—Kenyon College* of Sturges and Packard in 1860. Here for the first time appears "Dear Kenyon, Mother dear." There was a "Kenyon Orchestra" in those days, and it is still remembered for the good music it produced. In the sixties appeared the "Kenyon Glee Club," a name destined to a long and honorable life. It gave many concerts at Gambier, and ventured abroad as far as Sunbury. In the eighties the Glee Club was thoroughly organized, and Professor Streibert, who had recently come to Gambier, became its director in 1886. The love of music, and especially of singing, was widely diffused. Delta Kappa Epsilon and Alpha Delta Phi had their glee clubs, Psi Upsilon and Theta Delta Chi had quartettes, and Beta Theta Pi a sextette. Musical interest seems to have increased down to the end of the period. Excellent concerts were given, and from time to time visiting musicians found appreciative audiences.

During this period, with its small number of students, and multiplying athletic and social interests, the literary societies suffered a decline. In 1877 the *Kenyon Advance* said that for several years but little interest had been taken in them. Five years later it said, "The events of the present year have demonstrated pretty conclusively that the Literary Societies have ceased to benefit the students." The great majority of the members totally disregarded their duties. The "Open Meetings" of the societies, which had been held from a very early day, came to an end in 1883. Some of the students talked of forming a new society, to include all who were really interested in debating. The *Reveille* in 1885 published a memorial: "In Memoriam. Sacred to the Memory of the Philomathesian and Nu Pi Kappa Societies. Fell Asleep, A.D. 1884." In 1887 the *Collegian* said that they had "died out," and in the following year announced a meeting of students "to form some organization for a permanent literary society." This effort did not lead to the founding of a new society, but to the revival of Philo in October, 1888, when a new constitution was adopted, and regular meetings began to be held once more. In 1892 Nu Pi was revived, and thereafter the two societies carried on their work in a creditable manner for a number of years.

As in the fifties the increasing number of students first attracted the Greek letter societies to Kenyon, so in the eighties, when for a time Kenyon seemed to have recovered its prosperity, other fraternities established chapters. Beta Theta Pi dates from 1879, and Delta Tau Delta from 1881.

Theta Delta Chi, which had withdrawn from the college in 1861, returned in 1870, and again withdrew in 1899.

Through these years the *Reveille* pursued its way, with many interruptions. Now and again one, two, or even more, years would elapse without the appearance of this useful publication; to the great regret, no doubt, of contemporaries who were interested in Kenyon, and certainly to the regret of subsequent historians. Two causes principally account for these interruptions: the perennial inability of the managers to make the book pay the expense of getting it out, and the occasional indiscretion of the editors or contributors in making remarks about the faculty.

The *Collegian* suspended publication in December, 1860. It was not appreciated at its true value, for at the very time when there were more students than ever before, the number of subscribers fell so low that the magazine could go on no longer. From that time until 1877 the college had no magazine or paper of its own. The lack was in part supplied, from June, 1874, onward, by the admirable *Gambier Argus*, a local paper edited and printed by R. M. Edmonds. The *Argus* carried a "College Department," edited by college students, and this was the forerunner of the *Kenyon Advance*, which first appeared in October, 1877, beginning as a twelve-page paper, about nine and a half by thirteen inches in size. After a time it cut down the size of its pages, increased their number, and put on a light purple, or lilac, cover. (This color was probably meant to be "mauve.")* It was published monthly by the Senior class, to answer "the increased and

* Extract from the minutes of the faculty, October 13, 1870. "The President having stated that several persons who reside in Canada and England, upon whom the Honorary Degree of Master of Arts has been conferred by the faculty, have asked what is the authorized color for the Master's Hood, Mauve was adopted as the color for this purpose."

increasing demand for any news that will throw light upon the hitherto isolated college world." Doctor Bodine had recently become president, and had filled the students with his own hopefulness about the college. "*The Advance*," said the editors, "will present to you Kenyon as she is to-day, springing up with renewed life and vigor." It was an excellent college paper, a credit to its editors, and deserved much better financial support than it received. In 1881 the publication was transferred to a board chosen from the whole body of students, who carried it on for two years and then gave up the struggle.

In 1887 the *Collegian* appeared again, and it has continued to the present time. It retained the character of its predecessors, giving the news of the college, and publishing stories, sketches, poems, and other articles of more or less literary merit. To the historian of Kenyon College all these papers are of great value.

Copies of two occasional, anonymous publications of this period have come down to us. One is the *Kenyon Bomb Shell*, which in its day was regarded as highly offensive and reprehensible, but seems flat and harmless enough now. The other, the *Revile-Ye*, was edited by Ralph Keeler, '62. Keeler was one of the most lovable and interesting men that Kenyon has ever enrolled among her sons. He had rare gifts of humor. A very poor boy, he early joined a troop of negro minstrels that went up and down the Ohio and Mississippi Rivers, giving entertainments at the towns on the banks. He specialized as a dancer, and became very proficient. Having accumulated five dollars, he went to a Roman Catholic school in Missouri, and there received an excellent fitting for college. He entered Kenyon, maintained good standing as a scholar, and earned his own way by doing any work he could find. His good nature and irrepressible gaiety—which he often expressed by "dancing Juba"—endeared him to students and teachers alike. When he left college, at the end of his Junior year, he owed a large sum, but he repaid it in full ten years later, when he had established himself among the rising literary men of the country. The college gave him the degree of Master of Arts. He died in 1873, at sea, coming from Cuba. The *Revile-Ye*, therefore, was the work of a brilliant young man, and still, after the lapse of more than sixty years, it scintillates mildly.

Before athletics began to absorb so large a part of their attention, Kenyon students carried on, with great interest, a number of annual demonstrations. The first of these, and by far the most worthy, was the celebration of Washington's birthday. From early times the literary societies were wont to observe this day in some appropriate manner. It became customary to hold an open meeting, or "exhibition," on the twenty-second of February. The orator would address his lofty apostrophes to the "Father of His Country," and the debaters would present their views of the opposite sides of current political questions. In 1859 occurred what was termed the "First Annual Celebration of the Twenty-Second of February," and these annual celebrations continued, with but one break, until 1880. They were conducted by the two societies, each furnishing an orator. In 1862 several new features were introduced, one of which became very popular and continued as long as these celebrations were observed. The programme for that year reads as follows: "Morning Salute by Kenyon Artillery. Afternoon. Address by Hon. Chauncey N. Olds, Columbus. Evening. Illumination of College buildings, at 7 P.M. Exercises in Rosse Chapel, at 8 P.M." The morning salute by the "Artillery" continued to be announced every year until 1873, when the programme reads, "Salute, Kenyon Artillery???" In the following two years a like doubtful promise is made, and after 1875 there is no mention of a salute. The truth is that the "Artillery"—which was the famous and mysterious "Baby" which for the

past sixty or seventy years has appeared and disappeared
most unaccountably—had passed into one of its periods of
prolonged occultation. In 1870 it had made too much noise
one night, and the faculty had tried to get possession of it.
For several years an obscure border warfare was waged over
this matter, and the triple marks of interrogation indicate
that uncertainty which must always accompany war. Perhaps the "Baby" at this time suffered some obscure alterations of personality; for when, in 1877, the class of '79 got
hold of it, they discovered that whereas previously it had
been of the "smooth-bore" variety, it had now "got the
curve."

As to the afternoon oration, the experience of a few years
showed that nobody cared to hear it; therefore a free band
concert was substituted, and came to be one of the great
features of the day. The best bands of Columbus or Akron
were engaged, and people came in from the country to hear
the music. But it was the illumination of Old Kenyon that
attracted most attention. People traveled great distances to
see it. After the railway came to Gambier special trains were
run to bring over the Mount Vernon people. The printed
announcements gave the hours when trains left Cleveland
and Columbus. The *Argus* tells of the illumination in 1877,
and this may serve as a description of the principal features
that were repeated every year.

Early in the afternoon the front of the college began to change its
appearance, and by tea time all the windows were removed, the transparencies had been put in, and the usual display of curtains covering
the pictures was seen. Old students will remember the forlorn appearance of Kenyon, when the windows were covered with strips of carpet,
bed-quilts, green and yellow curtains, and the cords attached to them
were swinging to and fro in the wind. At seven o'clock the train from
Mount Vernon arrived, with a very respectable number of visitors.
It was a lovely night, and the splendid condition of the country roads
made it possible for a large delegation from the country to come.
. . . At a quarter past seven the bell tapped and the curtains

dropped. They came down very nicely. The band struck up a lively tune and drowned the burst of applause which arose from the throng when the beautiful sight was revealed. . . . It was a general success. There were some very handsome new transparencies. The Alpha Delta Phi Fraternity had one representing a Madonna. It was very chaste, very artistic. The Theta Delta Chi Fraternity had a very handsome, striking, new one. It represented a large, white cross, and an anchor, very artistically grouped. The Philomathesian Society had two new ones. There were several very comic pictures. At a little after eight Rosse Chapel was filled with an audience almost as large as that of Commencement day. At the proper time the music began, and the marshals conducted President Bodine and Dr. James to the platform. The orators appointed by the Literary Societies then addressed the audience.

Only a few of the windows had transparencies; most of them showed rows of lighted candles set along the sashes. Such illuminations were not without danger; and after 1881 the insurance companies put a stop to those bright exhibitions.

In the sixties and seventies the silly and discreditable custom of "boring the Seniors" was a source of much gratification to successive classes of Freshmen. At the conclusion of their last examination—or at some other equally unsuitable time—the Seniors, as they issued from Ascension Hall, were met by the Freshmen in fantastic array, and were compelled by custom, and by a pride that aped good nature or scorn, to stand and listen to whatever contumelious remarks might be addressed to them, in prose or verse, by these underclassmen. One is reminded of the Indian's stolidity before his tormentors. There was always a "bore song," which named, or plainly indicated, each Senior individually, and held him up to contempt or loathing for his unspeakable ineptitude of mind and behavior, or for the vileness and atrocities which— so the song said—characterized his life. These songs were often outrageous, and sometimes scurrilous. Public opinion at last turned against the custom, and about 1879 it died out.

As at most other colleges, there was at Kenyon for a good many years the custom of "burying" Euclid, or Homer, or "Balbus," or some other unloved textbook that had just been completed. Programmes of these exercises bore heavy margins in black, and were adorned with pictures of coffins and demons. These programmes were in what pretended to be Latin. There were formal orations, "dead marches," burial ceremonies; and generally some poet dropped a melodious tear in the form of a dirge. The "deceased," of whose future state no cheerful view was ever taken, was placed in a grave, or consumed upon a pyre. Sometimes the orations and lamentations were delivered from the top of the pillars at the entrance of the Park. Funny, no doubt, these obsequies were; but they staled with time, and the custom was dropped and forgotten.

It is not known at how early a date public dances were given by Kenyon students. In June, 1872, the Seniors had a "promenade concert" in the society halls, and this marked an era, for subsequent commencement dances were dated from it, as the "Second Annual Reception," and so on. The list of dances for 1876 may be taken as a sample of the early programmes. There were four quadrilles, lancers four times, eight waltzes, one galop, one mazourka, one schottische, and one Virginia reel. The dance ended at twelve o'clock.

In 1879 a "students' reception" was held at the society halls on the evening of the Twenty-second of February, after the exercises at Rosse Hall were ended. So successful was this reception that the programme for the celebration of Washington's birthday the following year announced a "Hop" with music by the Barracks Band of Columbus. In that year the twenty-second of February fell in Lent, and on a Sunday. The students preferred to hold the celebration, with its dance, on Saturday or Monday; but the faculty in the innocence of its heart, in order to avoid a desecration of

Sunday, moved it back to Friday, having for the moment forgotten the Table of Fasts. With but slight forethought the committee sent one of the invitations to Bishop Bedell, who was then at Cleveland. The college treasures among its most awesome documents the telegram received from the Bishop on the day before the appointed dance:

Prest. Bodine: Students invitation just received. Day appointed without sufficient consideration. Friday is Ember day, Fast day. Lent. I unconditionally forbid dancing. See article thirteen for faculty. G. T. Bedell, Prest. Board of Trustees.

Article thirteen, to which reference is made, provided that the Bishop's episcopal supervision and authority should be understood as embracing the spiritual interests of the college. The faculty at once replied that they had appointed Friday for the dance, in "pious zeal"—so they said—for the preservation of the sanctity of Sunday; the students had made all arrangements, had hired an orchestra, and had agreed that there should be square dances only. They therefore informed the Bishop that they could not retract their permission to have the dance. The Bishop answered: "Church institutions obey Church laws." He reminded the faculty that it is a universal rule to omit dancing in Lent. "Especially inopportune," he said, in view of the visit of the five bishops earlier in the year. For all that, the dance took place on Friday. Perhaps the faculty had misunderstood the students when they seemed to promise that there should be no round dances; at any rate, the printed programmes included many dances of that variety. The faculty confiscated the programmes, and informed the reception committee that there must be no round dances, and no music for such dances; and the dance must close at ten o'clock. Probably nobody was very happy over this dance: the Bishop was not, the faculty was not, and it is hard to imagine that the students were. This episode led to important results: it ended the celebration of Washington's birthday at Kenyon, and it nerved President Bodine to fight for amendments of the constitution which should limit the Bishop's power to intervene in the affairs of the college.

Washington's birthday generally falls in Lent, and at a season when only indoor amusements can be carried on. To avoid infringing the rules of Lent, and to make other exercises than dancing available, "Kenyon Day" was instituted in 1880, to come in the month of May and be celebrated with track athletics and ball games. In the evening Old Kenyon was to be illuminated, there were to be orations at Rosse Hall, and square dances might follow at the society halls. Kenyon Day was observed for six or eight years. Even after the illuminating of Old Kenyon was forbidden by the insurance companies many people came to see the games. Gradually the corners of the square dances became obtuse. In 1885 the celebration was put in commencement week, which does not seem to have been a happy change, for Kenyon Day did not long survive it.

Upon a general survey of this period one is impressed with the energy and spirit displayed by the students. Few in number as they were, they attempted to do everything that students in any college did; and what is more remarkable, they actually did it, always pretty well, sometimes admirably. Often Kenyon students were among the earliest to take up a new idea. They were publishing college papers, singing in glee clubs, playing in orchestras, carrying on dramatics, when in many Ohio colleges there was little or nothing of this. They tried every sort of athletics, and succeeded in making something of most of them. They took up baseball, football, and track athletics early, and got into the best and most exclusive Ohio college athletic associations "on the ground floor." What is it? Is it the air that blows over Gambier Hill that gives such vigor? Is it the spirit of the old bishop, first of Kenyon's race, that still resides in the foundations which he laid, and imparts to every succeeding generation something of his incomparable vim? What is it? Whence does it come? They may tell who can.

On the eleventh of March, 1892, Bishop Bedell died in New York, where he and Mrs. Bedell had resided since he resigned his charge of the diocese in 1889. He had been long an invalid. His body was brought to Mount Vernon, and the funeral procession made its way to Gambier along the road that leads over the hill and past "Kokosing," where the Bishop and his dearly loved wife had lived so long and so happily. The body lay for an hour in the parish house, guarded by officers of the Military Academy brigade, while all Gambier passed by to look on the venerable face of the man so universally loved. Probably at no other time has the village seen a larger throng of people, from the country, from Mount Vernon, from every part of the diocese and the state. After the service at the Church of the Holy Spirit the congregation filed slowly across the Park to the old church-yard, and there, with prayers and the singing of hymns, the Bishop was laid to rest beside his three children, where, not long after, his wife also was laid. This spot he had chosen, looking out over the valley, the river, and the hills.

Every Bishop of Ohio has been the devoted friend of Kenyon College, and has performed great labors in her behalf; but, except Bishop Chase, none has been so intimately occupied with her concerns as was Bishop Bedell. From 1859 to 1886 he lived at Gambier, and knew all that went on at the college. An extremely conscientious man, he could never relieve himself of a sense of the responsibility which—so he thought—his office as "prudential committee," and as supervisor of the spiritual interests of the institutions, laid upon him. He therefore intervened sometimes in the affairs of the college, and not always helpfully. No man could feel himself fully president of Kenyon College while Bishop Bedell was close at hand. During the Bishop's last ten years his health so far declined that he was not always able to give wise direction, and this fact contributed to the securing of the constitutional changes that limited the Bishop's control over the institutions. It would have been fortunate for Bishop Bedell if those changes had been made many years earlier, for his successor has found it possible within the limits of the revised constitution to render great services to the college. But Bishop Bedell, working under the conditions which—as he understood it—the old constitution imposed, did the very best that was in him to perform his duty, and to advance the interests of the school which he so dearly loved. Through the dark days, the long, discouraging years, he never doubted, never wavered, devised innumerable plans to help, secured large gifts of money, and himself poured out an unceasing stream of generosity. His title to the love and reverence of Kenyon College is secure; and that corner of the cemetery behind Rosse Hall, where he and his dear wife and children sleep, should be sacred ground to every Kenyon man.

CHAPTER XXIII

THE ADMINISTRATION OF PRESIDENT PEIRCE

DOCTOR PEIRCE was elected president of Kenyon College in March, 1896, and was inducted into office at the following commencement. He has held this office—formerly so transient—for more than a quarter of a century, and is the only president that the great body of the living alumni and friends of the college have known. In the midst of a period one cannot write as its historian, unless he be a prophet; for to understand what is about him he must look forward as well as backward; and Kenyon College is in the midst of a great movement, and the accomplishments of the past seem but preparatory to what will yet be done, if God continues His favor. Therefore one can now best treat of the years since 1896 topically, rather than in continuous narrative, and leave it to others, in days to come, to weave the whole into historical form.

The students were very much pleased when they heard that Professor Peirce had been elected president of the college. He was not then at Gambier, but they arranged a suitable reception for him when he should return. A yell of cheers, accompanied by the blare of horns and the explosion of giant firecrackers greeted him as he stepped off the midnight train at Gambier. The enthusiastic young men conducted him to a carriage and drew him up the hill and about town. The ceremonies culminated in front of Old Kenyon, where a vast bonfire with accompanying rockets and roman candles illuminated the scene. There were speeches, and yells, and all the informalities by which college students

PRESIDENT PEIRCE

register satisfaction. The gratification was not confined to Gambier; for letters, telegrams, and newspaper notices declared the approval of all who wished well to Kenyon.

If, as Kenyon's noble hymn says,

Life is vision close pursued by will,

then, surely, since the hour when he accepted the office there has been life within the head and heart of the president. As a persistent follower of the "gleam," he has seen much that it enfolded take shape and substance; and

Still the bright meteor allures.

Kenyon College at that time—certainly as represented by its board of trustees—had no definite programme for the future. It had lived through many difficulties in the past, and hoped to survive whatever trials might still lie before it. In those days, as at Rome during the Second Punic War, it was no small merit not to despair. The policy was, to keep things going as well as possible, trusting that something good might turn up. One of the trustees, when asked what ground he had for the belief he expressed that Kenyon would yet be a prosperous college, could say only that he hoped somebody, some day, would give it a million dollars. He admitted that he could not descry anyone hastening towards Gambier with such a gift.

The financial situation was bad. The new president was told that expenses must be held down to as low a figure as possible; and yet some of the chief hindrances to the growth of the college had resulted from the enforced parsimony of the past. The old dormitory was out of repair, heated by stoves in the rooms, without bathrooms and other conveniences that depend on a supply of water. Boys from the country and the smaller towns were used to such conditions, but not many city boys would endure them. In the catalogue issued in President Peirce's first year, out of sixty-five men in college only six were from large cities—two from Cincinnati, one from Cleveland, one from Columbus, one from Toledo, and one from Philadelphia. It was not reasonable or right to ask men to live in Old Kenyon. One of the first achievements of the new administration was to improve this building by introducing steam heat and bathrooms, and running water was supplied from a tank in the attic, to which it was pumped from cisterns. More thorough improvements were left for the future, but the building was rendered habitable and attractive. Improvements were made also at Ascension Hall, and steam heat was put into Bexley Hall. Thus, in a short time, with such money as the president could collect, the buildings were put in tolerable order. But in the meantime a calamity had befallen, in the burning of Rosse Hall, in June, 1897. The destruction was almost complete, and there was no insurance, for the college agent was shrewdly waiting to obtain better rates. A loss so large, so unexpected, and so unnecessary, was hard to bear with equanimity, since the building must be promptly restored, for it was the college gymnasium and auditorium. Money was got together in relatively small sums, and in June, 1900, the president was able to say that everything above the basement was finished and ready for use.

In 1901 Senator Marcus A. Hanna presented the college with money to erect an additional dormitory. He was at that time one of the most influential leaders of the Republican party, was regarded with great enthusiasm by many people, and had received a degree from Kenyon. He was present at the alumni dinner with Governor Nash, in June, and when called on to say something, he declared his intention to build Kenyon a dormitory. "And we will call it," he said, "the Politician's Barracks." The gift was timely, for increasing numbers had already strained the capacity of Old Kenyon. The cornerstone of Hanna Hall was laid November 8, 1902, on which occasion a special train brought many guests from Cleveland. The building was ready for occupancy about a year later.

In 1902 the Senior Class of Bexley Hall erected the beautiful Celtic "Prayer Cross" on the spot where Bishop Chase first held the services of the Church, after he had taken up his residence on the Hill.

In October of the same year was laid the cornerstone of the Stephens Stack Room, connected with Hubbard Hall, the library. James Pullen Stephens, whose name it bears, was a member of the class of '59. In 1901 he gave the college more than $17,000, endowing a fund for the purchase of books; and his prudent generosity in erecting the fireproof stack room saved the library from destruction a few years later. The next year Mrs. Lavinia C. Colburn of Toledo erected a building to house the theological library, which previously had occupied cramped quarters on the second floor of Bexley Hall. Colburn Hall is a memorial of Warren Colburn, Junior, husband of the generous donor, and of his father, Warren Colburn, whose textbooks in arithmetic were familiar to children before the Civil War. The building was dedicated November 10, 1904.

In 1905 the work of rebuilding Old Kenyon was begun. The superior conveniences of the new Hanna Hall made Old Kenyon seem rude and primitive in comparison. The first movement was made by the Delta Kappa Epsilon men. They proposed to furnish money for the renovation of the West Wing, and Alpha Delta Phi followed with a like proposition regarding the East Wing. These wings had been occupied by the fraternities ever since the close of the Civil War, and were held sacred by the older men, but were unattractive to Freshmen, who had no associations with them. Each fraternity undertook to pay to the college $10,000, the college to collect interest upon any unpaid balance. In return the fraternities were guaranteed the continuance of the old rates of room rent, and were granted the exclusive use of their respective wings, except that, if they should not need all their rooms, the college might fill the vacant ones with men chosen by them. The entire building was repaired, and very thorough work was done; for, while the venerable walls were left unaltered, nearly everything within them was made over or replaced. When, in 1907, the repairs were completed, Old Kenyon was virtually a new and modern dormitory, yet with the treasured associations of eighty years. The expense was heavy, exceeding $75,000. While this restoration was in progress repairs were made on Ascension Hall, and its walls, having a tendency to spread, were drawn together by tie-rods and braced with buttresses.

But it was not sufficient to restore old buildings. On the first day of January, 1910, Hubbard Hall, the library, burned to the ground with so fierce a fire that none of its contents could be saved. Valuable portraits and historical documents were destroyed, but nearly all the books escaped, being in the Stephens Stack Room, which withstood the flames that played up against it, and the brands that fell on its roof. Plans for a new building were drawn at once, but so slow were the builders, and so long was the college in getting money to pay for the work, that more than two years passed by before convenient use could be made of the books. The building bears the name of the Alumni Library, because the Alumni Association contributed a large part of the money; but the noble reading-room was built by Mr. David Z. Norton of Cleveland, and is called by his name.

In 1911 Cromwell Cottage, the residence of the president of the college, was begun, and also a house north of Rosse Hall for a professor. These were the gift of Mr. William Nelson Cromwell of New York. The house that stood where Cromwell Cottage stands was moved to a site near Sunset Cottage. It dates from 1834, but, being thoroughly repaired, it became almost new. The old building on Chase Avenue, where once the college store stood, and later Mr. French's store, was purchased, enlarged, and equipped as a college commons. This was a temporary expedient, to test the feasibility of thus providing board for the students; with the expectation that, should it be found best to establish commons permanently, a suitable building would be erected in the Park, to serve this purpose and to be a social center for the college.

In 1913 the renovation of Bexley Hall was begun. It had long been in a dangerous condition, owing to structural defects in the original work, and the wear and tear of seventy years, during which few repairs had been made. The beautiful exterior was not altered, except by rebuilding the oriel in stone instead of wood; but all the floor plans of the interior were radically changed. The original plan had provided on each floor six suites, of a study and two bedrooms each, and a large room for the chapel and library on the second floor in the middle of the south side. In the nineties a chapel was constructed on the first floor by throwing together the rooms in the northwest corner. In 1904 Colburn Hall took the library, and, in its basement, furnished bathrooms. The changes made in 1913 were most thorough. A cellar was excavated under the whole building, walls were reinforced, and new walls built, the Chapel of St. Mary was provided, and the Leonard Room, classrooms, and baths. The rebuilding was not completed until 1915, the students in the meanwhile being housed in Middle Hanna; but it required a considerably longer time to secure all the money necessary to pay for the work. Shortly afterwards the residence of the dean was extensively repaired and modernized. This fine old brick house was built in 1834 for Professor Sparrow. Here he lived until 1840, and after him came Doctor Bronson, Doctor T. M. Smith, Professor Henry Tullidge, Professor M. A. Tyng, Doctor Bodine, Doctor H. W. Jones, and others.

Thus within twenty years three new buildings—Hanna

Hall, Colburn Hall, and the Alumni Library with the Norton Reading Room and Stephens Stack Room—had been erected, beside two dwelling houses; and every one of the older buildings, except the Church of the Holy Spirit, had been extensively repaired, in most cases making what was equivalent to a new building. This was fundamental work that had to be done. It was, in a sense, preliminary work, without which the college could not expect to attract many students, or to care properly for them if they came. It was very thorough work, most of it planned and carried on under the exacting oversight of Mr. Charles F. Schweinfurth, the supervising architect of the college. It was immensely expensive work, and, except in the cases where individual donors gave new buildings, money had to be sought laboriously, and slowly gathered together. To this end the exertions of the president were incessant, and he was splendidly aided by Bishop Leonard, Bishop Vincent, Mr. James H. Dempsey, and others. The great services which, since the constitutional changes of 1891, the Bishop of Ohio has rendered to the seminary and college, although the limits of his official authority in their affairs have been very narrow, show that his predecessors in that office, since Chase's time, might, without any detriment to their ability to help, have been in like manner relieved of their autocratic power over the institutions; and this would have saved them much trouble, and would have left the guidance of affairs in the hands of those most competent to exercise it.

When Doctor Peirce became president, in 1896, there was a deficit of about $6,000 that had been incurred in meeting current expenses, and some of it was of several years' standing. The committee that informed him of his election advised him of "the necessity of rearranging the work of the college at the outset of his administration, so that the expense could be brought within the probable income." This could be

BISHOP VINCENT

accomplished, said the committee on finance, only by "some radical measures which we wish might be avoided, but which we believe are absolutely necessary in our financial condition." That is to say, there must be a reduction of the college faculty, and all the theological professors must do work in the college. These were retrograde steps, but by taking them the deficit was made to disappear, and in two years the receipts exceeded the expenditures by several hundred dollars. This was gratifying, but a policy merely of retrenchment could not but be disastrous. If the college was to live and grow, its expenditures must increase year by year; and this increase could be met only by a larger income from college fees, or by temporary subscriptions to meet current needs, or by gifts of permanent endowment funds. Recourse was had to all these expedients within the next few years.

In 1900 Mr. Samuel Mather offered to give, towards the permanent endowment, $10,000 for every $15,000 otherwise raised, until the total amount reached $100,000. Towards the $60,000 required in order to secure all that Mr. Mather offered, Mr. James H. Dempsey applied money that he had given and obtained to endow the Benson Memorial professorship of Latin; and in the course of time other sums were secured, and so the funds of the college were increased by $100,000, and for a time deficits disappeared, or were very small.

In 1904 Mr. Andrew Carnegie, having been told that Edwin M. Stanton had been a student at Kenyon, gave to the college the sum of $50,000 to endow the Edwin M. Stanton professorship of economics. Mr. Carnegie had served under Secretary Stanton in the time of the Civil War, and held him in admiration and reverence. Two years later he gave $25,000 to found scholarships "to enable such students as Stanton to continue their studies." In this year Mr. Carnegie visited the college. The students met him in front of Old Kenyon, and gave him a hearty greeting, which seemed to please him very much. He received an honorary degree at Rosse Hall, and delivered an address on "Stanton and Patriotism." On this occasion Colonel John J. McCook presented the college with a portrait of Stanton, painted by Mr. C. P. Filson, and Doctor George C. S. Southworth read an ode. Many people from all parts of the state were present. In the afternoon there was a great dinner at Rosse Hall, at which many speeches were made, and the Glee Club sang songs new and old, and merriment abounded.

At one time and another the college received considerable gifts from devoted friends. Mrs. Bedell left $30,000, of which $10,000 went to special funds, and $20,000 into the general fund, half for the college, half for the seminary. In 1909 Mr. Mather gave $100,000 to increase the salaries of the teaching force. This was a much-needed benefaction, and gave encouragement to men who had long been very inadequately paid. In 1914 Mrs. L. C. Colburn gave $20,000 to found a chair of homiletics at Bexley Hall. In 1916 the Reverend William Thompson, of the class of '58, left $30,000 towards the endowment of the presidency. In 1918 Miss Emma Watson of Steubenville left about $30,000 to the general fund. Through these and other gifts the endowment was largely increased, yet not sufficiently to meet the needs of the growing institutions, and for many years the college was carried along by annual subscriptions made to the general fund, or to some special fund. In 1906 Mr. Dempsey secured from alumni and others annual subscriptions amounting to $6,000 a year for five years; and similar subscriptions were obtained again and again. This was a very laborious and uncertain means of meeting expenses.

It was not current expenses alone that called for money. The repairing of Old Kenyon and Ascension had been possible only through drawing upon invested funds; and in 1906 it was found necessary to purchase Harcourt Place School, and again these funds had to supply the money. The funds were not used up, they were safely invested in buildings and grounds, but in this form they brought in but little interest. Thus the income of the college was diminished by at least $5,000 a year, "which must be at once replaced," said President Peirce in 1907, "if the college is to continue its work. I am firmly convinced that the time has come when in the mere spirit of self-preservation we must make an effort to add at least $200,000 to our invested funds." This then became the goal of financial endeavor; but it was not soon reached.

It was hoped that aid might be secured from the Rockefeller and Carnegie foundations, which were dispensing great sums of money for educational purposes. The "General Educational Board," in whose hands Mr. Rockefeller had placed millions of dollars, seemed friendly, and repeated applications were made by President Peirce and others for a donation to the college; but many years passed by before anything was obtained from this source. When Mr. Carnegie created his "Foundation for the Advancement of Teaching," the purpose of which was to grant retiring pensions to teachers in institutions of higher learning, he excluded from its benefits institutions "owned or controlled by a religious organization." Kenyon College was, and always had been, organically connected with the Protestant Episcopal Church, and loyal to it. Bishop Chase in his Deed of Donation had bound her to such connection and loyalty, and her original constitution had made the binding secure. Hobart College and Trinity College had manifested a like loyalty, but their loyalty was not specifically guaranteed in their constitutions; accordingly they were able to obtain the benefits of the Carnegie Foundation. So were many Ohio colleges that were in reality under denominational control, but were able to exhibit a constitution that did not specifically require such control. For a time hope was entertained that Mr. Carnegie might be induced to modify his requirements; but no such modification was made, and Kenyon College never derived any benefit from that fund.

Nevertheless, the effort to secure Carnegie pensions led to some good. It brought out the fact that Kenyon was burdened with "minute and complicated regulations and requirements" with reference to the composition of its board of trustees, from which such colleges as Hobart and Trinity were free. Many changes had been made in the constitution since it was originally drawn up by Bishop Chase and Charles Hammond in 1824, but these changes had made matters worse in this respect. In the beginning the requirements were very simple. Besides the Bishop, who was president of the college, there were but eight trustees, four clerical and four lay, all chosen by the convention of the Diocese of Ohio; but in 1912 besides the president of the college there were, first, the two bishops in Ohio, then ten other bishops of dioceses all the way from Pittsburgh to Iowa—twelve bishops in all, with the possibility of many more; certainly enough to frighten anybody except a very good Episcopalian. There were in addition six members, half of them clergymen and half of them laymen, elected, three by the convention of Ohio, and three by the convention of Southern Ohio, while five others were elected by five other diocesan conventions, one by each. Seven diocesan conventions were represented. With so many bishops and conventions governing her, it certainly looked as if Kenyon was tied and bound with the chain of ecclesiasticism. Besides these, there were six trustees elected by the alumni and eleven elected by the trustees, eight under one provision of the constitution and three under another. In all, there were forty-one members.

The bishops and delegates from outside Ohio had been brought into the board through an agitation that had gone on for many years "to increase the constituency of the college." They increased it only a little, and yet, up to 1906, the college had kept on in that direction, from time to time

amending its constitution so as to make room for more
bishops and more diocesan conventions. No one knows how
far it might have gone had not Mr. Carnegie awakened it to
a realization of the inexpediency of its course. Why, then,
pursue a policy that was both inexpedient, and, in a large
degree, futile? True, it was soon found that there was no
hope in the Carnegie Foundation, for it would extend its
pension provisions to Kenyon only upon conditions that
would have made her false to her whole history, and separated her from every tie of organic connection with the
Protestant Episcopal Church—conditions which she could
not accept; but now that their minds were turned in that
way, the friends of the college saw that the constitution of
the board of trustees could be greatly improved, and the
body be made much more efficient, by some radical change.
The Ohio bishops had always been a mighty tower of
strength to the college, but the other bishops, as bishops, had
not been of great help, though some of them as alumni had
been active in behalf of their Alma Mater. They could very
seldom attend meetings of the board, and could give little
thought to the affairs of the college. They must have found
their office burdensome. Again, diocesan conventions are not
qualified to exercise control over an educational institution.
Their time is occupied with other matters, and their
acquaintance with the needs of the college is small. It was
desirable that the college be released from the control of
these conventions. It was also desirable to eliminate from
the board all the bishops, serving as such, excepting those
from Ohio. A small, self-perpetuating board of trustees, with
the alumni representatives and the Ohio bishops, was the
ideal which President Peirce and others had in mind when,
in 1907, they procured the appointment of a committee "to
consider the constitutional changes that would be necessary
in order to place Kenyon in line to be accepted by the Carnegie Foundation for the Advancement of Teaching." It was

soon evident to them that Kenyon could not take a place in that line; nevertheless they reported a revised constitution, which was adopted by the board in Nevember, 1908. In May, 1909, the convention of the Diocese of Ohio ratified the new constitution, inserting, however, a proviso to the effect that any amendments must "receive the approval of a majority of the Bishops having jurisdiction in Ohio." The convention of Southern Ohio, having doubts as to the legality of the proposed changes, and fearing that they were in violation of the original trust, would not ratify until, after a delay of three years, the matter had been referred to Mr. Lawrence Maxwell, an eminent lawyer of Cincinnati, and he had declared that there was no legal or moral obstacle in the way of ratification, if the convention believed that the changes were desirable for the college. Thereupon the convention voted to ratify. Bishops Leonard and Vincent gave their approval, and in 1912 the new constitution came into operation. The controversy in Southern Ohio had been prolonged, and some bitterness had been engendered; and this was, for the time being, a disadvantage to the college. Although it was not so intended, yet the new constitution has so operated as almost to exclude clergymen—aside from bishops and the president of the college—from the board. Only one appears in the list as published in the catalogue for 1922-1923; and there are but two Bexley men there altogether.

In 1915 the "General Education Board" was asked to give $125,000 towards a total endowment of $500,000 to be raised by the college, but found it impracticable to grant the request. In 1917 it was asked to give $50,000 towards a new endowment of $250,000, but replied that no grants would be made during the war. When the war ended efforts were renewed to raise a large endowment, and this time the "General Education Board" was ready to help. It offered to give $75,000 if the college would raise $225,000 besides, the income to go to increase salaries; and when, by a splendid effort reaching to every alumnus, this was done, the "General Education Board" repeated its offer, the money to go this time towards the general endowment. All this was accomplished by the end of the year 1921-1922. Meanwhile, Mr. Archer M. Huntington of New York had given $50,000 for the encouragement of Hispanic studies. The assets of the institution, which in 1896 had been less than $600,000, now exceeded $2,000,000.

The completion of these funds opened the way for the beginning of a great building campaign. Mr. Mather in 1922 gave $100,000 towards the erection of a new dormitory, and accepted the chairmanship of a committee to secure another $100,000 for that purpose. This building is to be called Leonard Hall, and will be a memorial of Bishop and Mrs. Leonard. Plans have also been made, more or less definitely, for a science hall, and a building for the commons, both of monumental character. The thorough repair of Ascension Hall is planned, and a general heating plant, the gift of the alumni, will supply warmth to all the buildings in the Park. Two new houses for professors have already been built, and a third has been bought.

In the year 1900 Mr. H. N. Hills retired from his long connection with the Military Academy, selling his interests and belongings to Mr. C. N. Wyant, who had been associated with him in the management of the school, and to Mr. H. F. Williams, one of the instructors. These gentlemen as regents carried on an excellent and successful school. President Peirce said in 1905, "Under the present loyal management the Academy may be looked upon as an integral part of Kenyon College." Early on the morning of the twenty-fourth of February, 1906, the buildings of the Academy were totally destroyed by a fire of unknown origin. So rapidly did the fire spread that many of the boys, just waking from sleep, were cut off from access to the stairways. Most of them reached fire escapes, and got safely to the ground; but some leaped from windows and suffered severe injury. Three boys lost their lives. One of them reached a fire escape, but went back to get something from his room. Two, when the ashes were searched, were found, each within the frame of his iron bedstead: they had never awakened. This was an appalling calamity; and never has the Church of the Holy Spirit known anything so sad as the funeral of the three boys, in the early hours of a winter morning, their coffins ranged side by side before the chancel, while in the background of everyone's thought were the dozen boys that lay at Mr. Wyant's house, bruised, burned, and maimed.

With this fire the grammar school, which had been an important part of the college since 1824, and had at times been the largest and most successful part, came to an end. It was impracticable to rebuild and reëstablish it. The $35,000 received as insurance was far too little money to erect buildings of the modern type. The regents had dissolved partnership soon after the fire, and Mr. Wyant had taken a position in another school. Many authorities thought it inexpedient for a college to carry on a preparatory department. It was believed that private schools in the Middle West would be more ready to recommend Kenyon College to their graduates if it did not maintain a rival school. Such arguments restrained the trustees from making an immediate effort to secure money to restore the Academy, and experience has shown that the college does not need it.

At about this time Mr. Hills was obliged, for financial reasons, to give up Harcourt Place School; and the college purchased it, both to protect its own pecuniary interests, and to make sure that the property should not fall into the hands of persons who might put it to some objectionable use. It has since then rented it to those who have carried on the school. Financially considered, the investment has probably not been a good one; but considered socially, it has been of great advantage, bringing to Gambier many cultivated and charming ladies, and many delightful, animated girls.

The "French property," opposite Harcourt Place School, was purchased by the college upon the death of Mrs. French; for it was not thought safe to leave it to the chance of being bought and divided into small lots to be occupied by stores or dwellings. Besides, the house was useful as a dormitory while Old Kenyon was being repaired. Its destruction by fire in 1907 left the ground vacant, to be occupied some day—such is the hope—by an inn.

The "Harper Woods," ten acres in extent, west of Bexley Hall, were purchased in 1910; and here again the chief motive was to protect the village from being defaced by a row of insignificant buildings on the principal street. The college has been put to great expense, which it could hardly afford, in buying back property it once owned; and it may be put to yet greater expense if the inferior appearance of a considerable part of Chase Avenue is ever to be remedied.

By the removal of the hotel, and the buildings adjacent to it, in 1917, the approach to Gambier from the "Backbone" road has been made very beautiful. The substantial brick house built in 1832 for Professor Fitch, and long serving as a residence for the president of the college, was demolished to make room for Hanna Hall, and the small house facing it, the front of brick, dating from 1832, and the back part of stone, dating from 1827, was removed a few years later.

Kenyon College, being upon the top of a narrow hill of very porous stone, has always found a perplexing problem in seeking an adequate supply of water. We have seen how Bishop Chase's first care was to dig a well near the spot on which he purposed to build the college, and how, failing in that, he dug the well that is in the middle of the street, in front of the gates. For many years this well served a useful purpose, but it never afforded much water in a dry season, for it drains but a small area. A spring which still flows at the foot of the hill below Sunset Cottage, is said to have been used by students in the early days, when they occupied the buildings upon Wiggin Street. When Old Kenyon—then New Kenyon—was ready to be occupied, and the kitchen and dining-room were located there, Bishop Chase caused water to be hauled from the fine spring on the "academy grounds," and poured into the cisterns in front of the college. For a great many years an important source of water was the spring at the foot of the hill, east of Ascension Hall, near the road that leads to the railway station. The stones that walled it about may be seen between two tall sycamore trees which it still nourishes with its moisture. There must have been a well-worn path between it and Old Kenyon, trodden year after year by the feet of students, while their lips confessed their discontent at having to go so far for water.

When, in 1896, bathrooms and running water were introduced into Old Kenyon, the supply of water in the cisterns was inadequate to keep the tank in the attic full. In 1902 the trustees authorized President Peirce to have tests made, to see whether a sufficient supply of water could be obtained from wells driven into the gravel at the foot of the hill, on the west side. Since this gravel that underlies the surface soil in the valley is the source of Mount Vernon's abundant supply of excellent water, the experiment at Gambier was a hopeful one, and it met with success. The wells driven at that time, and since, supply water that has been declared by the State Board of Health to be as good as any in Ohio. A large part of the village uses this water. To the college it is of inestimable value.

Candles and lard oil lamps lighted the college until the time of the Civil War, and afforded the splendor of the early illuminations on Washington's birthday and other great occasions. The fuel was wood. Kerosene and coal succeeded these. When Bishop Bedell built the Church of the Holy Spirit he provided it with lamps, but his prophetic spirit led him also to enclose gas pipes in the walls. Natural gas came with the new century, at first a small and uncertain supply from shallow wells about Millwood, but soon abundantly, when strong companies, controlling great fields, took over the business. In 1921, when the price of gas became very high, the college substituted coal for heating most of its buildings, and in 1923 erected a heating plant near the railway track, to be thenceforth the great hearth for everything within the Park. At about the same time wires were brought into Gambier from Mount Vernon, and the college buildings were supplied with electric light. The college furnished the money for this transmission line, which is linked at Mount Vernon with the great system of the Ohio Power Company. An auxiliary plant at the water power house in Gambier keeps the lights going when, as occasionally will happen, the current from abroad is interrupted.

From behind Ascension Hall a belt of woods sweeps around Gambier like a huge, rudely shaped capital "C," encompassing the village except on the eastern side. About 1904 it was noticed that while the old trees in these woods were dying off, very few young trees were coming up to take their places. The State Department of Forestry was thereupon asked to take charge of these woodlands, and do what was necessary for their preservation. The Department planted thousands of young trees in various places, particularly along the western slope of the college hill. Here are now dense groves of young ash, tulip, and pine trees, and in many places about the Park are oaks, alders, birches, and cucumber trees, all of this planting. The annual burning over of the woods, that destroyed all the young trees and injured the older ones, was stopped, and the woods are now reproducing themselves in a natural manner.

Thus far we have been observing a remarkable course of improvement and growth in the buildings, funds, and physical possessions and surroundings of the college. Turning now to observe the increase in the number of students, we find the lines that trace this growth on the diagrammatic chart shooting up within the last few years to such unprecedented height that they have run off the chart altogether.

The enrollment at the college, which in President Sterling's time had risen rapidly from thirty-three to ninety-one, and had fallen again in 1896 to sixty-five, rose thereafter year by year until in 1905 it passed the high mark of 1860-1861 and registered one hundred and forty-eight students. This resulted from the labor of ten years in improving the college so that it might offer greater inducements to young men, and in advertising it incessantly in the most effective ways. While he was yet a professor Doctor Peirce had traveled for the college, visiting preparatory schools and prospective students; and this practice he continued and greatly extended after he became president. Every year schools were visited over a wide extent of country, acquaintances were formed with many citizens, teachers, and young men; addresses were made at teachers' institutes, and alumni gatherings, and sermons were preached in churches. College students were enlisted in this work, and sent out where they could be most effective. Influential newspapers were kept informed about what the college was doing. Both of the dioceses in Ohio were induced to hold conventions at Gambier. Never since the days of Bishop Chase had the college been brought so persistently to the attention of all who could be interested in it. The excellent performances of the athletic teams also had influence in drawing men to Kenyon. So the enrollment went on steadily increasing, and the present mark might have been reached by 1910; but in 1905 an event occurred that wrought the college great harm, and so set it back that ten years passed by before it had fully recovered.

SUNSET COTTAGE

THE DEANERY

CROMWELL COTTAGE

On the evening of Saturday, the twenty-eighth of October in that year, several fraternities held initiations. It was customary with most of them to appoint for each initiate some lonely spot where he must go and await in silence and solitude the arrival of the men who should take him to the chapter house. Stuart L. Pierson, a Freshman, was told to wait at the eastern end of the railroad bridge, near the foot of the hill. No one would have thought the place dangerous for such a young man, for on both sides of the track there was ample room for safety, and students sent there in previous years had not been hurt. Pierson was of an unusually mature mind, was clear-headed, athletic, accustomed to hunting and camping and taking care of himself out of doors. No train regularly passed there during the time that he must wait; but on this night a locomotive came from Brink Haven, going to Mount Vernon, and in some unexplained way Pierson was run over by it and killed. The engineer and fireman saw nothing on the track, and did not know of the accident until they reached Mount Vernon. When the fraternity men came to call Pierson they found his dead body. It was naturally the wish of his father, who had come to Gambier to attend the initiation, to return with the body to Cincinnati as soon as possible, that his wife might learn from him, rather than from the newspapers, the fact and manner of their son's death. The body was examined and cared for by a physician and an undertaker at Gambier, and was taken to Cincinnati that night.

This terrible death has remained a mystery. The boy's being on the track has never been adequately accounted for. The most satisfactory hypothesis is based on the fact that young Pierson was a very sound sleeper, and had been awake nearly all the previous night, waiting for his father's arrival from Cincinnati. He may have seated himself on an abutment of the bridge, and in the darkness and stillness of the night may have fallen asleep. Suddenly half-wakened by the sharp whistle of the locomotive as it approached the bridge, and blinded by the glare of the headlight, he may have sprung up, and—his mind being in a daze—may have started to run, and may have stumbled across the track and fallen. This explanation fits every fact that is known, and every probability. But the explanation that was immediately spread all over the world was that Pierson had been tied to the track to frighten him, the passage of the locomotive not being dreamed of. It was said that there were marks of ropes upon his wrists. The fact that the coroner, living at Mount Vernon, was not notified until after the body had been removed to Cincinnati, counted heavily in the mind of that official, and of many others, to confirm this theory. To those who did not know the persons concerned, and were ready to believe that college boys are criminally reckless in their initiation pranks, this explanation was very plausible. It was published everywhere as a statement of ascertained fact. But no one who knew the men of that fraternity chapter, and the physician, and the undertaker, and the president of the college who examined the body, has ever believed that the death was due to the boy's being tied to the track. The boy's parents never believed that story. Yet a sensation such as this can be but slowly allayed, and will never be forgotten. Newspapers in America and in foreign lands continued for months to speak of it; some eminent preachers told of it in their sermons; parents declared that never should their sons be sent to a college where it was the custom to tie Freshmen to the railway track. The enrollment at Kenyon immediately fell off, and went lower year by year; and not until ten years had gone by did it fully recover.

Other things contributed to this decrease in numbers. It was in the following February that the Military Academy burned and the three boys lost their lives; and a little later the French house burned down. Superstitious persons suspected that some kind of bedevilment or hoodoo was at work, and interpreted every untoward occurrence by that theory. Who knew what might happen next? Again, the rebuilding of Old Kenyon, since it threw students out of their rooms and subjected them to much discomfort and inconvenience, must have had influence in keeping men away. At last, in 1912, the tide turned, and in 1915 there were one hundred and fifty-one students at Kenyon. There were one hundred and fifty-two in 1916. In 1917, as the first effect of America's participation in the war, the number dropped to one hundred and fifteen, but then began to increase, and rose steadily until, in 1922, with the enrollment of two hundred and fifty students, the limit set by the trustees was reached.

At Bexley Hall the number enrolled did not vary far from twenty until the war began to draw students into the army, or take them out of the seminary before their courses were completed, that they might fill places left vacant by clergymen who had gone as chaplains, or as workers in some form of relief. For a year or two Bexley had but six or seven men, but in 1922 the number was fifteen, and there were also seven nonresident graduate students enrolled, candidates for the degree of bachelor, or master, of theology—a new and admirable extension of the seminary's work. Bexley graduates of this period are found in every part of the country. Missionary bishops have testified that they have no better men in their fields than the men from Bexley. They find them devoted, energetic, adaptable, and endowed with common sense. Though Gambier is a country village, yet Bexley men have succeeded as well in city parishes as men from other seminaries. Men of every school of churchmanship have come to Bexley, and all have found freedom of thought and action there. Four strong men in the faculty, teaching through long periods, have helped a whole generation of students to develop the best that was in them—Doctor Jones, who died in 1917, and Doctors Streibert, Davies, and Watson, who fortunately are still in the service. Bexley to-day, as in the past, educates about one-third of the clergy-men of the Diocese of Ohio. In the clergy list of that diocese for 1922 thirty-six men out of one hundred and one were from Bexley, and in 1923 there were thirty-six out of one hundred and eleven.

At the college slow but steady increase in the number of subjects taught, and in the number of teachers, has charac-terized this period. The chair of biology was added in 1902; chairs of history and of Romance languages date from 1903; that of economics and sociology from 1904. In 1918 a pro-fessorship of physics was created, separate from that of chemistry. Spanish now is taught to large classes by profes-sors on the Hispanic Foundation of Mr. Huntington. The number of assistant professors has increased from two in 1907 to five in 1922. The faculty, which in 1896 had but six members, now consists of twenty. Whatever machinery and forces may operate behind, the faculty of a college are the sharp edge by which the material is shaped. It will be the happy privilege of some future historian to write of the Kenyon professors of this period in terms as appreciative as those which in this book are applied to the professors of former generations.

During the last twenty-eight years the literary societies have at times been fairly active, and at times have exhibited few signs of life. The students in general have not been interested in them, and whatever activity they have had has been due to the enthusiasm of a few. For many years the Reverend Doctor E. M. Stires of New York has offered annual prizes for excellence in debating. The debaters, who are Juniors and Seniors, are supposed to represent the literary societies, and so these contests have kept alive the names of Philomathesian and Nu Pi Kappa. Mr. Ralph King of Cleveland has provided similar prizes for Freshmen and Sophomores.

In 1916 a chapter of Sigma Pi was organized. Since the

completion of Hanna Hall the South Division has been occupied by Beta Theta Pi, and the North Division by Psi Upsilon; Sigma Pi has the Middle. Alpha Delta Phi and Delta Kappa Epsilon have continued in possession of the two wings of Old Kenyon, and Delta Tau Delta of the East Division. The policy of the trustees which requires all students to room in the college dormitories is strongly supported by the public sentiment of the alumni and undergraduates, and will undoubtedly be maintained; therefore there can never be at Kenyon society houses in which students regularly reside. Yet most of the chapters own lodges. Delta Kappa Epsilon and Alpha Delta Phi continue to meet in their remote and ancient houses, which are viewed by their votaries with an admiration that cannot, of course, be shared by the world outside. Psi Upsilon owns the fine property at the eastern corner of Ward and Wiggin streets, which she uses as a social center, and a home for her alumni. Delta Tau Delta has a lodge in the woods northeast of Bexley Hall. Other fraternities are preparing to build.

Phi Beta Kappa has been an active society, holding meetings many times every year, at which have been read papers of interest and value. The Science Club was founded in 1911; and so excellent is the work it has done, that academic credit is now given for papers that evince unusual study and ability. The Edwin M. Stanton Civics Club was organized by Professor A. C. Hall in his department of economics and sociology. It flourished for a few years, and was a member of the Intercollegiate Civic League. The Chess Club and the Rifle Club owe their continuity and excellence to Professor Walton and Professor Reeves, respectively, and to the interest that a certain number of students will always be found to take in those fine recreations.

In 1907 Mr. Joseph H. Larwill, of the class of '55, founded the Larwill Lectureship, and thus conferred a lasting benefit upon the people of the college and village by affording them each year a number of excellent lectures upon a variety of subjects. Besides the single lectures, courses of lectures, provided by this foundation, have been delivered by President Charles W. Eliot, Senator Theodore E. Burton, Professor John W. Burgess, Professor George E. Woodbury, and Professor Irving Babbitt; and these lectures have been published. Ten courses of Bedell Lectures also have been given, making eighteen courses in all since this lectureship was established, in 1881. From time to time the students themselves, through the Assembly or through class organizations, have brought lecturers to Gambier, to speak in an informal way upon themes of practical interest.

Very great advances have been made in student self-government. In 1895 most of the students, with some members of the faculty, united in forming the "Kenyon College Senate," to be, as its constitution said, "an organization in which the authority of the student body shall be vested, and by which said authority shall be exercised." It was a federation of six "sections"—an athletic club, a tennis club, a dramatic club, a mandolin and guitar club, a glee club, and a lecture committee. This Senate soon transformed itself into the Assembly, which consists of all matriculated students and has for many years promoted and controlled most of the organized student activities. The name Assembly was adopted in the fall of 1895, when a new constitution was drawn up which conferred extensive powers upon an Executive Committee, and required that all disbursements of money be approved by this committee. The Assembly has been of the greatest benefit to the college, enabling the students to manage most of their common, or public, affairs efficiently. All the athletic organizations of the college are now under its control, and probably all other organizations soon will be. Every manager presents his budget to the Executive Committee, and this committee approves, or modifies, and votes the required money, which is paid by the treasurer on order of the chairman of the committee. This chairmanship has been held successively by Professor Reeves and Professor Allen, and the treasureship by Professor Walton; and to their constant interest and laborious services the Assembly is greatly indebted for its success.

In Kenyon, as in most colleges, there was, in the old days, much cheating in examinations; and although not all students cheated, still public opinion tolerated the practice, and no man lost caste by it, unless he was trying for honors, when, in the opinion of most, cheating was not sportsmanlike. In 1901 conditions in this respect were so bad that the faculty felt obliged to resort to new expedients of watchfulness. These expedients were disagreeable to professors and students alike. Some of the students were disposed to devise ingenious means of evading the stricter watch; but, on the other hand, many, when brought to think about the prevalent dishonesty, were ashamed. Said the *Collegian:* "Our dealings at home and abroad have been characterized by a spirit of honor. How are we to reconcile to this spirit these evils, this dishonesty, which we admit?" To a few upper-classmen, and in particular to Wilber L. Cummings, '02, and Albert G. Liddell, '03, is due the honor of leading in a reform which instantly proved effective and thorough, and has stood the test of more than twenty years. These men stirred up public opinion in the college and procured the signature of every student to a petition asking the faculty to introduce the "honor system" of holding examinations, to which they pledged their loyal support. This request was joyfully welcomed by the faculty, and a joint committee worked out the details of the Kenyon system of examinations, which was soon extended to tests and written lessons. The success of this honor system at Kenyon has been due to several causes. In the first place, the faculty attached no limitations, or "strings" to it. They said, "If we trust the students, we must trust them wholeheartedly, and they must see that we so trust them." Students, having once promised to be honest in their examinations, have not been asked to attach to their blue books a statement that they have kept their word; nor, as is the practice at some colleges, are members of the faculty present in the examination room, ostensibly to keep order, or to answer questions. In the second place, conditions at Kenyon have been propitious. With a small number of students, all living in the dormitories, a public spirit and opinion are generated which powerfully control individual standards and actions. This opinion has staunchly maintained the honor system, has reduced cheating to a very small amount, and has severely punished it when detected. The entire control of the examinations is in the hands of the Honor Committee, which consists of representatives of all four classes, appointed by the Assembly.

The Assembly also elects a Dormitory Committee, which consists of Seniors. This committee first came into existence to enforce the rules of the board of trustees with regard to intoxicating liquor in the dormitories. It is their duty to be vigilant in this matter, and, upon detecting any violation of those rules, to report the case to the Assembly and ask for a vote of censure upon the violators. The committee has generally been supported in such requests, and the formal censure of the Assembly is not lightly regarded at Kenyon. Manifestly, with students scattered all over the village, such a committee could exercise but little control; it is a *dormitory* committee, and can work effectively only when all the men live in dormitories. Even then, the public sentiment of the college must be the ruling power in this matter.

The Assembly appoints also a Commons Committee, representative of the students' views as to the board they get and the board they want. It has some authority in maintaining order, and occasionally seeks to restrain extravagancies in table manners. The Senior Council, of seven men, appointed by the Assembly, exercises supervision over a number of matters that require some authoritative direction, such as the annual cane rush.

Kenyon College is a very democratic institution, and the Assembly has made Kenyon safe for democracy. It has exercised a firm and beneficial control over many of the most important activities of the students, and yet has been, of necessity, responsive to their will. It has developed gradually, assuming one responsibility after another, changing its constitution from time to time to adjust it to new circumstances; and thus it is not an artificial, or extemporized creation, but a natural growth. It is a "town meeting" under ideal conditions, and affords to those who take an active part in it a capital training in practical political science. As affording preparation for performing the duties of a citizen it has possibilities not inferior to those of the old literary societies.

It is a custom at Kenyon to hold quadrennially a sham national convention, sometimes Democratic and sometimes Republican, to nominate a candidate for the presidency of the United States. These were first held with the thought that they would be instructive in the methods of carrying on national conventions; but the spirit of hilarity and extravagant burlesque generally so predominates that the educational advantage of taking part in them is but small. The Democratic convention of 1912 may be taken as a favorable example. There were present representatives of every state, "each wearing the customary garb of his state," said the *Collegian*, and added that "a noticeable condition was the predominance of the agricultural class." There were cowboys with belts full of pistols, and negroes of the minstrel show variety. Great efforts were made to unseat delegates because of their alleged former affiliation with the Republican party. There was hot contention over a resolution endorsing woman suffrage; but when this was carried, the convention voted to change the party emblem from a rooster to a hen. In making nominating speeches some of the delegates sought to reproduce the dignity and ponderous oratory of the Websterian era, others affected rusticity of speech, while the supposed cowboy style, punctuated with pistol shots, was exemplified by the western statesmen. As each orator named his candidate the roof of Rosse Hall was rent with howls of favor and disfavor, the band struck up its loudest strain, and the friends of the nominee paraded up and down the aisles. After many ballots, Woodrow Wilson was nominated, not without some extraordinary logrolling.

Interest in athletics has grown amazingly at Kenyon, as at every other college. *"Ad studium ad stadium aequaliter voco,"* says the inscription on the college bell; but it is hard to maintain equality of response. The athletic history of Kenyon has, for the last twenty-five years, been that of a small college, with great enthusiasm and inextinguishable hope, continually matching itself against large colleges. The "Big Six" was always, so far as size of institutions was concerned, a Big Five and a Little One; but in spirit and determination the Little One has been inferior to none of its larger brethren; and, in proportion to its strength, it has won probably more than its due share of victories in most branches of college athletics. In the earlier days of this period it was a formidable competitor with the largest Ohio colleges; and to-day no institution can be sure of an easy victory over it, or, indeed, of any victory at all.

Kenyon has always lacked money for athletics. Her body of alumni is small and not wealthy. The gate money for games at Gambier is of negligible amount, and, except when she plays football against Western Reserve, Kenyon draws no great crowd, and divides but a small sum with the home club. This game with Reserve has long been the great game of the year for Kenyon, and here she has won her share of glory. It is a custom almost equivalent to law at Gambier that every student shall go to Cleveland to see that game, and supply that audible appreciation which is supposed to be so helpful to a contending team. The railway fare between Gambier and Cleveland is high, and there have always been students that were unable, or disinclined, to pay it. For such the "Cannon Ball," or midnight through freight, has often provided a perilous passage. This train stops at Mount Vernon. It is partly made up of empty box cars and flat cars, and many an impecunious or adventurous student has beat his way to Cleveland on it, sometimes bestowing upon the trainman a small gift of cigars, or other commodities, to compensate him for his defective eyesight.

From the employment of professional coaches, partly paid by the alumni and students, and sometimes partly by the college, there has been a gradual advance to the present system of an athletic director, who is a full member of the faculty and is paid by the college. He has supervision over all athletic interests, and in the training of teams is assisted by coaches who are paid by the students and alumni.

Kenyon was one of the original members of the Ohio Athletic Conference, whose especial office is to maintain high amateur standards. From the first its representative has been Professor Reeves, who has for several years been president of the Conference; and his influence in behalf of pure athletics has been large. When the number of students at Kenyon declined, the exclusion of Freshmen from football worked disadvantageously to her teams, and there was a strong party that favored withdrawal from the Conference. The college faculty was opposed to such withdrawal, and passed a rule that forbade Freshmen to play, so long as they were forbidden by the Conference rules. In 1912 the situation became critical. There were in college but ninety-eight men, and of these thirty-seven were Freshmen. In response to a petition from the Kenyon Assembly, strongly presented by some of the undergraduates, the Conference granted to Kenyon permission to play Freshmen, until the time when she should again reach the enrollment—one hundred and forty-eight—which she had when she entered the Conference, in 1906. This permission showed the good will of the Conference toward its smallest member, but was of little use, for the college was hardly more successful when she played Freshmen than when she could not play them; and for the Freshmen the playing on the college team was bad, since it distracted their minds from their studies.

Canoeing, so popular in the eighties and early nineties, was continued until the destructive freshet of 1913. There was a canoe club, and a number of professors and students owned canoes, and kept them in a house built for them on the bank of the river. Men frequently dropped down to Howard, Walhonding, or Coshocton, generally sending the canoe home by the railway. Clear Fork, in Richland and Ashland Counties, and the Mohican through its whole length, revealed their beauty to the canoemen as they can to no one else. In 1913 the canoe house and most of the canoes were destroyed, and there has been little or no canoeing since. But the rivers are still there, as beautiful as ever, and some day this charming sport will regain the favor which it so long enjoyed and so richly repaid.

Interest in music and dramatics has increased greatly during the last twenty-five years. The "Kenyon Dramatic Club," consisting of some students and a few young ladies of the village, was in active existence until 1904 when the "Puff and Powder Club" was born—or, perhaps, more strictly, the first of a series of clubs, or groups of players, bearing that name. Its first play, "The Doctor," a farce by Charles Townsend, was presented February 16, 1904; and from that time to this the club has continued to afford pleasure and amusement to Gambier audiences.

In 1903, on the evening before commencement day, the Senior class presented Beaumont and Fletcher's play, "The Knight of the Burning Pestle," under the direction of the department of English; and such was the success of this play that the custom became established, and continued for many years, of the production by the Senior class, every year at commencement time, of one of the old dramas, or occasionally a new one that represented some interesting development of the dramatic art. These plays ran all the way from Gascoigne's "Supposes," and the original version of "Hamlet," to Bernard Shaw's "Devil's Disciple," and included plays by Shakespeare, Villiers, Sheridan, Pinero, and others. They were a notable feature of commencement week.

Meanwhile, various classes that were rich in dramatic talent or ambition have from time to time put on plays in excellent manner. Some of Gilbert and Sullivan's operas have been capitally produced. Two plays written by Mr. M. B. Long, '05, "A Stray Leaf" and "A New Commandment," found appreciative audiences. Recently musical comedies, written entirely, words and music, by Kenyon students, and presented by the Puff and Powder Club with elaborate staging and costuming, have displaced almost all other dramatic and musical performances, and have been presented in many cities of Ohio, winning much praise.

The chief musical organization has been the Glee Club, with which was long associated a Mandolin Club. Many concerts have been given at Gambier; and at the alumni dinners and on other cheerful occasions, the Glee Club has supplied or led the singing. The prosperity of such an organization depends upon the competency and zeal of its leader; and at Kenyon there have often been admirable leaders. In 1905 the Glee and Mandolin Clubs gave concerts in several Ohio cities, going as far as Columbus and Cleveland; and in the following years such a trip became the established custom, and other cities were visited, and even Newcastle and Killbuck were put to the test of appreciating college songs. A notable event was the joint concert at Columbus, in 1908, of the Kenyon Glee and Mandolin Clubs and the Amherst College Musical Clubs. Intermittently there has been a Kenyon Orchestra, for which the college has supplied from its students and faculty members a number of fine musicians, and the nonacademic portion of Gambier's population has also done its part.

The college choir has been composed exclusively of students. Its fortunes have paralleled those of the Glee Club, for the same singers have been in both, and generally both have had the same leader. At times the choir has attained excellence after its kind, and on special occasions has rendered such compositions as Gaul's "The Holy City," and Stainer's "The Crucifixion." There have been some fine musicians among the choir leaders, who have devoted great labor to producing music worthy of the services of the Church.

In 1908 Mr. Alfred K. Taylor, '06, compiled and published *Songs of Kenyon*, a handsome book of one hundred and fifty large pages. The editor gathered from every available source all the songs and tunes that had been sung at Kenyon in former years, and secured also the contribution of many new ones. Mr. Taylor's musical knowledge and taste enabled him to arrange the tunes most beautifully and effectively, and he and the Reverend Louis E. Daniels, Bexley '02, wrote new tunes. Probably no American college has a finer songbook than this.

Since its revival in 1887 the *Collegian* has continued to the present time. In 1904 a new editorial board changed the character of the publication from that of a literary magazine with some college news, to that of a college newspaper without "literary matter." Such it has continued to be, but once or twice has published a "literary number." The paper is under the control of the Assembly, the members of the editorial board work their way up, beginning as Freshmen reporters, the English Department scrutinizes every article, grades it and gives academic credit.

The *Reveille* has become a large, handsome book, full of information and pictures. Its value as a historical record continues to be great. For the historian of the college the *Reveille* and the *Collegian* are first-class sources of information. As he goes through them from their beginning in the fifties to their latest issues, he sees a vivid moving picture of college life as it has progressed from year to year. Great is the merit of editors and managers, who, for the benefit and honor of the college, have put so much hard work into these publications, and carried them on, often amidst difficulties and discouragements. There should be accorded them a very large and brilliant "K."

The chaplain of the college is also rector of Harcourt Parish. This fine, large country parish, with its three chapels, east, north, and west of Gambier, is in itself enough for one man to care for; and when, as has generally been the case, the chaplain has had one or two college classes to instruct in some part of the Bible, his hands have been full indeed. Half, or more than half, of the students are from Episcopal families, and most of these are communicants when they come to college. Next in number are Presbyterians and Methodists, and then follow representatives of most of the larger denominations, many of whom are communicants in their own churches at home; and it has seldom been the practice of a chaplain to seek to draw them from their fathers' faith. And yet, year after year, college men and Harcourt girls are confirmed in the Church of the Holy Spirit, and among them will generally be some that were negligent of religion when they first came to Gambier, but found in the services of that church something that drew and won them. "Compulsory Chapel" has always been a subject of grievous complaint on the part of some students; yet not many of the alumni as they look back regret that the rules of the college required them to spend a little time, Sundays and week days, in church.

The college has included in its curriculum a few courses of study in the Bible. For many years one hour a week of Bible study has been required of Sophomores, and, until recently, a three-hour elective, for one semester, in some part of the Bible, has been offered to Seniors and Juniors, and has found a respectable number of takers.

In most of the advances in religious activity the chaplain has taken the initiative, and generally there have been students that gave him a strong support. The Brotherhood of St. Andrew was founded at Chicago in 1883, and soon thereafter a chapter was established at Kenyon College. In 1904 this chapter had ceased to be usefully active, and was disbanded. In its place was organized a local society, the Kenyon Christian Union, to hold the ground until the Brotherhood might with advantage be revived. This service it performed. When Old Kenyon was remade the Theodore Sterling Room was set apart by the college to be used, under the chaplain's direction, for religious and social purposes. At that time the Brotherhood was reëstablished, consisting at first of K. C. U. men. Chiefly through their efforts money was secured, and the Sterling Room was furnished in a manner not surpassed by any of the fraternity parlors. Here they held their meetings, and entertained the college at many social gatherings. During part of the time between 1909 and 1915, when there were no services at the church in the evening, the Brotherhood held Sunday evening meetings at the Sterling Room, at which some Senior, or member of the faculty, would deliver an address. An earnest and capable director makes a live and useful chapter; and the Kenyon Chapter has from time to time had such leaders, and has then been an important factor in the life of the college.

Beginning in 1909 and continuing to the present time, a ten-minute service for college men has been held in the church at noon on week days during Lent. Many students have been glad to attend this service, which does not seem to lose its attractiveness as years go by.

From time to time the college has been visited by missioners, evangelists, and other religious workers. Father Huntington and Father Officer each came twice, and made a good impression on many students. Mr. Edward C. Mercer also, in two visits, aroused the students upon his special subjects. In 1913 Mr. Mercer said he believed that the Kenyon campus was a safer and more wholesome place for a young man than the home atmosphere of any town or city that he knew. Such visitors do good; but doubtless the greatest good is wrought through God's blessing upon the regular services of the Church, as carried on Sunday after Sunday, and day after day, at the Church of the Holy Spirit. The pulpit has not infrequently been occupied by invited clergymen; but the kaleidoscopic plan, so popular at many colleges, of changing preachers every Sunday, has never found favor at Kenyon, which still looks to its chaplain for the greater part of the preaching.

Towards the end of the college year there are two occasions that mean much to the Seniors. On the Sunday after Easter they attend chapel wearing their gowns, and just outside the door they pass between ranks of Freshmen who make an arch for them by crossing the canes which then, for the first time, they are permitted to carry. On the morning of the day before the Senior vacation begins there is the service of the "Last Chapel." The Seniors, wearing gowns, are conducted to their seats by the marshals, there is a printed programme of the service, special psalms, lessons, prayers, and hymns are used, and the president of the college briefly addresses the class. The Senior may have complained all through his course at being compelled to attend daily prayers, but he will hardly leave the church after this "Last Chapel" without some sentiment of regret that this component of college experience has now passed out of his life for ever.

Since 1896 the United States has engaged in two wars; one, the very small war with Spain, and the other the greatest of all wars. Kenyon College was not greatly stirred by the Spanish-American War. In May, 1898, five or six students enlisted in response to the call for volunteers, and about as many graduates of the class of '96, and a few others. Most of them were in the Fourth Ohio Volunteer Infantry. One of these men, Edward Darst Daily, of the class of 1900, died of typhoid fever. His name must be held in remembrance by his Alma Mater. All the others, having served faithfully, returned in November. To the undergraduates, and such of the graduates as came back to Gambier with them, a demonstrative welcome and supper were given. In proportion to the country's need, Kenyon did as well, and won as honorable a record, in this war as in any other.

The Great War had little visible effect upon the college until the United States became a participant. Some of the alumni, and a few men from the Hill, went to France to drive ambulances or trucks. There were alumni who enlisted in Canada or England. A "Kenyon Ambulance" was sent to France. Shortly before our declaration of war one hundred and ten students petitioned the trustees to apply for the establishment of a unit of the Reserve Officers' Training Corps at Kenyon, pledging themselves to take the full course of training. The faculty voted to admit for credit towards a degree the prescribed courses in tactics and military science.

Application was made accordingly at Washington, but the officials there were unable to give it attention. President Peirce, therefore, obtained the services of Captain Lanning Parsons, U. S. A., retired, to instruct the students in military drill. Meanwhile the United States had gone into the war, and a strong feeling of patriotic enthusiasm was felt throughout the college. A considerable number of undergraduates withdrew to enter the service. Some enlisted in the army, some joined the "mosquito fleet" at Portsmouth, New Hampshire; others went to some camp or school to take training preparatory to receiving an officer's commission. The policy of the college at this time was the same as in the Civil War; that is, to persuade the students to remain at their studies until it should become evident that they were needed in the service; and meanwhile to afford military training on the campus. The course of training was soon in full swing. Two hours a day, three days in the week, were devoted to military drill under the command of Captain Parsons. The field between the library and Ascension Hall was, on such afternoons, full of squads of men drilling under the instruction of students who had received training in the National Guard, or in some military school. Every day from sunrise to sunset the great flag floated from the college pole. Many students practiced rifle shooting under the instruction of Professor Reeves.

But the students were not satisfied with the amount of training they could receive at Gambier, and were leaving, one after another, to enter some training camp, or some branch of the service. In June President Peirce reported that nearly fifty men had left college to go to war; and some had gone into agriculture, a course highly approved by the government. To all who were thus taking military training, or had gone to the farms, the faculty granted leave of absence, with permission to make up the college work when they could. To Seniors who had enlisted, and to all who had entered an Officers' Training Camp, a full semester's credit was given.

Captain Parsons was called into active service in June, 1917. In the fall Major Harry P. Ward, O. N. G., took charge of the drill and the instruction in military science. That fall the *Collegian* printed a list of one hundred and seventy-three alumni and undergraduates who were in the service. Every week students were drifting out of college into the army. In April, 1918, the great "service flag" was hung in the chapel with two hundred and thirty blue stars, and three of gold. When, in the spring, Major Ward received his commission in the army, and left Gambier, no military man could be obtained to take his place; but Professor Reeves was put in charge of the battalion, and under his direction the drill and the instruction in military science went on.

In the summer of 1917 President Peirce became a member of the speakers' bureau of the American Red Cross. That he might speak out of a personal knowledge of the situation, he was sent abroad, in February, 1918, and spent four months in France. He inspected warehouses, hospitals, and the like, but beyond this, obtained permission to enlist as a convoyer of the "Rolling Canteen" service. He received the rank of first lieutenant, and was put in charge of the Franco-American canteen at Belleville, a suburb of Verdun. He was invited into the mess of the French officers there, and formed warm and enduring friendships with many of them. The Germans were still pressing the siege, and French troops were passing through Belleville every night and morning, to and from the front. To supply them with food, coffee, and cigarettes was the work of the canteen, and Doctor Peirce came into close contact with thousands of these soldiers. Thus equipped to tell Americans about war conditions in France, and the work of the Red Cross, he returned just in time for commencement.

In the fall of 1918 a unit of the Students' Army Training Corps was established at Kenyon College. Here, as in most other colleges where the S. A. T. C. held sway, the memory of it is a nightmare. The government, having discovered that college life and training produced the very best material to make into officers, proceeded to wipe out nearly every feature of that life and training which had produced such admirable results. The *Reveille* of 1919 contained an article on the S. A. T. C. written by a student who had been through it, and setting forth the students' view:

Smashing practically every precedent and tradition that Kenyon ever boasted, the Kenyon unit of the Students' Army Training Corps, beginning operations on Monday, October 1, 1918, lived through the signing of the armistice with considerable loss of morale, and culminated upon government orders in its demobilization on Saturday, December 14, 1918, to the extreme satisfaction of faculty, students, and alumni, alike.

An impressive ceremony was witnessed by a large gathering of people on the second day of the unit's existence when the company was formed on the campus between the Alumni Library and Ascension Hall, and formally inducted into the service of the United States, President Peirce and Lieut. Searle M. Brewster making inspiring addresses.

The non-commissioned officers, with the exception of Sergeants Weida and Brewer, who had attended O. T. C. at Fort Sheridan, Ill., the previous summer, were picked from those having some military experience before entering the unit; and the machinery for turning out good soldiers under the most trying conditions, that of drilling but two hours a day, while the remainder of the time was taken up with academic work, was put in motion. The company was divided into platoons of five squads each, besides the detail squad, those men who were over twenty-one. The men were then assigned to quarters, averaging four men to one room, and physical examinations held.

Shortly after the unit was mobilized an epidemic of the widespread Spanish influenza gained a foothold and remained for six weeks. Because of the fact that there were four, and sometimes five men in one small room, and as the men were crowded into the Philomathesian and Nu Pi Kappa literary society rooms each evening for two hours' study, the epidemic spread with amazing rapidity. Ultimately the West Wing was converted into a hospital, and the "Flu" victims were there isolated, but not until they had had time to pass the germs on to others. Finally, when all the patients were removed to the hospital, conditions were bettered. Eight men in the company acted as nurses, and two professional nurses were secured. Soon the wave had reached and passed its crest under the careful guidance of the graduate nurses. During the epidemic two of the unit, Verner Lee Hulse, and Neal Jones, succumbed to the dreaded disease.

Imagine, Mr. Alumnus, the Commons being turned into a mess hall on the cafeteria plan, with no table-cloths and no napkins; the divisions being divested of all furniture and made barracks; The Alumni Library being a study hall where all men marched to study when they had no classes, and no one being allowed in said "Barracks" except for a few minutes at noon, and just before and after supper. Imagine Kenyon men tumbling out of bed at 5:45 in the morning to the call of a bugle, and "standing reveille" a full half hour before breakfast, making their beds, sweeping out their rooms before breakfast, the rising bell being rung only in case of a fire or fire drill! Truly the government turned things topsy-turvy.

To First Lieut. Brewster, commanding, is given the honor of making the unit what it grew to be—the best unit for its size in the whole S. A. T. C. Kenyon may well feel exceedingly fortunate in having such a man to command its "first army corps."

As far as the S. A. T. C. in Ohio is concerned, taking Kenyon as representative, it was not a success. Academic work was practically useless, as it was being constantly interrupted when the military establishment "ranked" the college authorities, and whatever academic work was done was of a negligible quantity. (Abridged.)

The officers of the S. A. T. C. were exceptionally good men, and were respected and liked by the students and the professors. They were, First Lieutenant Searle M. Brewster, commanding, Second Lieutenant Lawrence B. Maplesden, adjutant, Second Lieutenant John J. Kindell, rifle instructor, and Second Lieutenant Jesse C. Williams.

The service flag as it now hangs in the church bears four hundred and thirty-five stars, eight of them of gold. These eight gold stars are for Alfred L. M. Gottschalk, '96, Corporal Leonard Sherburne Downe, '09, Major William John Bland, '10, Sergeant Ralph Waldo Wyant, '10, William Webster Sant, '14, Corporal Richard Charles Marsh, '15, Sergeant Walter Henry Endle, '17, Sergeant Rollo William Stevens, '17. These names are inscribed on the bronze memorial tablet placed in the Church of the Holy Spirit by the brother alumni. Bland and Marsh were killed in battle. Downe, Wyant, Endle, and Stevens died of disease, in the service. Sant, serving with the British troops in Palestine, in Y. M. C. A. work, died at El Arish. Gottschalk was lost at sea. Bland and Sant were Kenyon's two Rhodes scholars, and splendidly filled out Cecil Rhodes' ideal. Bland's course at Oxford was brilliant. He became president of the "Union," the only foreigner that ever held that office, which also is to be attained only by a man of extraordinary force of character and forensic ability. Sant came to Oxford just after the war began, and was impelled by his sympathy with the cause of the allies to devote himself to the service of the British troops long before his country entered the war.

The brevity of America's participation in the war forbade that many of the men new to the army should attain high military rank; but Kenyon men fared well compared with others in this respect, and a number of them received war crosses—French, Italian, Belgian—and British and American decorations. Four hundred and thirty-five men is not far from one-half of all Kenyon men of military age.

Instantly upon the signing of the armistice the students lost all interest in military matters, and wanted only to have the S. A. T. C. come to a speedy end. They were therefore much disquieted upon learning that the board of trustees had voted that a unit of the Reserve Officers' Training Corps should be established at Kenyon, and systematic military drill be continued under an officer appointed by the government. This was something they would not endure, and they threatened rebellion if the board should carry out its purpose.

A compromise was effected, in accordance with which the R. O. T. C. was established, but was to come to an end at commencement time, 1919. Lieutenant Colonel R. W. Boughton, a West Point man, was detailed by the War Department as commandant, and if anyone could have reconciled the students to military drill it was he; but neither at Kenyon nor at any other college did this training meet with favor, the whole country was swept by antimilitaristic sentiment, and the R. O. T. C. went out of existence in June.

When peace returned Kenyon quickly recovered its place in that course of development along which it had been moving when the war began. Its recent increase in numbers does not seem to have been due to causes generated by the war, for the enrollment had begun to increase in 1912, and had continued to mount up very steadily for three years at a rate which, had it been maintained, would have brought the college, not later than 1922, to its present limit of two hundred and fifty students. And there is no reason to doubt that it would have been maintained, if the war had not intervened; because the growth from 1912 onward was the due reward of the fortitude with which the president and the board of trustees had met the disasters of 1905 and 1906, and had, year by year, made the college, in equipment and efficiency, a better place to educate young men. Formerly nearly every man that came to Kenyon had to be sought, or, at least, his inclination to come there had to be encouraged; but now men are coming who were never heard of until they made application. Enrollments may fluctuate in the future as in the past, but Kenyon seems now to have attained what she never had before, a dependable constituency of sufficient magnitude to keep her classes filled without the incessant labor of campaigning for students which has hitherto been necessary. Out of sixty-four Freshmen in the class of 1924, forty-five assigned as their main reason for coming to Kenyon the personal influence of Kenyon men, fathers, or brothers, or friends, or interested alumni. In the class of 1925 fifty out of eighty-five came for the same reason. Thus from sixty to seventy per cent of her ingathering is, so to speak, self-sown; and this is a proportion that should naturally increase.

It is with no self-denying ordinance that Kenyon has chosen to be a small college. There are conditions that make it improbable that great numbers of students will ever come to her. The fact that she is situated in a very small village, near no large city, and that she offers only a simple college course, with no adjuncts of musical, or commercial, or advanced scientific training, will not bring her into favor with the multitude in these days. Her character as a college of the Protestant Episcopal Church gives her no added attraction to those whose denominational views differ from hers. But she accepts these limitations and believes in them; and to discard them would be to break with her entire history. Indeed, they are to her sources of strength. She has her definite, well-known character, and is unique among the colleges that are her fellows. In a time when nearly every college in the Middle West is coeducational, or provides a department for women, Kenyon remains a college for men only, and will not change. Again, Kenyon is wedded to the dormitory system. Only under stress of the recent very rapid growth in numbers did she, as a temporary measure, permit students to room in the village; and that necessity passes away with the building of Leonard Hall. All her major distinctive features were imposed upon her by her founder, Bishop Chase, with or without his intention.

In a college of two hundred and fifty men, all living together in three adjacent buildings, and dining together at the commons, there is, to some extent, a breaking down of social exclusiveness, a compulsion to know every member of the group, and an opportunity to become acquainted thus with men of many sorts, and to be broadened by such acquaintance, and made more capable of dealing with men in general. It is the firm belief of virtually all Kenyon men that the compulsory dormitory system has had that good effect. In such a college public opinion develops and is powerful; and there is room for influence and leadership. In such a college tradition is strong and insistent. No sensible person will say that the public opinion of Kenyon College is always what it ought to be; or that her traditions do not hand on a good deal that is foolish, and some things that are bad. But on the whole her public opinion has been a force for that which is reasonable and good; and the intermingling of wheat and tares in college traditions is not more perplexing and discouraging than in the traditions of society in general. Kenyon is a democratic college. We have seen how, through the Assembly, a large degree of self-government is successfully carried on. The thoroughgoing "honor system" has done more than secure honesty in examinations; it has bred a spirit of mutual trust in all the relationships between faculty and students, so that espionage and minute supervision of conduct are unknown. This has its disadvantages, and does not always work well; but Kenyon believes that it tends to the development of self-control and manliness.

The Hill, overlooking the beautiful valleys; the trees, the lawns, and the Path; the buildings; the close contacts of a compact community of young men; the spirit of democracy; the influence of the Church, exerted especially through its services; all these, working together, give Kenyon a character of her own, and produce a type of college life not just like that which is found elsewhere. She has her defects and her failings; but she has excellences that are rare. Men can learn Latin, and physics, and all the other disciplines, in other colleges as well as at Gambier. They can elsewhere form as strong, as ennobling friendships, and find as high an ideal of life. They may come under religious influences that make as powerfully for righteousness and devotion. In this college or in that the total effect of the institution may be as good as that of Kenyon. But she has a character of her own and an influence that entitle her to no inferior rank among the colleges that educate and build up men; and this is her excuse for being, this gives her a place such as no other college can exactly fill, and which could not be empty without loss. This unique character and influence justify all the labors and sacrifices and gifts which for a hundred years devoted men have made for her.

THE END

APPENDICES

APPENDIX I

BISHOP CHASE'S "DEED OF GIFT," OR "DEED OF DONATION"

THE original of this, the fundamental document in the history of Kenyon College, is in the college library, at Gambier (K. Ch. 231127b). It is endorsed—evidently in haste—in Bishop Chase's handwriting, "Original Copy of Deed [&] schedule of Property given in London." It is accompanied by a note to Lord Gambier, on a separate sheet of paper, as follows:

My very Dear Lord.

The inclosed is the Original which I drew up & got Mr. Pratts Secy. to copy *last Novemr.* I have always considered it as in Your Lordships hands. Please to retain it; and have the goodness to certify on the back of the Copy (in another cover) that it is a true transcript of the one in your Lordships hands: & much oblige your Lordships sincere friend & very

Huml Ser
PHI'R CHASE

This note is endorsed, "Copy of a Letter to Lord Gambier about the Deed of Gift 1824." Evidently Lord Gambier did not retain the original. He may have preferred to keep the copy which Mr. Pratt's secretary had made, which was probably in a more business-like shape, and better spelled and punctuated.

So far as is known, this Deed of Gift has never been published in its entirety, and the Schedule has never been published at all. The original is written in Bishop Chase's hand, on eight pages of paper, sewed together with thread. The following is an exact copy, so far as such a copy can be made in print.

THE Bishop of Ohio, United States, North America, now in England, will give his landed property, situate neer the Village of Worthington, township of Sharon, County of Franklin, State of Ohio, and all the buildings, and property thereunto pertaining, as described in the annexed schedule, to the Society or School, or Theological seminary, for the education of young men for the Christian ministry, to be organized by the Convention of the Protestant Epis-

copal Church in the said state of Ohio, according to the plan, or outline stated in his printed letter to the Right Rev. Bishop White of
Philadelphia, dated the 23d. of September in the year of our Our
Lord one thousand eight hundred and twenty three (—a copy of which
accompanies this—) as nearly as may be consistently with the funds
obtained.

The Bishop of Ohio will also give his library consisting of about
seven hundred volumes, mostly on divinity, (—the catalogue of
which is also annexed) *provided*, that the said School or Theological
Seminary be legally incorporated by the Legislature of the State of
Ohio and that the act of incorporation contain a clause to the following effect, namely—"that all acts and proceedings of the sd. school
or Theological Seminary shall forever be in conformity to the Doctrine discipline, constitution, canons, and course of study prescribed
by the Bishops of the Protestant Episcopal Church in the United
States of America; and, on proper evidence of a default thereof, that
the Right Rev. the Bishops of the Said American church or a majority of them as a Committee of the incorporated Institution of the
General Theological Seminary of the said Church in the City of New
York, or elsewhere, shall have power to institute an inquiry at law,
and to see that the will and intention of the founders and donors
of the said school or Theological seminary in Ohio, be Fulfilled:
Provided also, that the sum of Ten Thousand Dollars or upwards be
given in England for the maintenance of the said School or Seminary
in Ohio by one or more Benevolent persons.

It is understood that the monies collected for the above purpose
are to be deposited, by permission, in the hands of the Right Honorable Lord Gambier, and not to be transmitted to America, until the
said School or Theological Seminary, shall have been, according to
the said plan, duly and legally incorporated, and a title of the said
landed and other property and Library, in good faith, given and
executed to the said School or Seminary; of all which the Honorable
Henry Clay, of Kentucky shall be considered the Judge.

It is also understood, that, should the Convention of the Protestant
Episcopal Church in the State of Ohio, prefer any other place to
that of the Bishop's residence, and will give or cause to be given
another plantation or landed property, equal, or superior, in value,
buildings, conveniences, & stock, then, in that case, such plantation
and property may be received in lieu of the one promised & given by
the Bishop as above; & not otherwise; and of this the Honorable
Henry Clay above named shall also be the Judge.

It is further understood that the Bishop of Ohio, with his family, is to reside on this plantation and occupy the Mansion House as usual, during his life time, as a part of his Salary for superintending the School or Seminary, as also his Successor in office: And should the present Bishop of Ohio depart this life, leaving his Wife a Widow, or before his children come of the age of twenty one years, a reasonable allowance shall be made for their maintenance from the funds of the Institution: of this also the Honorable Henry Clay above named, shall be the Judge: and in case of his failure so to do by death or otherwise, the Judgment of the Gouvurnour of the State of Ohio for the time being in all the above particulars shall be taken

PHILANDER CHASE

London Nov. 27th.
Ad 1823.

Bishop of the Protestant Episcopal Church in the State of Ohio, N. America

A SCHEDULE

of the Landed and other Property alluded to in the annexed instrument of Donation

THE Plantation consists of One Hundred & Fifty acres of good land: about 40 acres under good fence and cultivation: About 16, but partially cleared: the residue 95 covered with forest trees, affording abundance of fuel: and from some of which is usually made four or five hundred pounds weight of Sugar, for family use

FRUIT Trees About 60 apple trees, large and very productive. Above one hundred young standards set out in an orchard the most *apple.* of which in bearing. & a great part of which are ingrafted from the finest fruit.

Peach About one hundred young and old; from which in some years there is produced many hundred bushels of the most delicious fruit.

Buildings —

A substantially framed building of wood well covered and painted white main body on the ground 36. by 26 feet well *Proprietor's* finished above and below *House —* Annexed buildings not so well finished—they are a kitchen store and dining rooms: and a wash-house
A well of pure water is conveniently situated

There is a well-finished Cellar under the main building 26 by 36 feet The building in all its apartments is well glazed.

Farm house for a Manager　About four hundred yards from the proprietor's house is the house for the manager. This also is of wood and painted white: has three rooms two below and one above the whole well lighted.—a Cellar underneath and a neat yard in front well set with forest trees black locust, honey locust, & Sugar trees.

Barn —　The dimentions of the Barn are 46 by 36 feet with 17 feet posts—sides well covered with boards and the roof with shingles.

annexed is a shed and granery and a small carriage house.

The yards round about are sufficiently numerous well divided for a good stock of Sheep Cattle & Horses.

Live Stock

Horses Sheep hogs & Cattle　Two good horses—about 150 sheep—the same number of swine great and small and about 25 head net Cattle; beside a large quantity of poultry.

Bees　A few hives of Honey-bees are placed in a convenient bee-house on the premises.

Some general remarks.

THE House built for the proprietor of the above premises is situated back from the public road leading north and south from Worthington to Columbus: and is exactly eight miles and a half from the latter and one half mile from the former. Columbus is the seat of government or the town where the State Legislature hold their annual session. Between the mansion house and the road is situated the Orchard of Peach and apple Trees intermingled above described. Next to the house however between it and the fruit trees is a thick row of young forrest-trees from fifteen to five & twenty feet high: among the branches and over the tops of which are spread a great number of wild grape-vines, which coming up naturally were suffered to grow on this row of forrest trees in front of the house about 300 feet in length to the north & to the south. forming an arbour majestic and graceful to the beholder and peculiarly refreshing to the family in a warm climate in summer.

NOTE. This is a schedule of the property both real and personal, as nearly as I can remember, alluded to in the annexed instrument of donation. One item however I forgot when stating the number of acres. There is one hundred and fifty acres of the original plantation; but of this one one has been sold to a Mechanick who has partly & I believe for the most part paid the condition money One hundred Dollars, and when he shall have completed the payment will be entitled to a deed.

PHILANDER CHASE

the proprietor of the above premises now given on the conditions set forth in the act or instrument of donation accompanying this.
London Novr 27th AD 1823.

P.S. It may not be thought irrelevant to mention the following fact.

Commissioners having been appointed by the Legislature of Ohio to survey and report the practicability of, a canal to connect the *Lake Erie* with the waters of the *Ohio river;* the same has been done within the two last past years. The route of the Canal, (I was informed by one of the Commissioners with whom I had a personal interview before I left Ohio) will be up the Sandusky and down the valley of the Sciota Waters: in passing to Columbus it will touch the western end of the above described Plantation. P. CHASE

APPENDIX II

OLD KENYON

KENYON COLLEGE is a notable structure. Bishop Chase, believing that he was building for the ages, planned upon a very large scale, procured the most noted American architect of his time to draw the design, and, despite much opposition, would have the walls of stone only, "such as the nature of so glorious an Institution required," he said; and that, too, in an age when brick was almost exclusively the material of which colleges in this country were built. Of course, the occurrence of excellent stone right on the side of the hill where the college was to stand had something to do with his decision.

Bishop Chase visited Washington in the early months of 1826, and it was probably then that he met Charles Bulfinch, who had designed the State House and Faneuil Hall in Boston, and was at that time architect of the national Capitol. Thus Old Kenyon has very distinguished affinities. As originally planned it was a much more spacious building than that which we now see. It was to be shaped like a gigantic H, each wing containing five divisions, while the middle part—the cross-piece of the H—contains but three. Thirteen divisions, each with twelve rooms, would accommodate nearly five hundred students; for the Bishop intended that there should be three in each room, sleeping in a three-story "bunk."

After the laying of the cornerstone, June 9, 1827, the work went forward rapidly. It is remarkable that a sufficient force of stonecutters and masons could be gathered together in the depths of the forest. The lower six or eight feet of the front of the middle divisions show rather crude work, but there was improvement soon. The south wall is an impressive piece of stone work. The walls are more than four feet thick at the ground, and become but a little thinner as they ascend. Bishop Chase, in his *Defence against the Slanders of the Rev. G. M. West*, says that he followed the advice of the best architects in making the walls so thick, and that he also had "local reasons." "I thought myself justified in using all the means that God had given us, to guard against the dreadful effects of hurricanes, so frequent in our country." He took pride in the topmost range, which consists of very large stones. "The walls are massive, exceedingly well put together," he wrote to Lord Gambier. "The roof, on account of the elevated site of the college and its consequent exposure to the violent winds of our country, has more timber in it, and is put together with more appropriate firmness, than most things of the kind in America; the steeple is in good proportion, high and beautiful."

The building was under roof in June, 1829. Philander Chase Freeman, who graduated in September of that year, says that he lived in the college the last three months of his Senior year. He must have been the first, or among the first, to occupy it; and it was then far from completed. The next year Bishop Chase and his family took up their residence in the basement of the West Division, and in the fall many of the students were occupying rooms in the building. For lack of money Bishop Chase was able to complete only the middle part of the college. At that time an area ran along the north side, giving light to the basement windows, which were then of full size, as anyone may see who will go inside and look. The steps leading to the divisions bridged this area. There was a door at the south end of the middle hallway, with steps down to the ground.

Bishop McIlvaine procured the necessary money, and at once set about building the wings, but upon a much smaller scale than the original plans called for. To his architect—whoever he was—are due the admirable bull's-eye windows. In November, 1834, the *Gambier Observer* noted that "one wing of the college is completed (east) and the other almost ready to receive its roof." In October, 1836, it spoke of the "west wing of the college building recently completed."

Old Kenyon has been many times repaired. In 1841 President Douglass replastered and renovated the middle divisions, and tore down the three-decker berths that Bishop Chase had provided. In 1848 a new roof was put on, of shingles, as the first had been. In 1866 extensive repairs were made. At that time the plain wooden pyramids on the roof were replaced by the elaborated ones of galvanized iron with which we are familiar, and the slate roof, with its display of the name of the college, was put on. It would not cost a great deal to remove those red slates that spell the name, and put gray ones in their places; and it would be a most happy thing if the sheet iron pinnacles were replaced by stone pyramids, after the original design. Later repairs have been described in Chapter XXIII.

In the catalogue for 1836-1837 for the first time the number of each student's room is given, and this continued until the catalogue for 1870-1871, when, for some unknown reason, the printing of the numbers ceases. It was not renewed until 1907-1908, when the building had been entirely made over on the interior. For the intervening twenty-six years it is impossible to tell, from the catalogues, where any man roomed. The old numbering, from 1837 to 1871, was entirely different from that now in use. Each division and wing was numbered separately, but all after the same system. As one stood at the outside door, on the first story of any wing or division, and looked in, the more remote door at his right—concealed by the stairs —was numbered 5. Opposite it was 6. At the observer's left hand was 7, and at his right—at the foot of the stairs—was 8. Number 9 was at the head of the stairs on the second floor; 10 was opposite it, and so on. The bull's-eye rooms of the two wings were 17 and 18. Numbers 1, 2, 3, and 4 must have been reserved for the basement. The knowledge of this old numbering seemed to have been lost, but it has, by a great deal of inquiring, been worked out as given above— correctly, it is believed. A list of the occupants of any room between the years 1836 and 1871 can now be made out. Unfortunately, most of Kenyon's very famous men left college before 1836. The persistent tradition is that Edwin M. Stanton lived in the west bull's-eye room; but the west wing had not been built when he left college.

For further information about Old Kenyon consult Index.

APPENDIX III

ASCENSION HALL

WITH the increase in the number of students under President Andrews' administration, the need of additional buildings became pressing. Old Kenyon and Rosse Chapel were all that the college had. In 1854 President Andrews began to call the attention of the trustees to these needs, and in 1855 the board appointed a committee to prepare plans for such buildings as were deemed necessary, select sites for them, and estimate their cost. The next year the board resolved "that it is the purpose of the Trustees to collect in the diocese $12,000 towards the erection of another edifice for Kenyon College, and that the two Literary Societies be invited to invest (so soon as the Board shall collect the above amount) the sum of $4,000 each, to provide rooms for their proper use in the same building." The effort to collect $12,000 in Ohio does not appear to have been very strongly urged, for nearly all the money for this building, except what the literary societies contributed, came from the East. Bishop McIlvaine, secured most of the money from members of the Church of the Ascension, in New York, as has been told in Chapter XVI. In 1857 a plan and elevation of the proposed building were drawn by W. Tinsley, a prominent architect, and were adopted by the board. The work was done piecemeal, as money came in sight. At first the building committee was authorized to let the contract for the basement, at a cost not exceeding $4,000. The cornerstone was laid, June 30, 1857, with impressive ceremonies, and an address was delivered by Bishop McIlvaine, standing upon the wall. In 1858 John Johns of Baltimore left the college $15,000, and this, or part of it, was used to put Ascension under roof. In the fall of that year the outside of the building was finished, and a flag was flying from the roof. In January, 1860, the north wing and central part were completed. The south wing was finished off gradually, as the rooms were needed for class and administrative purposes; indeed, it can hardly be said that even yet it has been brought to a proper completion.

The contractor for this building was Mr. William Fish, who, to obtain stone, opened a quarry of olive shale two miles northeast of the college. The same stone was also used for the Church of the Holy

Spirit, the Quarry Chapel, "Kokosing," and some foundations. The quarry was exhausted in constructing these buildings. Mr. Arora Buttles was the unofficial, but most useful, supervisor of the building of Ascension Hall.

The literary societies had contributed largely to the building fund, and were permitted to finish off their rooms as they thought best. Each spent two or three thousand dollars in this way, with the understanding that it was to have the exclusive use of its hall. In 1875 the college claimed the right to hold certain exercises in these halls, and the societies denied the claim. The question was submitted to several prominent lawyers—John E. Mitchell of Columbus, Moses M. Granger of Zanesville, and James D. Hancock of Franklin, Pennsylvania—who gave their opinion that the right of the college to use the halls without consent of the societies was exceedingly doubtful in law, and at any rate unjustifiable morally.

For further information about Ascension Hall consult Index.

APPENDIX IV

ROSSE CHAPEL. ROSSE HALL

WHEN Bishop Chase was in England he found no one more ready to aid his cause than Miss Duff Macfarlane, daughter of the Bishop of Inverness, and a warm friend of the Marriotts. Through her the dowager countess of Rosse became interested in the Bishop, with the result that she sent him, first £200 to aid his work, and subsequently £100 more for his private use. The Bishop writing to her to express his thanks, said:

"Instead of using this for my own personal benefit, I could wish your Ladyship's consent that it might be applied towards the erection of a modest yet convenient chapel for the use of the seminary. And here a thought strikes me with so much pleasure that I entreat your Ladyship will not forbid its indulgence—that the chapel may be called after the name of the donor. . . . Though the sum, the use of which I am now considering, may seem small in your Ladyship's eyes, yet with *us* it will be great indeed. It will lay the foundation on which, encouraged by this munificent example, others may be disposed to erect and complete the edifice. Methinks I see this lovely spectacle rise to my view, and quickly filled with devout worshippers from the 'sons of the soil,' all in successful training for future ministers of the blessed gospel of salvation. Amidst our wild woods, where so lately were heard only the war-whoop of the savage and the howlings of the forest wolf, will be sung the sweet songs of Zion, mellowed by the controlling power of the pealing organ." (K. Ch. 240501.)

When the college grounds were mapped out, Bishop Chase selected for this chapel a most beautiful location, on the western side of what was planned to be "Bexley Square," on the highest ground in the Park, overlooking the valleys east and west. Here he proposed to erect a noble building after the gothic order, as he understood gothic. It was to be one hundred feet long and sixty-six feet broad, with a chancel forty feet deep at the western end, and a tower ten feet square at the eastern end. The Bishop estimated that the chapel would accommodate nine hundred and forty worshippers, allowing six square feet of floor for each. It would be, he said, "unpardonably criminal were I to let my infidelity proceed to such length as to carve out a scanty plan for the House of God—a place too small to accommodate an audience suited, in some degree, to the greatness of our plan. (*Defence against the Slanders*, etc., p. 29.)

The cornerstone was laid May 4, 1829. In this stone were placed, "in a sealed vessel," various documents, and also this statement: "This Edifice, erected to the glory of God through Jesus Christ our Lord, of which the cornerstone was laid on the fourth day of May A.D. 1829, is called ROSSE CHAPEL of KENYON COLLEGE: the Faculty and Students of which for the time being are as follows: [sixty-eight names follow]. The chapel has its name from the Right Honorable Lady Countess Dowager of Rosse, she having been its first donor in the sum of one hundred pounds sterling, to commence its foundation.—The remainder of the expense was defrayed from benefactions subsequently made by the truly benevolent in England and Ireland." The Bishop's hopes for money were disappointed, and he was able to carry the work no further than to the top of the basement, and lay the timbers to sustain the first floor. He also accumulated much material—stone, brick, wood—towards its completion, but most of this was devoted to other uses after his departure from Gambier in September, 1831.

Bishop McIlvaine completed the chapel on a reduced and altered plan. The new design was probably drawn by Charles Romanoff Przriminsky, the architect of the old Trinity Church in Columbus in 1834. The designs of the two buildings were very similar, and in the Kenyon catalogue for 1834-1835 Mr. Przriminsky is named as "Teacher of Modern Languages." Bishop Chase was not pleased with these alterations. He said, rather bitterly: "Again, its size was large, and would occasion too much expense; therefore the chancel (another Episcopal appendage) must be cut off, though double the sum necessary to continue *that* be expended in excavating a basement story after the walls had been built up solid to the floor, and the sleepers laid." The cornerstone, he said, had been laid in the wall of the chancel, and was dug up when that part of the foundation was removed. (*Reminiscences*, first edition, p. 782.) A small part of the chancel was left, to serve as a vestry, a door opening into it behind the pulpit.

By the end of 1834 Rosse Chapel was "nearly enclosed," and the following year the chapel services of the college were transferred from the Old Seventy-Four to the basement of the new building. Shortly thereafter hard times fell upon the country, money could not be obtained, and for several years little was done towards finishing the chapel, although occasionally, in favorable weather, exercises were held in the great upper room. In 1844 the women of Harcourt Parish held a fair to raise money to complete the chapel. This fair, said the *Western Episcopalian*, "came off quietly, soberly and advisedly," and "by entirely honest and laudable methods" more than $200 were obtained. (What sort of fairs did those ladies usually have?) The building was consecrated June 21, 1845. Five or six years later the flat ceiling was found to be inadequately supported, and had to be propped with long timbers, whole tree trunks with the bark on. Some of these sprouted and put forth leaves; which was regarded as a good omen. In the fall of 1852 the roof and ceiling were repaired.

Rosse Chapel was not an attractive place of worship, having been finished off within with but little regard for the beauty of holiness. It is significant that talk about building a new church seems to have begun shortly after the arrival of Bishop Bedell, who, like Bishop Chase, had an eye for beauty. In 1869 he began to build the Church of the Holy Spirit. Perhaps it would have been better if he had reverted to Bishop Chase's original plan, and employed a competent architect to carry it out, with such changes as a better knowledge of gothic might suggest. It is not known who Bishop Chase's architect for this building was.

After Rosse Chapel ceased to be used for religious services there was not much that could, with a good conscience, be done with it. Its name was changed to Rosse Hall, but it was not deconsecrated, and its sacred associations clung to it. From time to time there was talk of converting it into a library and museum. In 1884 it was partially fitted up as a gymnasium. On January 25, 1896, the building was secularized by the college chaplain, acting under the authority of Bishop Leonard. The following year it was destroyed by fire, leaving little more than two walls standing. It was soon rebuilt in its present form, and fitted especially for use as a gymnasium, auditorium, and hall for social purposes.

Rosse was sixteen years building; it could not be comfortably heated in the winter; its roof nearly fell in; after it had been in use —partial use—for little over twenty-five years, it was abandoned as a church and was given over to profane uses; it burned down; it has never been very well suited for any of the purposes to which it has been put; its first builders gave it wooden pediments, its second builders a metallic cornice. An unlucky building, surely. Nevertheless, once there were many who associated it with the most sacred experiences of their lives, and to-day there are many who associate it with their merriest hours. And it has been, and is, a very useful building.

For further information consult Index.

APPENDIX V

THE LIBRARIES

BISHOP CHASE realized, perhaps as much as anyone of his day, the importance of a library in a seminary of learning; therefore a prominent part of his appeal in England was for books to supplement his own collection of about seven hundred volumes which he promised to give. This appeal met with a generous response, and hundreds of books were from time to time sent across the Atlantic, from private and collegiate libraries, to find lodgment, first in the Bishop's house at Worthington, and afterwards in one room and another at Gambier. At Worthington pupils were set to cataloguing them, and they were kept in Mrs. Chase's room. She was the first librarian. At Gambier the library was kept in a room in the West Division of Old Kenyon. A second appeal to English generosity, made by Bishop McIlvaine in 1835 brought nearly two thousand more books. In all, there were in 1836 more than four thousand volumes in the library, many of them very learned, and of great value to theological scholars, some of them rare and costly. There was a fund of $1,000 for the increase of this library, given by Mr. Peter G. Stuyvesant of New York in 1833. In 1845 the library, being distinctively theological, was removed to Bexley Hall. It consisted then of about 4,500 volumes. George Thompson, a theological student, numbered them "by sections and by shelves," and made a list of them. In 1850 the Reverend Doctor Anthon of St. Mark's Church, New York, gave $1,000 from the estate of Charles D. Betts, of which he was trustee, the interest to be used for the purchase of books. By means of this "Betts Fund" have been purchased probably not less than $5,000 worth of books, and the money is still there. Mrs. Bedell, who died in 1898, left $5,000 to the Bexley library fund. In 1902 Mrs. Colburn of Toledo built Colburn Hall for the theological library, and the books were removed to it in 1904. The catalogue for 1922-1923 announces that there are about 12,000 volumes. Bishop Bedell, Bishop Leonard, the Rev. W. C. French, the Reverend D. B. Ray, and Doctor H. W. Jones made large and valuable contributions of books.

For books of a "secular" character, whether light or serious, the students, for sixty years, depended mainly on the libraries of the literary societies. These libraries together contained in 1835 more than 2,500 books; in 1872 they contained nearly 10,000. Their rooms were in Old Kenyon. In 1865 President Short founded the library of Kenyon College, procuring about five hundred books for that purpose. Bishop Bedell took great interest in this library, and in 1867 he obtained from Mr. Frank E. Richmond of Providence a gift of $5,000, known as the Hoffman Library Fund, the interest to be used in purchasing new books for it. In 1881 the literary societies were barely alive, and their libraries were merged with that of the college. In 1886 the books were removed from the rooms in Old Kenyon and Ascension in which they had been housed, to the newly erected Hubbard Hall. This building was enlarged in 1900 by the addition of the Stevens Stack Room, to which most of the books were transferred. Hubbard Hall was destroyed by fire in 1910, but the fireproof stackroom preserved its contents in safety. Hubbard Hall has been replaced by the Alumni Library, with its beautiful reading-room, Norton Hall.

For further information consult Index.

APPENDIX VI

THE OLD HOTEL, OR "KENYON HOUSE"

THE four houses that Bishop Chase erected on Wiggin Street, for the temporary accommodation of the students, were all of the same dimensions, twenty by thirty-eight feet, and two stories high. One of them, with additions at the rear and a porch in front, still stands in its original place, on the north side of the street, between Mr. Scott's store and the Psi Upsilon grounds. East of it stood the second house, long known as the Lurkin house, from the name of a family that once lived there. This house is still on the original spot, but has been turned around through ninety degrees, and what was its front has been joined to Mr. Scott's store, of which it is now the back part. Opposite it stood, until the early eighties, the third house, which was for many years part of the earlier "Scott's store," and is now part of a stable on the Academy grounds. These three houses survive and are still in use. The fourth house stood west of the third and opposite the first. At a little distance west of this fourth house, and about thirty feet back from the street, stood the hotel, built in 1829 or 1830. "It is two stories high," said Bishop Chase, "having two convenient rooms below and five bedrooms above." This hotel was not large enough to accommodate all the people that came to attend commencements or diocesan conventions; and at such times the men used to sleep on the hay in the loft of the barn near by, leaving the bedrooms to the women. After the students had been removed to Old Kenyon, some additional accommodation was provided by putting beds into the upstairs rooms of the fourth house above mentioned, the downstairs rooms being used for a shoe shop and a carpenter's shop. At some later time this fourth house was moved to the west, in front of the hotel, and the two buildings were joined, and made one, and constituted the wooden part of the old hotel, which hundreds of Kenyon men will remember. The gable of the rear part rose a good way above the ridge of the roof of the front part, and anyone could see that these were two buildings put together. The brick part of the hotel seems to have been added about 1854. The whole was torn down in 1917. This history of the old hotel is partly conjectural, but is corroborated by all obtainable evidence, and is probably correct.

For further information consult Index.

APPENDIX VII

THE COLLEGE STORE

IN Bishop Chase's time there was, on the spot where the college commons building now stands, a composite structure, partly log, partly frame. This was the college store, where goods of all sorts were for sale, most of them having been hauled over the mountains in wagons, from Philadelphia. The early account books of this store have been preserved, and one is surprised at the number and variety of things that could be bought. Groceries, dry goods, hardware, cutlery, chinaware, clothing, jewelry, books, stationery, and medicines, are some of the main genera, the species of which are innumerable. The display of swansdown, sateens, silk vestings, cassinet, broadcloth of various colors, silks, and ribbons, suggest that even in that primitive age the young men of the college and the young ladies of the vicinage were not unmindful of their appearance.

The log part of the store, originally a dwelling, is said to have been built by Isaac Dial for Warner Terry. When Mr. Terry left Gambier the house became a blacksmith shop, and here—as Doctor S. A. Bronson long remembered—was held a session of the diocesan convention of 1827, on the afternoon of September sixth. Later it became the store, and soon was rendered more convenient by the frame addition. After a few years, when a new store was built, which is now Mr. Stoyle's residence, adjoining his restaurant on the north, the old store was removed, and the log portion, after several journeyings and sojournings, at last found rest in the spot where it now is, in the northern part of the village, on the Amity road, as the middle part of the second house beyond the Harper woods. It has been weatherboarded, so that the logs are not seen, but their presence is betrayed by the deep doorways and window frames. This is undoubtedly the oldest house in Gambier, and it has an interesting history.

For further information consult Index.

THE LITERARY SOCIETIES

THE records of the Philomathesian Society begin as follows: "At a respectable meeting of the students of Kenyon College, assembled in the Recitation Room, on Thursday May 10th, 1827, for the purpose of forming a Society, Mr. Nathan Stem was called to the chair, and Henry Dickinson was elected Secretary." This was at Worthington. On the thirtieth of June seventeen names were enrolled.

For about one year weekly exercises were held in the "log cabin recitation room." After the removal to Gambier the society met in the old dining-hall, near the present gates, and the members were summoned to attendance by blasts of a horn. The room was used for many purposes, and the Philomathesians desired a hall that they could call their own. They received permission to put up a cabin at the corner of Brooklyn and Ward streets, and began to fell trees for that purpose; but upon learning that the Phi Phi Alphas, a grammar school society, were to share the use of the building which they were laboring to erect, they lost interest in the project, and decided to remain at the old dining-hall.

In 1832 Edwin M. Stanton, a Sophomore, became a member of Philomathesian; and being even then a candidate for immortality, he presented the society with a fine, large, leather-covered record book, with his name as donor stamped upon the side. At that time the country was rent with political discussions, President Jackson's anti-nullification policy having general support at the North, and being opposed by the South. The debates of Philomathesian were fervid, for there were members from both sections of the country. The first page of the Nu Pi Kappa record book tells what happened, as viewed from the southern side. "In consequence of the misjudged and censurable conduct of certain members of the Philomathesian Society, a party spirit was excited, dividing the Society into Northern and Southern, and making it advisable, and almost necessary, for individual improvement, and well being of the whole, that a separation should take place."

The separation took place on the twenty-third of June, 1832, with the consent of the faculty. A toss-up as to which should retain the name Philomathesian resulted in favor of the Northern society. Funds and property were amicably divided. Thirteen men formed the new society, to which they gave the name Nu Pi Kappa. Eight of the thirteen were from Maryland, four from Virginia, and one from Connecticut. It does not appear that the five or six men from Mississippi and Louisiana joined them. In November the society resolved that "agreeable to the wishes of the Philomathesian Society, we elect members hereafter only from the slave-holding states, this resolution being understood to include all those born in the Southern States, and that it should only hold its force so long as circumstances render it necessary; but that it be understood as having no reference to foreigners."

The two societies seem to have pursued their ways most of the time in a friendly spirit. Each contributed an orator annually to enrich the exercises of commencement. There was another literary society, the Phi Phi Alpha, which originally consisted of grammar school pupils; but when these pupils entered college they brought their society with them. Phi Phi Alpha supplied orators to the commencement stage in 1831 and 1832, but thereafter disappeared. Its most distinguished member was David Davis, of the class of '32. In 1834 Philo and Nu Pi held a joint exhibition, entertaining their audience with six orations; and once or twice thereafter similar exhibitions were held; but for the most part the societies held separate exhibitions. The chief matters of interest at the regular meetings was supplied by the debates, or "forensics," as they were called.

The mutual cordiality of the two societies was broken for a time in 1836 and 1837, when "members upon both sides carried arms, ready for attack or defence; but there is no record of the spilling of blood." In 1840 there was a remarkable exhibition of friendliness on the part of Philo towards its rival. With the decline in the number of southerners in the college—from twenty-seven in 1832 to eight in 1840—Nu Pi Kappa was reduced to a very small membership, and was in danger of extinction. Therefore at its request, in July, 1840, a conference of committees from both the societies was held, and certain recommendations were presented to Philomathesian, which were adopted by that society. An agreement was made that all students entering college the following autumn were to be requested to join Nu Pi Kappa. Beginning with the class entering in 1841, students were to be divided in equal numbers between the two societies. As a means of immediate relief, members of Philomathesian were to

be "permitted to volunteer to aid the Nu Pi Kappa Society (if necessary) in the performance of duties, until such time as they should
have members of their own sufficient to discharge the same. Provided
that not more than ten be permitted to volunteer at a time, or for more
than one year." Thereupon, ten members of Philomathesian (*not*
including R. B. Hayes) went over to Nu Pi Kappa, to aid it for one
year. This transfusion of blood, with the arrangement for equal
membership in the future, saved the life of Nu Pi Kappa. Thereafter
the societies were not divided by geographical or political lines.

Both societies had rooms in the basement of Old Kenyon. With the
new life that poured into the college in the fifties, and the larger
ideas and ambitions thus engendered, there came a desire for better
quarters. At first they planned to erect separate halls, but subsequently they entered into agreements with the college whereby they
were to have rooms in the proposed Ascension Hall. For further
information consult Index.

SOURCES

Manuscript.

The Records of the Board of Trustees. Minutes of the Faculty of Kenyon College. Various other records and documents, at the office of the college treasurer in Gambier.

Collections of hundreds of letters and other papers, at the college library; especially the Chase, McIlvaine, and Allen collections, designated respectively, "K.Ch.," "K.McI.," "K.Al."

Records of the Philomathesian and Nu Pi Kappa societies, and other college organizations, at the college library.

Printed.

Catalogues of the college and seminary, at the college library.

President Peirce's reports to the trustees, and letters to the alumni, at the President's office.

Many pamphlets, at the college and seminary libraries; generally in bound volumes of miscellaneous character. Chiefly to Bishop Bedell is due the preservation of this invaluable material. Especially useful for this history are the following: "A Letter on the Subject of Going to England for the Relief of the Protestant Episcopal Church in the State of Ohio, addressed to the Rt. Rev. Bishop White"; "Bishop Chase's Defence against the Slanders of the Rev. G. M. West" in which will be found detailed descriptions of all the early buildings; "The Rev. B. P. Aydelott, in answer to the Rt. Rev. P. Chase"; "A Reply to the Charges and Accusations of the Rt. Rev. Philander Chase," by the Rev. William Sparrow; a circular, dated at Gambier, July 14, 1831, printed on two pages of a four-page folder, and signed in autograph by Bishop Chase; "The Professors of Kenyon College. A Letter addressed to Bishop Chase," July 25, 1831, printed on two pages of a four-page folder; "A Statement of Facts and Circumstances relating to the Endowments of the Theological Seminary of the Diocese of Ohio," by the Rev. S. A. Bronson, D.D.; "A Memento to the Donors and Founders of the Theological Seminary, etc.," by the Rev. S. A. Bronson, D. D.

Journals of the Conventions of the Diocese of Ohio, at the seminary.

Files of Publications.

The *Reveille*, the *Collegian*, the *Kenyon Advance*, the *Gambier Argus*, the *Philadelphia Recorder*, the *Gambier Observer*, the *Western Episcopalian*, the *Standard of the Cross*. All these may be found at the college, or seminary, library, except the *Kenyon Advance*, of which, unfortunately, there is no file at Gambier. The author is under obligations to Mr. Charles H. Wetmore, '69, of Columbus, for the use of his file. There is no complete file of the *Gambier Argus* at Gambier, or, so far as is known, anywhere. This was an extremely valuable paper for the history of the college, and it is hoped that the file may be completed by gifts from persons who have copies.

Scrapbooks.

There are at the college library many scrapbooks, containing letters, programmes, newspaper cuttings, and the like. Far the most numerous and important of these is the set compiled by Doctor E. C. Benson. From 1872 to 1897 he gathered almost every programme, or announcement, or newspaper article that had anything to do with Kenyon or Bexley, or any of their alumni. Besides, he collected many programmes, etc., of earlier date. All these he pasted into a series of large scrapbooks which are a mine of information, much of it not now obtainable from any other source. Since Doctor Benson's death Mrs. Devol and Miss Hicken, librarians, have collected similar material, and other persons have made contributions.

Photographs.

Besides two or three valuable pencil sketches that have come down from early times, the college has, at its library, a large collection of photographs. Many of these are pictures of presidents, professors, and students. Particularly valuable are the photographs of Gambier and the college buildings and grounds, taken in the fifties by Professor H. W. Smith. These came to the college as a gift from Mrs. Levi Buttles. Mr. Crowell, a Mount Vernon photographer, beginning in the sixties and continuing for many years, took Gambier pictures, of which the college now owns many negatives, chiefly through the generosity of his successor in the Mount Vernon gallery, Mr. Wagoner. Mr. Peter Neff, '49, during a long residence in Gambier took many photographs which have been given to the college by his son of the same name. In the nineties, and later, there was a photography club in Gambier. From this club have come to the college many photographs and negatives. Other pictures have come from other sources.

Books.

Bishop Chase's "Reminiscenses." The lives of William Sparrow, Henry M. Stanton, Henry Winter Davis, Heman Dyer, Henry Livingston Richards, and Rutherford Birchard Hayes contain much that is interesting concerning early days. "America and the American Church," by Henry Caswall, is extraordinarily valuable for the years 1828-1831.

To no single source, except the Chase letters, is the author more indebted than to the Kenyon Book, published by President Bodine in 1891. Here one may find conveniently reprinted, many early documents, or parts of such documents, and many letters containing reminiscences of old students, and a great deal of general information. Here is much information that would not now be obtainable had not Doctor Bodine taken pains to collect it and print it in his book.

INDEX

ACLAND, Sir Thomas and Lady, Bishop Chase visits, 29.

Adams, C. W., 38.

Allen, Alexander V. G., 168; describes Kenyon College in his day, 177-180.

Allen, Benjamin, his kindness to Bishop Chase, 64.

Allen, R. B., 281.

Alpha Delta Phi, 183, 244, 250, 259, 279.

Alumni Library, 226, 260, 262, 296.

Ames, John G., 231.

Andrews, John W., 184, 225.

Andrews, Lorin, elected president, his qualifications and experience, 154, 156; growth of college under, 166, 167; strong faculty under, 169; enters army, 187, 188; his military services, illness, death, and burial, 189, 190, 192, 223, 313.

"Appeal," pamphlet commending Bishop Chase's cause in England, 25, 26.

Artillery, Kenyon, see "Baby."

Ascension Hall, why built, 313; money to build, 155, 313; plan of, 155; cornerstone laid, 313; completed and in use, 155, 313; stone of which built, 313, 314; halls of literary societies in, 182, 314; grammar school pupils quartered in, 201, 210; dilapidated condition of, 226, 250; improvements in, 258; re-

paired, 260, 264, 269; Appendix III.

Assembly, The, 280-283, 289.

Athletics, in general, 181, 232; great interest in, 239, 240, 284; on Kenyon Day, 253, 274, 280; lack of money for, 284; Ohio Athletic Conference, 285; director of, 285. See also Baseball, Boating, Canoeing, Football, Gymnasium, Tennis, Track Athletics, etc.

BABY, The, 248, 249.

Bache, Benjamin F., 131.

Badger, Norman, 133.

Balliol College, 177.

Bancroft, L. W., 199.

Baseball, 181, 240, 241.

Bates, Cyrus S., regent of grammar school, 219, 222, 237.

Bedell, Gregory Townsend, 64.

Bedell, Gregory Thurston, rector of Ascension Church, New York, 155, 189; in controversy with college faculty, 203, 204; his generosity, 205, 206; connection with building Church of the Holy Spirit, 207, 208; president of board of trustees, 209; active in helping college, 216, 217, 218, 221; enjoins a dance in Lent, 223, 253; resignation of, 227; his position in Gambier, 234; extends the Path to Bexley Hall, 234; his services to the college, his death and burial, 254, 255, 319, 320.

excellent faculty, 99; charter amended, providing for separation of college and theological seminary, 128, 129; a new Kenyon College created, 131; entire change of faculty, 131; D. B. Douglass becomes president, 133; buildings and grounds improved, 134, 135; matriculation introduced, 136; disorders, 137; decline in attendance, 138; S. A. Bronson becomes president, 139; allied with Evangelicals, 144; T. M. Smith becomes president, 152; proposition to suspend, 154; Lorin Andrews becomes president, 154; a period of prosperity, 155, 156; causes of growth in the fifties, 166, 167; examinations, 170, 171; daily chapel, 171; faculty and students in 1859-1862, 177-180; effects of the Civil War upon, 187-190; Charles Short becomes president, 193; increasing prosperity, 193; charges against the faculty, 194; J. K. Stone becomes president, 194; theological controversy with calamitous results, 195-203; E. T. Tappan becomes president, and great hopes are aroused, 200; the faculty rejects the advice of the trustees regarding giving degrees, 204; faculty protests against cutting down expenses, 207; name legalized, 209; the faculty protests against rules made by trustees, 215; W. B. Bodine becomes president, 214; visit of bishops to, 216,

217; decreased attendance, 221; the power of the Bishop of Ohio over, 222, 223; few endowed chairs, 224; at lowest ebb, 228; T. Sterling becomes president, 228; a period of transition, 233; W. F. Peirce elected president, 231; a good college, 238; energy of the students, 253, 254; its condition in 1896, 257, 258; faculty reduced in numbers, 263; increased attendance, 274; diminished attendance, following the death of S. L. Pierson, 276, 277; increased attendance, to the limit set, 277; increase in the number of professors and studies, 278; student self-government, 280-283; conditions during the Great War, 292-298; its distinctive attractions, character, and influence, 298-301.

Kenyon College (the building), designed by Charles Bulfinch, 87, 310; cornerstone laid, 68; work on, 69-71, 310; middle part nearly completed, September, 1829, 80; students transferred to, 81, 82; Bishop Chase and his family take up residence in, 82, 311; not very comfortable, 82; cost of, 87, 96, 112, 115; completed, 121, 311; first illumination of, 122; middle part renovated and supplied with furniture, 134, 311; illuminated in honor of President Andrews, 154; its many facilities, 155; theological students in, 159; its "philosophical apartment," 170; rooms